W9-BIK-821

More advance praise for Bob Mayer's *Power Plays*

"Bob Mayer's techniques have made me a believer. I've seen him solve sensitive problems time and again, and I'm delighted that Bob is sharing his methods in his new book."

> —*Jeff Scheinrock*,
> vice chairman, finance and strategic planning,
> Packard Bell

"*Power Plays* is the ideal how-to-negotiate primer and a must-read for every dealmaker or dealmaker-to-be."

> —*Al Lapin, Jr.*,
> founder, International House of Pancakes;
> past president, International Franchise Association

"No magic elixirs or mumbo jumbo: just straight-talking, easy-to-understand, easy-to-remember, and easy-to-use principles of persuasion and negotiation—secrets I've seen in action when Bob Mayer has successfully negotiated for me."

> —*David Crosby*,
> singer/songwriter

"Professional women now have a playbook for survival and success in today's ever-competitive workplace. Bob Mayer's *Power Plays* will really help level the playing field."

> —*June Nichols Sweeney*,
> second in command,
> U.S. Small Business Administration
> under Presidents Reagan and Bush

Power Plays

How to Negotiate, Persuade, and Finesse Your Way to Success in Any Situation

ROBERT MAYER

TIMES BUSINESS

RANDOM HOUSE

Dedicated with love
to the memory of Anne and Franc Mayer
Mom and Dad, I miss you so

and to my wife,
Bev, for more reasons than I can count

ACKNOWLEDGMENTS

From when we first spoke, Karl Weber of Random House referred to *Power Plays* as "our book." Karl, thank you for sharing my enthusiasm and vision.

Thanks to Beverly Pennacchini for her insightful editing in the book's early stages.

CONTENTS

PART III Hard Bargain: Winning When the Score Is Kept in Dollars

PART IV The Deal-Maker's Playbook: Low-Impact, High-Yield Tips, Tricks, and Tactics

INTRODUCTION

So You Want to Tilt the Playing Field

Some will say that this book is a primer on how to be manipulative.

More importantly, others will say this is a book about how not to be manipulated.

The fancy footwork and magic moves for outgunning, outmaneuvering, and outnegotiating the other person are all here. So are techniques for developing life skills that will dramatically enhance your chances of professional success and personal satisfaction.

Life today is highly competitive. More than ever, the name of the game is *results*.

Authors, whether they be academicians or pin-stripe guerrillas, have responded in kind:

There are *hard-bargain* books. But life is difficult and demanding enough, without having to spend your days browbeating or bulldozing someone else to get the results you want.

There are *soft-touch* books. But if you focus primarily on cooperation, you may be exploited in the process.

A one-dimensional approach just doesn't cut it in today's supercharged business environment.

Today's super negotiator is a problem solver who seeks hard-bargain results while using a soft touch.

Part 1, *Soft Touch: Finessing, Influencing, and Persuading Others,* is about getting things to go your way more easily more often. This part *is not* about being a "softie." It *is* about how to read people, how to influence their decisions, and how to deal with their resistance while winning their cooperation and support. It *is* about finesse, the art of the velvet glove.

Part II, *Trouble Shooting: Settling for More,* is about what works—and what doesn't—when you are up against a stone wall . . . or when your ideas are being rejected . . . or when you are confronted with hostility and anger. It will teach you how to be an uncompromising compromiser. How to finesse people who would rather be right than reasonable and stand up to people you can't stand.

Part III, *Hard Bargain: Winning When the Score Is Kept In Dollars,* explores the art and psychology of the rough and tumble—terms, price, conditions. Here is the iron fist for those times when you need to become a "take no prisoners" opportunist.

Part IV, *The Deal-Maker's Playbook: Low-Impact, High-Yield Tips, Tricks, and Tactics.* It's not enough to know *how* to negotiate; you must also know *what* to negotiate. So here it is. Real world deal-making without chiseling, offending, or embarrassing anyone—including yourself. You'll find step-by-step "how-tos" and "what-tos" for 36 common negotiating situations—everything from buying a car to leasing an apartment. From finessing an increase in salary to influencing the outcome of a contested divorce. From going toe-to-toe with the IRS—or an insurance claims adjuster, or someone who owes you money—to how to ace a job interview, buy a franchise, or negotiate your way out of debt.

This book is a compendium of possibilities.

Many of the possibilities have been drawn from recent advances in the fields of psychology, linguistics, trial advocacy, sales, and management communications. They represent the cutting edge of the art of performance.

Other possibilities are as old as the teachings of Buddha, Zoroaster, and Confucius.

There are also possibilities of my own—the result of thirty years in the trenches as a transactional lawyer representing thousands of clients, both big (foreign government agencies and megacorporations) and small, famous (some of the world's best-known actors, authors, and athletes), and infamous, negotiating deals on everything from amphitheaters to Zero aircraft.

And then there are the tricks, the possibilities I picked up from studying the world's master dealmakers—the street and bazaar merchants of Bombay, Cairo, Istanbul, and Shanghai.

All are possibilities, because the same problem may call for different answers at different times, depending on who or what is involved. Human behavior can't be reduced to recipe cards. There is no one-size-fits-all approach.

Possibilities are collectively referred to as "persuasive principles" or "negotiating principles." Many could just as easily have been labeled "leadership principles" or "conflict management principles," because they affect behavior. The same concepts that will give you a competitive advantage in business can be used to help you get along better with your family, friends, and neighbors.

The choice is yours. It's all here—everything you need to know to be an impresario of influence or just one hell of a better negotiator.

■ ■ ■

Tom, an investment firm manager, was looking for a college student to work for him during summer vacation. My son, Steve, was looking for summer employment in finance. The match was made.

"You know, Bob," Tom told me, "Steve is coming here to learn about things like index arbitrage and option contracts. But you and I both know that learning about those things is not nearly as important as the *real* lesson that can be learned here. All of my people are bright, industrious, capable, and well informed. Yet, somehow, a handful of them are making fortunes while others are 60ish junior executives just surviving. If Steve can understand why that is, then this will be the most valuable summer of his life."

We all know people like Tom's *survivors*—people who are talented, personable, and reasonably successful at what they attempt. We also know other people who, although neither more talented nor more personable, always seem to make things happen. They are the power people, deal doers—the *winners*.

More often than not, the big difference between the winners, the survivors, and the losers is the way they interact with other people. This book's *relationship strategies* can go to work for you immediately, connecting you more persuasively and effectively with people in every relationship and every situation.

PART I

SOFT TOUCH
Finessing, Influencing, and Persuading Others

1

WINNING IS A MINDSET
The Great Wallenda Effect

Being at the top of your game begins with seeding your psyche.

Being a winner is not what you *do* but what you *are*. By *being*, you will *become*.

A loser will dwell on failure. A winner will visualize attainment. By internalizing success, you develop a winning mindset. With a winning mindset, you will act and react with a *winning reflex*.

A winner knows that having a victim's mentality is self-defeating behavior. It will portend rejection or victimization. The self-assured person expects to succeed—and does.

Sound trite? No question about it. Nor is there any question that winning is a head game. For superior results, you have to *expect* and *get* the best from yourself.

Karl Wallenda, the greatest of the Great Wallendas, was the finest high-wire aerialist of all time. Failure was beyond Karl Wallenda's contemplation. He spoke of failure for the first time only weeks before plummeting to his death from a slender cable suspended between two resort hotels. The dramatic correlation between one's confidence and one's performance is now referred to by psychologists as the "Wallenda effect."

Winning is being willing to *take risks*.

3

Does taking risks mean setting the goal of buying half of Rodeo Drive for no money down? Or better yet, becoming general manager of the universe?

No. It means mentally going the extra distance. It is *stretch programming* your mind with can-do goals. You can't steal second base and still keep one foot on first.

Winning means you must be willing to *try*—

To *test*—

To *move on* with it.

The young comedian playing to a backyard audience of my friends knew he had bombed. He'd gotten no laughs, few chuckles. After considerable coaxing, he reluctantly took my check. That was then. Now, Bob Saget is the first television star to ever have two concurrently running hit TV shows: *Full House* and *America's Funniest Home Videos.*

Winning is learning to *tolerate mistakes* you may make along the way.

There are people who can instruct you how to build your body, train a dog, or close more deals. They can give you pointers on how to be more effective in what you do. But to be a winner you have to *think* and *believe* that you are a winner, and what goes on in your head is a do-it-yourself project.

Winning begins with your inner self.

MEET LANCER

lancer

The secrets of how to influence others—the persuasion progression—are contained in the acronym l-a-n-c-e-r.

linkage
alignment
needs
control
evaluation
reading

2

LINKAGE
The Stealth Factor

Dancer

Shaping tone and mood, personalizing, establishing rapport, developing a positive aura, creating involvement, and causing the other person to identify with you—all of these create *linkage:* a critical personal interfacing that makes it possible for you to lead and persuade.

To have the charisma of a super negotiator, there are seven secrets you absolutely must know about.

1. Engage in Cerebral Foreplay

In years past, I looked to the Far East. Principles that Lao-tse preached to his followers in China's Valley of the Han three hundred years before the birth of Christ were used to explain the concept of linkage. Fortune-cookie wisdom reinforced this theme: "A man whose face is without a smile should never open a shop." "He who goes softly goes far."

Taking a more contemporary approach, I now call on the teachings of a modern sage—sex expert Dr. Ruth Westheimer.

Doctor Ruth views the mind as an erogenous zone: "The only real aphrodisiac is the one between your ears." Great lovers know that *how* it is done is as important as *what* is done.

6

Cerebral foreplay is an integral part of the persuasion process. It is the soft-touch shaping of how the other person feels about you. People will react to the way you act. Good feelings yield good deals. Agreements are made not just on the basis of reason and facts but on whether the deal *feels right*.

Negotiate Friendly. Your approach should be first as a person, then as a negotiator. View the other person as a challenge, an opponent, rather than an adversarial enemy.

As our fax/e-mail/cellular telephone world becomes more uniformly high-tech, a *soft touch* will make the competitive difference. Treating the other side to a $12 lunch today may be a more persuasive tactic than making a $12,000 concession tomorrow.

Here's an example from a moment of business crisis and tragedy.

It was the tender side of the "Delta Plan." "A state-of-the-art blueprint . . . to follow in the aftermath of a disaster," reported *The Wall Street Journal*.

"Within hours [of a Texas jet crash in which 137 people died], Delta had dispatched employees to be with every [victim's] family." Delta's strategy was to treat "the victims and their families with all the compassion a corporation can muster."

The result?

"Later, many victims found it difficult to sue a friend. This early bonding . . . was part of Delta's claims-control strategy. And it has been extraordinarily effective."

2. Hit the Ground Walking

Underwhelm Your Opponent. More often than not, you will want to demonstrate that a low-key style is the order of the day. Relaxed people will be less resistant to you and your ideas.

Practice tip: People who are sitting down are more easily persuaded than people who are standing up.

Lighten Up. The people you want to influence will be defensive or receptive, depending on how they read you. Schmooze for a while about the weather, the traffic, Sunday's ball game, the trivia question you missed last night, some mutual acquaintance. Accept or offer a cup of coffee. Tell a joke. Icebreakers shape a persuasive climate.

To look "warm and approachable," businesspeople of both sexes should, according to the *Los Angeles Times,* wear pastel rather than white shirts and should "discard their three-piece suits and tie shoes for less formal blazers and footwear." It also helps if they "put aside their sleek eel-skin briefcases and carry well-scuffed ones."

3. Personalize the Process

Have you noticed that negotiations conducted over a shorter period of time are always more competitive? They are. The reason? The negotiators are less able to *humanize* the other side through personalization techniques.

Personalizing means speaking for yourself rather than your company. Which is more persuasive? "*Karen,* I would like to tell *you* about a deal *I* can make for *you*" or "*Acme* has a proposal that *it* would like to make to *Apex.*"

Professional communicators personalize constantly. Television news team members call each other by their first names more than we mere mortals do. Their highly personalized dialogue—"Fine reporting, Mary Ann." "What has happened in sports today, Ted?" "Is it going to rain tomorrow, Pete?"—gives viewers a sense of ease and commitment. All news shows are pretty much the same in format and content. We tend to choose *our* team by how we *feel* about its players.

Lee Iacocca didn't appear in Chrysler television commercials because of his charisma or stage presence. He spoke for the corporation because marketing experts wanted Chrysler to personalize its outreach to potential customers.

A Lesson from Jerry's Kids. The annual Jerry Lewis muscular dystrophy telethon doesn't cut it as even mediocre entertainment. Its unrivaled success is repeated year after year because the telethon's outreach and cause have been super *personalized.* Our telephone pledges are not to a charity that is as faceless as Standard Oil but to Jerry himself. When "Jerry's kids" are introduced to us on television, we relate to flesh-and-blood victims of the disease rather than statistical data or nameless photos.

The personalizing strategy works in reverse, too. T. Reynolds, an IRS agent, had maneuvered one of my clients into a full-court press. Our conversations had always been cordial, but with a standoffish "Mr. Mayer"/"Mr. Reynolds" sort of way. When I finally had occasion to send him a letter of agreement, I asked his first name. "Just address the letter to T. Reynolds," he replied. Internal Revenue agents use only a first-name initial on business cards and correspondence. When they speak, it is for "the Department" or "the Service" rather than for themselves. Similarly, in most jurisdictions, police officers do not have their first names on their ID tags.

Their strategy is *depersonalization*. The more detached the officers or agents, the less likely they are to be guided by their emotions and the more likely they are to do their job "by the book."

4. Establish Rapport

Trust and credibility are essential ingredients of the persuasion progression. Without these ingredients, negotiating would be nothing more than discussion, because commitment would always be in doubt. No wonder it is common to hear businesspeople talk of needing a *high comfort level* with the folks on the other side.

Where did your dentist go to school? How did he or she rank in dental class?

A full 50 percent of all practicing dentists were in the bottom half of their graduating classes, but patients concern themselves instead with whether they like the dentist *as a person* well enough to let that person put a high-speed drill into their mouth.

Trust and credibility are established through reputation and expertise, but most often through rapport. The other person is more likely to be persuaded if he or she likes you. People keep going back to the same barber, accountant, dentist, or lawyer because they like that person.

People will like you if you are sincerely interested in them and their problems. The fellow with problems at the office will give those problems a higher priority than a famine in Somalia, a volcanic eruption in Colombia, or an earthquake in Kobe, Japan. Why? Because those problems at the office are *his* problems.

Give other people a sense of genuine self-importance and they cannot help but like you. Talk to people about themselves and what they are interested in and they will listen for hours, and you will be liked for having picked such interesting subject matter.

Acknowledge people who have done something that is genuinely worthy of accolade. Better yet, acknowledge their achievement in the presence of someone who knows them.

Use your business letters to express interest in some nonbusiness aspect of the addressee's life. How did he or she enjoy the well-earned vacation or the daughter's graduation or the home games of the division playoffs? Pick up the telephone now and then and keep the dialogue on a strictly personal level by not uttering a single word of business.

Don't overdo. Putting on your negotiating personality doesn't mean making the other person your new best friend. It means not allowing that person to be a stranger.

Never, *never* be a "junk bonding" phony. "He complimented me on my looks and my intelligence," testified a Prudential Bache vice president who, after being wined and dined and showered with flowers, made a $2 million loan to Barry Minkow, the kingpin of ZZZZ Best carpet cleaning. Two days later, the price of ZZZZ Best stock "was falling through the floor."

Minkow, who was trying to negotiate a loan from a client, met with me on several occasions. Trying to make me his new best friend, Minkow told me that he thought so much of my work that, for the next deal, he would like to use me as his lawyer. No wonder Minkow was once lauded by President Reagan for his "entrepreneurial vision."

Tactical rapport is understanding that your problems and needs are usually both boring and of little consequence to the other person, their own problems and needs, however, are of paramount importance. As Mel Brooks puts it, "Tragedy is if *I* get a hangnail. Comedy is if *you* slip on a banana peel and die."

Sorry. When it comes to establishing rapport, only your mother really cares about how wonderful your new minivan is—or how much you enjoyed the authentic luau you went to in Kona—or how exhausted you are from all those holiday parties.

5. Create a Positive Aura

Persuasion is a function of attitude. Positive attitudes produce positive results; negative attitudes produce hostility.

A positive attitude will be reflected in your approach. Your voice, demeanor, and attentiveness should communicate concern, empathy, understanding, and a desire to work side-by-side rather than toe-to-toe.

Before you can control others, you have to be able to control yourself. Sure, it's tough to be positive when your opponent is a sour, cantankerous deal-crippler. Sure, it would be self-satisfying to tell an irascible and abusive ass to take his proposal and shove it up his briefcase. But is losing the deal a luxury you can afford? Is being negative going to maximize your chance of success?

Do people tell you that your outspokenness and candor are "refreshing"? That's what they told me. In fact, I was so busy being "refreshing" that I failed to appreciate that the difference between an honest but negative comment and *applied people sense* is called "tact."

In personal relationships, occasional outbursts of aggression or an unkind word will penalize you a few strokes. They are not terminal. The relationship can be patched up at another time and the game resumed.

In a business relationship, the penalty is the game. You do not have the luxury of being able to react rather than act.

Be true to your commitments. Pay attention to the little things; through them, other people read you. If you are not punctual in keeping appointments, are remiss about returning phone calls, or don't send the letter you promised would be in tonight's mail, you are transmitting a negative message that you cannot be relied on to carry out your end of a bargain.

6. Create Involvement

A Shirt Story. Macy's is Macy's. Neiman-Marcus is something altogether different. Macy's hangs most of its sport shirts on racks. Neiman-Marcus, true to its upscale image, displays its shirts in fingerprint-free glass showcases.

I confess. On a number of occasions I have purchased a Neiman-Marcus shirt even though I knew it really wasn't right for me. I did so because I was either too embarrassed or too cowardly to let down the saleslady who was so nice about refolding and repinning the five other shirts that didn't fit. I knew she was being paid for her exemplary effort but somehow, because of her *involvement,* I felt compelled to buy at least one shirt even though it wasn't a GQ perfect fit. To buy nothing would have been a rejection of a very nice person rather than a rejection of Neiman-Marcus inventory.

A Shaggy Dog Story. We wanted to buy a family dog. The cheapest part of owning a dog is the purchase price. I decided that if I was going to go through weeks of training and years of expense, I might as well get a best friend with some status. And so I was off to buy a Soft-Coated Wheaton Terrier.

I telephoned the local Wheaton guru and was told that, "if approved," I would be number thirty-three on an "adoption" list that several Los Angeles breeders drew from as litters were born. I could expect a call in about seven months.

"Seven months!!"

In a calm voice, the guru whispered that actor Henry Winkler was now number six on the list. If anybody would get "cuts" in line it would most certainly be the Fonz.

Being status dogs, Wheatons are not available for viewing in mall pet shops which are reserved for spaniels, collies, labs, poodles, and other species of lesser status. So, a week later, I again telephoned the guru and explained that my kids had never seen a Wheaton. Could I show them her dogs so that they could share my anticipation and excitement?

On Sunday afternoon, the family descended on her. We admired her house. We admired her kids. Most of all, we admired her dogs. I had a bouquet of flowers delivered afterward to thank her for being so kind.

A week later I got the call: a Wheaton puppy was available.

Time flies but it isn't super-charged. Congratulations were in order! I was now Number One!

Why?

Because I was no longer a statistic. I was a real, honest-to-goodness person who had taken the quantum leap from being "number thirty-three" to being "Bob." My relationship had changed through *tactical involvement.* Poor Henry Winkler, just a face on television, had slipped to number seven in the Wheaton standings.

There you have it: the pitfalls of modern-day shirt shopping and a shaggy dog story to boot. All to demonstrate how critical it is to get the other person involved with you and your situation. To not allow yourself to be a situation in the abstract.

To create interaction by asking for the other person's advice, help, assistance, suggestions, opinions, or anything else which causes them to become involved in the scenario being played out.

7. Establish Identification

As our lives become more harried and complex, we rely more and more on our gut feelings and intuition. How you *feel* about people is what you *believe* about them.

We are usually comfortable doing business with people with whom we can *identify.* We agree more readily with them and tend to be more receptive to their suggestions and ideas.

- For Cary Grant, a lack of identification barred him from appearing in commercials. "Would you believe we couldn't find a single company in America that wanted him?" reported a specialist in matching celebrities with advertisers. "Nobody identified with Cary Grant. He was too erudite, too sophisticated."

  Your partiality toward an entertainer is largely based on being able to identify with that person. Mel Gibson is richer and handsomer than you, Goldie Hawn is cuter and more effervescent. But even though they are larger than life, you can *relate* to them in a way that wasn't possible with Cary Grant. Mel Gibson and Goldie Hawn are more real than Cary Grant, more the way you could imagine yourself being. Mel and Goldie project a "call-me-by-my-first-name" way with which you can identify.

- For Nancy Kerrigan, the elements for identification were all there. She is beautiful. Her mother is legally blind. Her rival, Tonya Harding, was implicated in a plot to destroy Nancy's knee and career. No wonder one of the largest television audiences ever tuned in to the winter Olympics to cheer her to victory.

  But then it happened. After finishing a too-close-to-call second to 16-year-old orphan Oksana Baiul, the world eavesdropped on Nancy's sore-loser remarks about the Ukrainian gold medalist's cosmetics.

  A few days later, after the announcement of a multimillion-dollar Disney deal, eavesdropping television cameras picked up Nancy's complaining about having to ride with Mickey Mouse in a Walt Disney World parade arranged in her honor: "This is so corny. This is so dumb." Suddenly, the millions who had adored her weren't so sure they wanted to be like Nancy Kerrigan.

- For Muhammad Ali, the power of identification was in his bragging that he was the Greatest with a flair and bravado that showed he was not taking himself all that seriously.

- For Ronald Reagan, the power of identification was in his sweeping the country to achieve the largest landslide ever tallied by a nonincumbent presidential candidate. Many people who voted for President Reagan were more in tune with Walter ("Fritz") Mondale's politics. They agreed with Mondale but identified with Ronald Reagan because they *liked* him.

- For Reverend Jim Jones, the power of identification was in being able to lead nine hundred and eleven of his faithful Jonestown,

Guyana, followers into mass suicide by simply asking them over a loudspeaker to drink cyanide-spiked Kool Aid. His mind-boggling abuse of power was possible because his followers mistakenly believed he was concerned and cared for them.

■ ■ ■

We will identify with another person if that person seems to care about our needs, wants to help us solve our problems, seems to have the ability to make things come out right, and is like us as we are now and at the same time resembles how we would like to be.

Dancer

Linkage: People want to do business with people whom they like and with whom they feel comfortable. Linkage strategies are designed to humanize negotiations, bolster credibility, create a negotiating comfort zone, and make the other person more receptive to you and your ideas.

3

ALIGNMENT
Soar Points

Being persuasive does not mean standing up to another person nor does it mean countering with a force of your own. It means moving with and using the other person's energy. It means *aligning* yourself with—rather than resisting—that energy.

Once a crucial personal interface has been established, take advantage of it and build on it with the *soar points* in this chapter. *Soar points* are alignment tricks that are neither resistive nor combative but which advance the persuasion progression by reinforcing linkage, preventing resistance, harnessing the other person's energy, and shaping a pattern of agreement.

Here are twenty-four soar points that will make a major difference in your effectiveness in dealing with people.

Reinforcing Linkage

1. Don't complain or sulk. *You are unfair and unreasonable, you are not dependable* and similar utterances are guaranteed to curdle even the sweetest deal.

2. Don't look back. People look back only to criticize. Your goal is an agreement, not an admission or apology. If you talk about

15

who did what to whom, you are sabotaging any chance of an understanding.

3. Avoid absolutes like *always* and *never*. They beg for rebuttal. Rarely will anyone *always* or *never* do a given thing.

4. Is there a major negative drawback in what you want to propose? You may have a professional, legal, or moral duty to mention it. Besides, even a morocco-bound, gilt-edged, hand-tooled obligation lacks commitment if it has been unwillingly created.

5. Pointing out *selected* negatives in what you have to suggest stimulates confidence and increases rapport. Without being told, everyone knows that next year's model will be an improved version, that styles are not a constant, and that the discounter on the other side of town charges less. But a clothier who tells you that the suit you are trying on will never fit properly no matter how much the tailor alters it will earn your confidence for life.

Preventing Resistance

6. Emphasize the aspects of your proposal that the other person seems to like. By stressing spheres of compatibility, you will encounter less resistance to your ideas and less likelihood that conflict will dominate the negotiations.

7. A radio advertiser claims that they can give you the "verbal advantage" in dealing with people because a "powerful vocabulary gives a powerful impression." But when rapport is important, talking down to the other side doesn't work. Nor does pontificating. Nor does having a holier-than-thou attitude. Nor does demonstrating what you perceive as your intellectual superiority. What does work is speaking to the level of the person you wish to influence.

8. Create hypothetical experiences. *Suppose we were to . . .* or *Let's assume . . .* hypothetical experiences cause involvement, and involvement is the persuasive forerunner to change.

9. Act in a self-assured manner. Don't be defensive and don't apologize for your requests. Statements like *I really don't like*

asking you to do this but . . . forecast and prompt a negative response. Projecting weakness encourages the other side to become more forceful and domineering.

10. Avoid judging other persons' actions or thoughts. Judgmental words—*wrong, stupid, bad, crazy, foolhardy,* or *ill informed*—promote defensiveness and resistance.

Harnessing the Other Person's Energy

11. Let the other person know that their feelings and thoughts are as important as yours. Go a step further and sincerely solicit their counsel and input, making the other person part of a collective nonadversarial effort. Give incoming suggestions the status and dignity of a viable alternative; never summarily reject them. Maybe they can be improved on, to emerge as real possibilities.

12. Build on the other person's words using *their* vocabulary. Make *their* thoughts and words the bridges to meaningful negotiations. A pro will cross these bridges. An amateur will burn them, putting up walls in their place.

13. Suggest scrutiny of your ideas. Allow them to be tested by fair and logical examination. *What do you think of this idea? Do you see anything wrong with this possibility?* Ask how your suggestions can be altered to be more compatible. Acknowledge that you understand a critical comment, but do not take the criticism personally, no matter how pointed it may be.

14. Don't maneuver the other person into a corner by pointing out discrepancies and showing them to be a liar. To do so is an invitation to fight. Instead, go to the pros' script: *You've said X and you've said Y. They are at odds with each other. How can we resolve these inconsistencies?*

Shaping a Pattern of Agreement

15. Be persuasive one on one. Trying to persuade more than one person at a time only brings additional egos, roles, and needs into the game.

16. An approach that moves from agreement to agreement will produce better results than an approach that moves from conflict to agreement.

17. If you cannot agree on specific major issues, then seek an agreement in principle that can be a bridge to further discussion.

18. Express your positions as *feelings*. Expressed *feelings* are irrefutable. A statement that *Your price is not fair* is attack-provoking. It rejects the seller's notion of worth. *I don't feel the price is fair,* instead of asserting a position, relates *feelings* that the price is unfair. How can anyone find fault with feelings? If I tell you I *feel* happy, you cannot tell me I am wrong. If I tell you I *feel* sad, you cannot correct me. If I *feel* that your price is not fair, how can you tell me that those are not my feelings?

19. When you must take a poke at a problem, offset it with a pat on the back. *Sandwiching,* a tactic of praise followed by criticism followed by praise, is so commonly used as a technique that most people will feel manipulated by its use. Starting with criticism followed by praise reinforces linkage by making the other person feel you are part of the same team. People liking the *pats* will do everything possible to eliminate the *pokes.*

20. Avoid hype that only builds false hope. Be conservative in your projections. Surpass those conservative projections, and you become a star. Fall short of an optimistic forecast and you will be called *unreliable* on a good day and *defendant* on a bad one.

21. General praise ("Good presentation, Jan") comes across as an expression of good manners. Specific praise ("Jan, I was particularly impressed with the way your presentation compared . . .") reinforces linkage because it sounds less manipulative and more believable.

22. Asking "What is your problem?" weakens linkage by making the other person feel inadequate or lacking.

23. It is rare that someone will admit that they were being unreasonable. Asking "Why can't you be reasonable?" is a question which will weaken linkage and invite conflict.

24. A linkage rule of thumb: If saying it will make you feel good, then don't say it unless it will make the other person also feel good.

lancer

Alignment: To capture an elephant in the web of a spider, you must use the energy of the elephant. In the persuasion progression, alignment techniques play against and harness the other person's energy while establishing a pattern of agreement.

4

NEEDS
Making Your Ideas Irresistible

It is only after I have read, identified, and stimulated your *needs* that I will be able to energize our discussions while irresistibly presenting my ideas to you.

Think about the choices you make:

- Is your car the cheapest automobile that you could find?
- Is your blue sweater the least expensive blue sweater sold in the mall?
- Do you get your haircuts only at a shop that offers the best deal?

Your answers are "no" because price is only one factor in how we make choices.

Although it was disguised as a cable television program, it was really one of those half-hour long infomercials for a self-improvement videocassette. Viewers would dramatically increase their persuasive abilities by calling the toll-free number and ordering the secrets of how to push the other person's "motivator buttons."

Motivator buttons???

If you ever took Anatomy 1-A or peeked when you were in the shower, you know that none of God's children has these features. What then are we talking about?

20

Other people's *needs* are their motivator buttons.

The attributes of your proposal that best satisfy other people's needs—your proposal's *sweet spots*—are the "push."

Advertising agencies are in the motivator button-pushing business. They get paid to tell us how their clients' products or services will satisfy our needs. Masters of manipulation, like the infamous Joe Hunt, founder of the Billionaire Boys Club, who are expert at pushing motivation buttons know that when we are satisfying our needs we are guided by our emotions rather than our reason.

Although not all people behave the same way in the same situation, certain motivator buttons are common to us all. Here are four of the most important.

1. A Sense of Goal Attainment

Here's the goal attainment story in "sable black" and "cotillion white."

General Motors, knowing that a Cadillac must be more than transportation if it is to command top dollar, includes among its DeVille colors gossamer blue, autumn maple, chamois, and silver frost. Sounds pretty luxurious.

On the other hand, Chevrolet, which has a more functional image, has a very similar palette without the uptown names: light blue metallic, maroon metallic, yellow beige, and silver metallic.

To persuade a customer to shell out the bigger bucks, the Cadillac dealer must focus on those motivator buttons that a Cadillac pushes best. For some purchasers, a Cadillac's ability to satisfy the need for self-actualization—personal goal attainment—justifies its price.

Growing up, I lived on the same street as Jake, a retired butcher shop owner. Jake seemed to spend most of his waking hours waxing the paint and polishing the acres of chrome on his black 1953 Cadillac. When Jake needed to go somewhere, he would take his old Plymouth. The neighbors speculated that Jake just didn't want to get the black Caddy dirty or dinged. I often wondered why Jake would buy such an impressive car and then let it sit in his driveway. Today, I understand what was so curious to me then.

For years, Cadillac marketing reminded Jake (and us) that "You know you have arrived when you arrive in a Cadillac." Cadillac wants its cars to be perceived as something more than mere status. A Cadillac is to be perceived as *the* Lifetime Achievement Award you (or Jake) present to yourself.

The need for a sense of goal attainment is the need for self-actualization: to be able to accomplish the big things we set out to do in life and the smaller things we set out to do in negotiations.

2. A Sense of Belonging

"On big-city playgrounds, the athletic shoe of choice is currently the Nike Air," reported *The Wall Street Journal*. "Reebok, hoping to regain lost ground, is fighting back . . . giving away samples of its newly designed shoes to a 'core' group of trend setters."

Reebok knew that kids wanting to emulate their peers would flock back to Reebok. The kids' need for belonging was there all along, but Reebok created a new way of satisfying that need. Even as adults, we don't outgrow our need for a sense of belonging.

The need for a sense of belonging is the need to be accepted by our peers.

3. A Sense of Security

As a devoted fan of the television series *Cagney and Lacey*, for years I watched the Laceys struggle to make ends meet. Good fortune was finally theirs. An entire episode was devoted to the Laceys' bickering about how Harvey's profits from the long-sought "big job" should be used.

Mary Beth was practical. She was all for saving the money for a rainy day. Harvey? He was enticed by big-ticket luxury items and the accoutrements of the grand life. The Laceys were fighting because of their dramatically differing personal needs.

Was Mary Beth security-oriented because of years of insecurity had created an obsessive need for accumulating and preserving money?

Was Harvey's need for status and a feeling of personal worth overshadowing his need for financial stability?

What was important to Harvey would have been meaningless to Mary Beth. To predict and persuasively shape Mary Beth's behavior—to push her motivator button—you would have had to read her individual and compelling personal need for security, and speak directly to that need.

A "benefit" that doesn't correspond to a need is not a benefit at all.

The need for a sense of security is the need for stability, predictability, and safety: a deal that "feels right," a retirement program, job tenure, money in the bank, insurance, an employment contract.

4. A Sense of Self-Esteem

Imagine that you are part of a consumer panel and are looking at watches. Here are two candidates for your consideration:

- Watch A is enclosed in a lightweight, slim, waterproof resin case. This quartz watch has state-of-the-art accuracy, a stopwatch, an alarm, a lighted display, and a calendar. You can purchase this watch for $35.

- Watch B is enclosed in a heavy, stainless steel, waterproof case. This watch tells the date and the time. Because it is a self-winding mechanical timepiece, it is less accurate than Watch A. You can purchase this watch for $1,150.

Which watch would you select?

As you have probably already guessed, Watch A is picked from any number of popular and inexpensive watches that are available just about everywhere.

Watch B is a Rolex Oyster Perpetual Date Chronometer.

If you are buying an accurate timepiece, then objectively Watch A is the appropriate choice, hands down. A Rolex *is* handcrafted and takes months to create, but, according to a leading Rodeo Drive jeweler, the movement is "obsolete—it's not quartz. There is a fluctuation of two to three minutes a month—if you are lucky. But it's *the* watch."

Style? The Rolex has a number of worthy, less expensive imitators.

Investment? Stainless steel is not a precious metal, and a watch is not really an investment. (It depreciates in value and pays no dividends or interest.)

Comfort? Other watches are stressing that it's in to be thin, but a Rolex is so bulky that custom shirtmakers know to leave an extra half-inch of fabric in the Rolex owner's left cuff.

Look at the Rolex advertising. What does it tell you? Rolex doesn't proclaim itself a status symbol. Instead, it tells you that Rolex watches are worn by the well-known. By the bold. By the adventurous and athletic people with whom we would all like to identify. Our self-esteem is enhanced through identification and emulation.

If a Rolex were just a timepiece, it would have gone the way of the slide rule—another example of obsolete technology.

Our sense of how we appear to others is *status*. How we appear to ourselves is *self-esteem*. A Rolex buyer's need is not the need to own a timepiece. It is the need to own a "feeling better about yourself" piece.

The need for a sense of self-esteem is the need for a feeling of competency and personal worth, a need for status, a need to be recognized and appreciated.

Party Time

You are a caterer and have been negotiating a contract for a large corporation's annual dinner party. The price and menu have both been modified several times. Yesterday, the customer told you, "There is fierce competition for the job and you must improve your price."

Should you:

- Continue to negotiate?

- Hold firm?

- Request verification of the competition's prices?

- Try some other tack?

The best answer: find out what your customer likes about your company and your proposal. These are your client's motivator buttons—the needs that you are able to satisfy better than your competition.

The chances are that the reliability of your company, or the appearance and demeanor of your white-gloved food-service personnel, or your incredible hot hors d'oeuvres will be much more important than a modest price differential. Besides, if you allow price to be the sole basis of persuasion, the most persuasive caterer in town will always be the one with the lowest price.

Winning the contract depends on understanding why this customer has chosen to negotiate with *you*, bypassing all those other caterers in the yellow pages.

Another situation: You own a small lodge in Montana and are expecting a telephone call from a movie production company asking you to quote your "best price" for providing accommodations for a cast and crew for several months while they are on location.

Would you be best advised to:

- Quote high?

- Quote low?

- Quote in between?

- Quote nothing at all?

Your best bet would be to quote nothing at all. Even though you may not need additional information, tell your caller that you want to get much more information regarding your prospective guests' specific needs.

By understanding the production company's needs—its motivator buttons—rather than its requests, you will be in a position to persuade rather than just bid.

lancer

Needs: In the quest to satisfy our needs, we are guided by emotion rather than reason. This quest for satisfaction energizes the persuasive process. The art of influence is the art of stimulating, reading, and then satisfying other people's conscious or unconscious urges for feelings of goal attainment, belonging, security, and self-esteem.

5

CONTROL
How to Listen so People Will Talk and Talk so People Will Listen

There is a quantum difference between the power of speech and the power of persuasion. Speaking is about giving out information. Persuasion is about getting through. It is about *control*. It is about engineering consent.

The persuasion progression is advanced not by monopolizing a conversation but by controlling it. How and where you make your shot will predetermine how it's returned by the other player.

Actions control reactions.

When and how a suggestion is made or a question is asked will determine the other person's response.

Persuasive Listening

As a *persuasive listener,* you reaffirm and galvanize alignment by becoming the speaker's advocate and adding something new and positive to the speaker's argument.

26

Handing the speaker ammunition will cause him to look at you not as an enemy but as a collaborator in a common mission. You can never be faulted for trying to understand the speaker's position, and you will be credited for helping to improve it.

Speaker: Hey, I am so jammed up I can't even guess when your order will be finished.

Listener: I understand that you are backlogged and cannot commit to a completion date. With the Labor Day weekend coming up, you will be even further behind schedule.

By bringing up the Labor Day holiday, you have purposefully strengthened the speaker's case. Rather than resisting, you have aligned yourself with the speaker through agreement. Later, with rapport established, you will be in a better tactical position to point out the failures, weaknesses, and problems associated with the speaker's position.

Persuasive listening is occasionally, *but infrequently interrupting to let the speaker know you are tracking the conversation.* Limit these unobtrusive interruptions to inquiries that *clarify* what is being said or briefly *acknowledge* that what is being said is understood although not necessarily agreed to.

Persuasive listening is helping the speaker clarify his or her ideas by repeating back or paraphrasing from the speaker's perspective what has been said. *I think I understand what you are saying, but I want to make sure I know what you mean* . . . .

Persuasive listening is knowing that there is a difference between listening and concerned listening.

Television interviewer Gary Collins's guest, a well-known celeb-hairdresser, was discussing why women tell their most intimate secrets to their hairdressers. Women open up and reveal all because their hairdressers show *special concern*—achieved, he explained, by making the customers more beautiful as they speak.

A prominent UCLA professor of medicine counsels his students to show special concern by sitting at the head of the patient's bed and touching them while listening. By standing, or sitting at the foot of the bed, the physician appears less concerned and more positioned to exit than to hear.

Working without a desk, former talk show host Arsenio Hall hunched on the edge of his chair when he visited with guests. This physical demonstration of special concern was Arsenio's method of creating instant intimacy with his celebrity interviewees.

Persuasive listening is listening out loud. It is active listening. A pro, whether a physician, hairdresser, or television talk show host, knows that there must also be a showing of special concern, an indication that you want to connect because you care about the other person's point of view and feelings.

Talking out loud is a habit. Listening out loud is an art.

On-Ramping

It's still rude and must be the exception, not the rule, but sometimes you just have to interrupt the other person. Maybe it's to keep a meeting from going into overtime or to derail a runaway mouth. No one likes *hear-to-eternity* rambling that turns five minutes of information into a dissertation best timed with a calendar.

Tell someone to "get to the point!" and they will respond "I'm getting to the point!!"

Television interviewers are taught that the best way to interrupt is through the alignment tactic of agreeing with what the speaker is saying. A polite *yes* or *absolutely* is a *verbal on-ramp* into the ongoing monologue. *On-ramping* should be used only to *sharpen the focus* of a drifting and undirected speaker or to *introduce your point of view*.

Practice tip: Want to introduce your point of view without being defensive or sounding like a buttinsky trying to get in your own four cents? Use a *yes/and* combination instead of the reflex word *but*. "*Yes*, deliveries are running late, *and* the reason is we have a new, more exacting quality control process."

If that doesn't work, you can always resort to a simple "Excuse me" spoken in an agreeable tone of voice.

Questions That Guide and Direct

Conversations are controlled by the *listener* through the use of questions.

Notice the course changes in the following conversation between a show production manager and her costume maker, which I overheard in Las Vegas. While using the costume maker's energy, the manager skillfully guided and directed the dialogue through the use of questions that brought *her* focus and *her* ideas into the conversation.

Manager: Do I understand you correctly when you say *the costumes can't be ready by the 15th because you don't have orange taffeta and because your seamstresses are fully scheduled?*

The manager's question focused the dialogue on a single issue—the availability of taffeta and seamstresses.

Manager: Are you in effect telling me that *if I can get orange taffeta delivered to you by Monday and if your seamstresses work overtime, the costumes can be ready by the 15th?*

The second question directs the costume maker toward the manager's solution: The manager will make sure the taffeta is at the costumer's workshop by Monday, and the seamstresses will work overtime.

The Power of Suggestion

Whether you are a know-it-all or, even worse, a tell-it-all, it's a mistake to always be right.

Hidden suggestions are not communicated as suggestions. Instead, the other person "discovers" an idea in your hidden suggestion and proposes it back to you with an unjustified pride of authorship. At a minimum, hidden suggestions preserve linkage and alignment by keeping you from sounding like the person who has an answer for everything:

- *I don't know what I would do if I were you. I had a customer with a similar situation a few years back and he . . . .* (The customer's solution is the hidden suggestion you are offering.)

- *I read an article the other day and the author thought it would make sense if . . . .* (The author's thought is the hidden suggestion.)

- *Some people think that the wisest thing to do in this market is to . . . .* (The other person should then suggest to you the solution that you said other people are using.)

Being able to introduce a good new idea into a conversation is an art. Unconscious leads and hidden suggestions will not meet the same resistance that a suggestion on the conscious level would encounter.

Channeling

The dessert cart was docking at the table where I was having dinner with business associates.

Our waiter, an exponent of the "life is to be lived" school of indulgence, described in teasing detail the mousses, cremes, and pastries. My real dilemma had to do with Doc Gitnick. For years he has been reminding me that the best dessert is a nice piece of broiled fish. Having a skinny physician can sometimes be a curse.

Not being a group to walk away from temptation, we happily indulged while speculating about what a life it would be if cholesterol and caffeine were essential nutrients.

But wait a minute. Just as the check arrived, we noticed the same waiter bringing fresh boysenberry tarts to another table. Asked why *we* were never offered the tarts, he replied, "We had so few left, that we saved them for those patrons who specifically requested them." The regulars knew to ask. We did not. The waiter's *channeling* stratagem was to communicate a limited menu.

Presenting your proposal in a limited-menu fashion will direct the other person's thinking to your presented choices rather than to other possible alternatives: *It seems to me that there are really only three choices . . . .*

I Heard You Twice the First Time

It's a matter of simple economics: Talk is cheap because the supply is far greater than the demand.

The less you say, the more people will remember. The more concisely you are able to communicate your thoughts, the greater the likelihood you will be able to get a *yes*. If your proposal will take a great deal of time and effort to understand, its chances of being turned down for all the wrong reasons are greatly enhanced.

Think back to those teachers and professors whom you considered great. They were great because they were able to capture and hold your attention while presenting their thoughts. Executives who want to be more effective are being tutored to pepper their speech with action verbs, sensory images, pregnant pauses.

They are being taught that to simply express an idea or situation *is* power.

They are being taught that the rules that got them an A in high school grammar and the rules of breakthrough communicating are not the same.

They are being taught that persuasion is not about what you *tell* the other person—it's about what the other person *hears*.

They are being taught if you haven't struck oil in the first few minutes—*stop boring!*

THE MESSAGE IS . . . YOU!

Think back: Was it a fund raiser, a political candidate, or a membership drive spokesperson—the "when will this be over?" speaker—who left you bored and edgy? The speaker who never ventured away from the lectern. The speaker who glanced back and forth between pre-prepared remarks and the audience. The wooden speaker who spoke in a dry, lifeless monotone.

Imagine: That same speaker is making the same remarks while moving around the room, interacting, and linking with the audience. The speaker is *in touch* through eye contact, facial expressions, and vocal intonation.

Now ask yourself: Which of the two presentations would motivate or move you? Persuade you? Convey commitment, belief, and enthusiasm? Reflect credibility and sincerity? Demonstrate warmth?

Whether your audience is many listeners or only one, a well-crafted argument or proposal is not enough.

Content is what is in the eyes (and ears) of the beholder. Content is a totality made up of word signals (the text of your remarks) and body signals (your demeanor, gestures, pitch and tone of voice, rate of speech, and energy).

Body signals will have a far greater impact on the listener than word signals. *Words* impact the listener's *intellect. Body signals* impact the listener's *emotions* because they reveal not only your doubts, fears, and deceptions, but, more importantly, the kind of person you are. In the persuasion progression, *you are both the messenger and the message.*

Practice tip: Your eyes are the magnets that will cause the listener to connect and stay connected with you.

Prioritization Tactics

Which part of your presentation will be best remembered: the beginning, the middle, or the ending?

People remember only what is simple and meaningful—*and* pushes their motivator buttons. Listeners remember the *first* and *last* parts of a presentation better than the middle. The first part is remembered better than the last. Game control requires *prioritizing* your presentation accordingly.

An Oscar for Best Original Screenplay went to John Patrick Shanley for the movie classic *Moonstruck.* Here is one of its many memorable moments:

Priest: What sins have you to confess?

Loretta (Cher): Twice I took the name of the Lord in vain, once I slept with the brother of my fiance, and once I bounced a check at the liquor store but that was really an accident.

Priest: What was that second thing you said, Loretta?

Please Return Your Mouth to Its Full Upright Position

When do you stop talking?

You stop when you have finally asked the other person for a commitment on the major issues.

Do not repeat yourself.

Do not resell.

Do not rephrase.

You will have an urge to talk—

It is easier to manage sound than silence.

We mistakenly believe that the more we say, the more we influence. But probably nothing you can say will improve the silence. By anxiously sweetening your proposal before there is a response, you are only bidding against yourself.

If the response is a question, keep your answer short and to the point. As empathic as you may feel, don't express your *"I know that it is a difficult choice you have to make"* feelings.

Control: The persuasion progression is advanced by having a winning mindset; establishing linkage; aligning yourself with the other person's energy; pushing motivator buttons; controlling dialogue by guiding the other person to your thoughts through questions and suggestions; controlling yourself by presenting your ideas in a clear, succinct, prioritized manner; and knowing when to stop.

6

EVALUATION
Finders Keepers, Losers Beepers

lancer

Your medium or mode of communication is in and of itself a negotiating tactic.

It's a new age. Telephones are in briefcases, airplanes, cars, and shirt pockets. Telecopiers are becoming household appliances. E-mail is a part of our daily lives. Each communications medium comes with its own built-in implicit message.

Want your proposal to deliver this implicit message: *This is it. Take it or leave it?* Then writing may best serve your purpose. Fax traffic arrives with the implicit message that its text has a special importance and immediacy. Regular mail may convey a more laid-back message: *There is no rush.*

If feedback is more important than the implicit finality of writing, then an interactive medium—a meeting or phone call—will be your medium of choice. Initiating a live conversation conveys a *Let's talk about it* message. Investing the effort of arranging and holding a meeting sends a stronger message that there is a desire to talk things out.

34

"If the Phone Doesn't Ring, It's Me"*

When you place a call, you have a major advantage: Knowing you will be on the telephone, you are psyched up and prepared to negotiate.

But a phone call may, on balance, be to your disadvantage. You can't read body language through a telephone receiver, and it is easier to be fooled or misled when your full sensory abilities can't be used.

Ask yourself: Is there a possibility that your phone call will more readily prompt a negative response? Since the other person is looking at plastic and a telephone cord instead of flesh and blood, it is far easier to say "no" telephonically than in person.

Your call also makes it all too easy for the other person to verbally walk out of the conversation: "I was just running out the door to a meeting when you called . . . ," "Sorry, but I can't talk any more right now, I have an incoming call from London. . . ."

Ask yourself: Is it important to explore needs and interests in a lengthy, more fluid dialogue? It takes much more patience and effort to be a good telephone listener. Does what I have to say require a high degree of concentration which may be too difficult in a telephone call?

Ask yourself: Will I be able to resist the pressure to respond, which is inherent in a telephone call? A few moments of silence in a meeting is a few moments of silence. On the telephone, a few moments of silence is an eternity.

Ask yourself: Will a more personalized strategy better advance my cause? Will a telephone conversation be more stressful or less? Telephone conversations are briefer and therefore more competitive than face-to-face dialogues. Meetings take time and effort to arrange and attend, but by their nature, they are chattier and less structured.

Ask yourself: Will the person I am calling be curt because I have interrupted what he or she is doing?

I Just Called . . . To Say . . .

Once you have decided to go it by telephone, make sure you have thought out what you will say and how the other person can be expected to respond. Insulate yourself from diversions and distractions.

---

*Title of a song recorded by Jimmy Buffett.

Telephone calls are prone to shortcuts, so make sure you have all the necessary data and information in front of you. Nothing should be left to guesswork. A few notes to yourself will ensure that you will receive all necessary information and ask all pertinent questions.

Practice tip: To confirm that you have been getting through, conclude the telephone conversation by reviewing the points that were agreed on. Your follow-up letter summarizing those points will help reinforce the other person's telephonic commitments.

I Am in Receipt of Your Proposal, I'll Waste No Time Reading It

I handed my client, the late comedian Jackie Vernon, a rather wordy and complex contract I had received. As "Mr. Excitement" perused it, he glanced up and said, "Bob, the trouble with Hong Kong is I can never seem to find Chinatown."

In every fat proposal, there is a thin proposal trying to get out.

A persuasive proposal is one that sets forth your *best* ideas rather than all of your ideas.

Today's executives are learning how to avoid *read it and sleep* letters and written proposals. They are learning that the best way to make sure that a written proposal is summarily rejected is to leave nothing out.

They are learning that emphasis is no longer on dangling participles, prepositional phrases, fragmented sentences, subordinate clauses and legalese, but on simple letters containing short sentences and paragraphs.

They are learning that *technobabble* or any part of a presentation not serving a clear purpose belongs on the cutting room floor.

Evaluation: Expediency, convenience, and effectiveness are not the same. The right tactic may be to initiate a call or it may be to postpone accepting a caller's invitation to talk. And then it may be to send a fax. Or call a meeting. Or send a letter.

7

READING
People Are an Open Book

The art of winning begins by reading yourself. It is advanced by knowing how to read others. To persuade you, it is not enough to know *who* you are. I must also know *what* you are.

An accomplished people reader knows that there are two eternal truths.

Eternal Truth No. 1: The Other Person Is Not You

Each of us has our own reality. No one functions in the abstract, and we view things as *we are* rather than as *they are*.

Your every word, your every gesture, your every movement passes through the other person's filters. These filters include personal values, impressions, backgrounds, prejudices, likes, dislikes, experiences, feelings, and expectations.

Do you hear what I hear? Because no two people have the same filters, thoughts transmitted may not be the same as thoughts perceived. This truth is the spawning ground of much tragedy and almost all comedy. ("Help the Old Ladies' Home." "Blimey, I didn't know they were still out."—*Me and My Girl,* a 1937 musical.)

37

Perceived differences, which are *people* differences rather than *substantive* differences, are the barrier between one person's thoughts and another's. To persuade and influence others, you must come to grips with a problem as *they* perceive it. You must deal with *their* reality.

The art of reading people begins with understanding that the other person is not you, will never be you, and cannot be read as if they were you.

Eternal Truth No. 2: People Conclude Facts from Their Gut Impressions, Perceptions, and Assumptions

As kids, we found that the comics were a good way to learn how to read. Even if we didn't understand all of the words, we could track the story line once we knew the signs. Villains were the ones who seemed always to be in need of a shave, smoked stubby cigars, and wore dark clothing even in the dead of summer. Heroes, on the other hand, were a clean-cut, wrinkle-free lot with straight noses and the proper attire for every occasion.

As adults, we still allow symbolism to define the other person. We assume character traits from initial impressions.

But impressions are only temporary. They are assumptions based on clues of bearing, speech, dress, demeanor, and grooming. You may later discover that the persona projected was a facade and that the clues you were reading were false leads.

The "ol' country boy" may be a Wharton MBA trying to make you the expert, hoping you will grant concessions or make suggestions contrary to your own best interests.

Politicians, wanting us to perceive them as having a commanding presence, seldom wear suits with patterns, and their shirts are always white or blue. Neckties are most often maroon. Executives who pay hundreds of dollars to learn what to wear and how to act are taught that a blue suit projects a more authoritative impression than a brown one and that there is such a thing as a "power suit."

Reading people is about developing insight that goes beyond the "obvious."

Not everyone has a sixth sense. But if I cannot read you, how will I know how to persuade you? How will I know how hard to bargain with you?

Will a simple agreement suffice, or do I need a lengthy contract filled with onerous compliance and enforcement provisions?

Can I rely on you to adequately and promptly satisfy my critical requirements? Would I be better off not even getting involved with you in the first place?

People threaten, manipulate, care, evade, help, demean, and disrupt. They become reclusive, rigid, flexible, obsessive, demanding, self-righteous, nurturing, and supportive. From this human chaos emerge individual readable patterns. These patterns are our *way*.

To know the kind of person you are—to read you—I must know your way. To know what will motivate, aggravate, stimulate, or appease you, I must know your way. To know how you will manage and resolve conflict, I must also know your way.

We do not have the same way when we deal with our bosses that we have when we deal with our children. We do not have the same way when we are worried, desperate, or tapped that we have when we are in command of our lives. We do not have the same way when we feel rejected and emotionally let down that we have when we feel good about ourselves.

Our way is a function of our perceived goals, needs, dependencies, and circumstances. Our way is the roles we play, our personality traits, our long-ago-forged core tendencies, and how we go about satisfying our perceived needs.

To forecast and manage the behavior of the people you wish to influence, you must first read their way.

Reading the Roles People Play

A physician's bedside manner, a salesperson's charisma, a spouse's attentiveness, a parent's supportiveness, a police officer's authority, an entertainer's flamboyance, a mâitred's graciousness, a teacher's restraint, an executive's decisiveness, and a sergeant's bravado are, to a large degree, role playing.

As role players, we deliver those qualities and characteristics that we expect from ourselves and others expect of us. How we see ourselves is often a reflection of how we believe others see us.

By our nature, we tend to play to our audiences. Agents act more like agents when their principals are present. Young lawyers drop their voice an octave when conferring with clients. Texans who never ride horses wear cowboy boots when they go to conventions in Los Angeles.

Walt Disney World's very grand Grand Floridian resort does not have a single "employee" nor do any of the people who work there wear "uniforms." Clerks, bellhops, maids, and everyone else who draws a paycheck are "cast members" who dress in "costume." Reinforcing the notion that everyone is a role player and the Grand Floridian a stage, Disney management prompts choreographed conduct from well-scrubbed and eager-to-please personnel who play to rave reviews.

Jerry Rubin, in a spectacular and dramatic way, was the personification of role reversal. As the consummate role player, Jerry understood and delivered what his audiences wanted.

His audience in the 1960s and 1970s was the national press. As founder of the yippies and a Chicago Seven conspirator, his stage was the seven o'clock news. His was the rebel's role played out in tie-dye shirts and bandannas.

In the 1990s, he was my client. But now his audience was his hundreds of nutritional product distributors. He played an entrepreneurial role (earning him upward of $70,000 a month) in three-piece navy suits, white shirts, and nondescript ties.

Roles lead to predictable responses, actions and reactions—they too are part of our way.

People conform to the roles they play. They are what they do.

Understanding how people view their role at any given moment enables us to understand their motivation and forecast their behavior. We respond to situations differently throughout our day as we take on our various roles: a boss, an employee, a customer, a supplier, a Disney "cast member," a parent, a neighbor, or a friend.

Reading Personality Traits

As he walked along the path, the boy spotted a struggling scorpion lying on its back.

"Please turn me over, or I will surely die," begged the scorpion.

"If I do, you will sting me. Then I will be the one to die," the boy replied.

"No. No. I could never sting someone who saved my life," pleaded the scorpion.

As the boy turned the scorpion over, he was stung.

"Why did you do that? You promised!" the boy sobbed.

"You knew what I was when you picked me up," replied the scorpion as he ran beneath a rock.

An uncaring person with a history of overreaching and taking advantage of others isn't going to turn over a new leaf come dawn.

A person who is stingy and penurious today will not be a big-time spender tomorrow.

The impatient person who screams at your receptionist for being put on hold or who flies off the handle at a busboy who forgets to bring his coffee is not going to be any more tolerant or understanding of you once the contract is signed.

We are creatures of habit, and our readable habits are stronger than our sense of reason.

Our values, our notions of right and wrong, our religious convictions, our sense of heritage, and our regard for our fellow humans are fixed. These character traits are so defined and crystallized that no matter how bleak or bright our situation, they are a constant facet of our way.

DEAR ABBY:

Several months ago, a prominent Louisiana physician choked to death while dining . . . in a room filled with physicians! It was the third such tragedy in as many years. . . . In all three cases, the victims, programmed since childhood not to show distress in the presence of other diners, left the table without giving the slightest indication that there was a serious problem.

Some personal qualities are so ingrained that they can't be "bought" at any price.

William Murphy, an unemployed mechanic, anonymously returned a found wallet but held onto the lottery ticket inside until he learned it was worth $5.6 million. "I thought of keeping the whole thing," Murphy admitted, but "that's not the way to be."—*People*.

These long-ago-forged character traits that transcend the circumstances of any given moment in time are our *core tendencies*. They are both the axis and the essence of our way. How we interface with other people is primarily influenced by how we read their core tendencies.

It never happened before or since: an insurance adjuster wasn't requiring documentation to justify my client's personal injury claim. It wasn't important to the insurance company that Vincente Minnelli was

Liza's father, Judy Garland's husband, or the Oscar-winning director of *Gigi*. What was important, I was told, was that "Minnelli's reputation for honesty precedes him."

Reading Needs

As we saw in Chapter 4, everyone has a minimum daily requirement of needs.

Our way is a function of our conscious or unconscious urge to satisfy those needs.

Your ability to recognize and read the other person's needs is the critical element in pushing motivator buttons and making your ideas irresistible.

Include Him Out

My friend "Don" is a brilliant lawyer—a lawyer's lawyer in every sense of the word. He is the man other lawyers call on when they have a thorny legal problem. He is the man always nominated first to head up an academic bar committee.

But alas, Don can bore you to tears if given half a chance. At his best, he is ten thumbs and a trick knee—the Sheik of Geek. Don is an unpressed collage of colors, patterns, and seasons. In a brown sweater, he closely resembles a mud slide. He is the personification of the short-sleeved wash-and-wear dress shirt, the polyester suit, and the unbuttoned button-down collar.

Don's blond desk is so old that any day it will change from outdated to fashionable Art Deco. Half the plants in his office are dying. The other half are plastic. Don is central casting's notion of couch potato plain and Norman Rockwell placid.

Then there is Howard, whom I have known for years. By his own admission, Howard is one of the world's worst lawyers. He brought up the bottom of his class at a fourth-rate night school. Howard is unrealistic about life, himself, and his cases. The fact that he graduated and passed the bar exam after only three tries is still one of life's great mysteries.

Howard is debonair, athletic, authoritative, well-groomed. He may even hold a black belt in savoir faire. Howard is pure *pow!* The colored

Jockey poco brief and the three-piece pinstripe were designed with Howard in mind. His car, a black Bimmer, shines like obsidian. Howard has a leap-tall-buildings persona. If Don and Howard were attending the same dinner party, Don would bag scraps for his dog and Howard would bag three new clients.

Although we do not judge books by their covers, we do judge people by our first impressions of them. Those first impressions are our assumptions of their ways.

Don gives a first impression that he is lackadaisical, disorganized, passive, and inefficient. Howard projects reliability, credibility, efficiency, trustworthiness, and authority.

The art of reading people is the art of looking beyond the apparent and beyond the assumed. The art of knowing how people are read is also the art of being "well read" by others—of *influencing how you are read by them*.

Ways are not limited to people. Businesses, communities, social groups, religious orders, and political parties also have predictable and readable ways. Their ways are keyed to a need for recognition, acceptance, status, and the money to remain viable.

■ ■ ■

Reading other people's *fine print* is looking and listening for their body signals, their hidden word messages, their primary ideas, their priorities, and their pronoun clues.

Looking and Listening for "Tells"

Body signals, our silent language, are so universally understood that people of every tongue and culture have cried and laughed with the likes of Buster Keaton, Harold Lloyd, Charlie Chaplin, and Fatty Arbuckle, who could move, entertain, arouse, and excite without ever uttering a word.

Body signals are clues to how the other person is receiving, making sense of, and accepting what you have to say. Because they are largely subconscious and are so difficult to control, con men appropriately term them *tells*.

U.S. Customs agents are trained to give more credence to defensive body signals than to a written customs declaration. Interviewers for a major Ivy League university are asked to evaluate a prospective student's self-confidence based on the applicant's choice of interview seating.

Raising your Eye-Q: Almost all mannerisms are important. Alertness to "tells," zooming in to *read* the other person's fine print.

- Does the other person choose to sit directly across from you, indicating confidence, or at an angle, indicating uneasiness?

- Has the other person loosened a shirt or cuff or removed a jacket, an indication of feeling comfortable with you?

- Are there nods of approval? Are there disapproving headshakes?

- Have you said something that has caused the listener to smile in relief?

- Are the other person's arms protectively folded across the chest? Are the hands open and relaxed or clenched?

- Is the other person avoiding eye contact?

- Are there signs of tension: compressed lips, strained laughter, blushing, giggling, staring? Is the person fidgeting?

- What are the other person's eyes telling you? (People who are lying tend to blink more and have more dilated pupils.)

- Has the speaker's tone of voice become shrill and belligerent? (People who are lying tend to speak in higher pitch.)

- Is a "final offer" being made with deliberate certainty, reinforced by the speaker's leaning forward and establishing eye contact? Or do the expression and tonal inflection show a laid-back lack of commitment?

■ ■ ■

"Well, you've heard it with your own eyes!"—*Howard Cosell.*

LOOK for congruence. Monitor continuing body behavior; don't rely on any single gesture. Is the verbal consistent with the nonverbal? Are individual body movements confirming or canceling each other?

BEWARE of the *offensiva del sorriso*—the "smile offensive." Is the signal being transmitted a true reflection of the person's feelings and attitude, or is it a contrived signal?

THINK about whether *you* are being *well read* by the speaker. What signals are you transmitting with your arms, hands, face, legs, and body?

Looking and Listening for Hidden Word Messages

Only the foolish man hears all that he hears.—*Ancient proverb.*

The other person's messages can be real, true, and reliable, or they can be lures, cover-ups, and decoys.

A world-class people reader sees and hears more than the other person's words and more than the message that the other person is intending to convey. Construing words literally or accepting the other person's messages at face value is not effective people reading.

A teenage girl tearfully tells her boyfriend, "It doesn't matter." Are we to believe that it really doesn't matter, or that it matters a lot?

"Incidentally," "by the way," and "as you already know" sound casual and incidental but usually introduce statements that the other person wants to downplay or sneak by.

A friend tells you, "You are 100 percent correct in what you are saying, but . . . ." Does that friend really feel you are 100 percent right, or are you just being softened up for some bad news?

"I'll give it my best." "I will try my hardest." These statements are clues that the speaker is presupposing a high probability of failure. Only a speaker who says "Yes, I will" is programmed for success.

Statements that start with "Don't be concerned, but . . ." or "You have nothing to worry about . . ." mean only one thing. There is something to worry about up ahead.

Looking and Listening for Primary Ideas

Knowing where the other person is coming from is knowing how to read his or her primary needs, desires, and concerns. It is being able to separate the detailed, supportive, or tangential part of the other person's message from the part that is pivotal to reaching an agreement.

In college lecture classes, most of us would take page after page of notes. A good student, we thought, was anyone who had a big stack of spiral notebooks filled up at the end of the semester. My roommate, Hal Beral, would go through an entire seventeen-credit semester with just a few spiral notebooks. Years later, Hal's friends are still deliberating: Was Hal a great listener because he was a straight-A student? Or was Hal a straight-A student because rather than taking dictation he was listening for what the lecture was all about?

Looking and Listening for Priorities

Being sensitive to word patterns and timing patterns is part of a relatively new discipline known as *conversation analysis*. Conversations, even small talk, are never as random or disorderly as they may seem.

Quick! Make a short list—say, five items—of foods, vacation spots, or television shows.

Did you list the items randomly? Or in the order of your personal preferences? In all probability, the person with whom you are negotiating will present or specify issues in an order that is consistent with his or her own priorities or desires.

Points that you may consider *throwaway points* or of secondary importance may be *primary points* to the other person. Learning to look and listen for what the other person considers critical will enable you to discover motivator buttons or to grant or request concessions accordingly.

Looking and Listening for Pronoun Clues

Somehow I just can't help myself. When I agree with the position taken by a client, I usually will advocate the position with phrases like "*We* just can't accept a penny less than . . . ." But when I am dutifully following a client's instructions and those instructions are not totally to my liking, then my subconscious inclination is to say "*He* won't accept a penny less than . . . ."

Whether we are spouses, lawyers, agents, partners, or employees, we all throw off pronoun clues. The verbal or written pronouns that people use are both a forecast of the response they are expecting and a reflection of their own degree of commitment to their asserted position.

Wishful Listening

On Black Monday, the stock market had its second worst crash in history. The next day, the media featured scores of financial prophets and prognosticators.

Those who had just gotten clobbered hearing only what they wanted to hear, were quoting the pundits who were now predicting that the ferocious bear market would be short-lived and that good times were around the corner.

Those who had sold before the crash reinforced the wisdom of their decision by quoting what they had wanted to hear: post crash forecasts of impending disaster, and advice that the best survival strategy was to be half in cash and half in canned goods.

> As might be expected, people who plan to vote for Bush on November 8 thought, by a lopsided 20 to 1, that he won the debate. This general pattern was the same for Dukakis' supporters . . . .
> —Los Angeles Times.

Investors and voters. Each were advocates of and listeners to only what they wanted and needed to hear. When we listen selectively, we are not really listening at all.

One Hundred Words from the Eskimos

When all your faculties are being utilized in the listening process, you are in what psychologists call *complete attendance*.

The average person talks at the rate of 120 words per minute, but can hear and comprehend 600 words per minute. We have the extra capacity to listen to speakers' words as well as their tells, hidden word messages, primary ideas, priorities, and pronoun clues. Each of us has the capability to be in complete attendance.

Just Say Snow. A native Southern Californian, I have never taken the time to learn how to appreciate snow. I acknowledge that it makes all the difference on a Christmas card or television holiday special, but somehow for me the real stuff means only wet feet, bulky clothes, slippery streets, and a runny nose. My feelings about snow can be easily summarized in a single word.

Eskimos are at the other end of the snow "attendance" scale. An Eskimo's snow sensitivity is so keen that, according to *Time*, "He has one hundred words for snow—such are the subtleties he detects in its color and tone and depth and temperature." If I were an Eskimo, I would be ninety-nine snow words short.

Reading: To be able to persuasively present your ideas and prevent resistance, you must read how the other person makes decisions. How they make sense of things. It may not be the same as how you make sense of things. Each of us is pre-programmed to act and react in accordance with the roles we play, our personality traits, our core tendencies, and our needs.

Amateurs will listen to someone else talk only because they know their turn is next. World-class listeners will listen to someone else talk to gather "fine print" clues that can be used to influence and persuade.

8

LANCER
Postcards from the Top

The soft-touch, low-impact methodology of the persuasion progression takes you over the top. The secret of your success is readily recalled in the "breaking through" acronym, LANCER.

Linkage is a *personal* interfacing that encourages the other person to be receptive to *you* and to your *ideas.* Shape your negotiating environment—tone, mood, and attitude—through rapport, personalization, identification, and involvement.

Alignment tactics harness the other person's energy while establishing a *pattern of agreement.*

Needs must be identified and stimulated. Pushing motivator buttons will *energize* discussions while making your ideas irresistible.

Control the negotiating dialogue through *persuasive listening* and questions. With linkage, alignment, and control firmly in place, present your proposal in a succinct, prioritized manner.

Evaluation of communication options enables you to determine which media will best advance the persuasion progression.

Reading the other person is ascertaining how roles, personality traits, and core tendencies will impact decision making. Reading their "fine print"—tells, hidden word messages, priorities, and pronoun clues—provides ongoing feedback as to how you and your ideas are being received.

49

Lancer: A Step-by-Step Progression?

The persuasion progression cannot be segmented. It has neither discernible tiers nor distinguishable boundaries. Masters of persuasion are weavers. The result is a tapestry that blends, bonds, and relies on each and all of the contributing elements. Read the other person while establishing linkage. Align while evaluating communication options. Control dialogue while identifying needs.

It's Not Over Even When It's a Done Deal

After you have gotten a nod of acceptance, don't validate the wisdom of the other person's decision by making reinforcing comments (*That was a wise choice* or *You got an incredible deal*). It will only make the decision suspect.

If you have gotten the nod on primary issues but there are still unresolved minor points, sometimes—and this is always a judgment call—it may make sense to leave those *micro negotiating* points for another day.

Letting the deal set gives the other person a chance to become comfortable with it, or to act in reliance on it by planning a vacation or raising the cash to do business with you. Confront the minor issues too early, and you risk their becoming deal breakers.

The persuasion progression isn't about dumping everything on the negotiating table at once. Each new point raised is an excuse for the other person to go back and revisit terms previously agreed on.

Practice tip: Sometimes it makes good sense to nail down what you have so skillfully achieved in a letter agreement or getting signatures on a deal memo before forging onward to conquer new micro-point territory. With important points solidly "in the bag," you have tactically positioned yourself to press for those lesser terms without risking the ground you have won.

A *cautionary note:* You can never really be sure when it's over. One of my clients owned one of the country's biggest automobile dealerships. On the other side of the negotiations was Tokai Bank, a Japanese bank that takes special pride in its image.

I had negotiated the reduction of my client's personal guarantee obligation to the bank from about $11 million to $1.5 million. A nice two days' work. My client and the bankers willingly signed a letter of agreement.

Less than two weeks later, the Tokai senior vice president who had signed the deal announced, "No matter what it costs, the bank is going to worm out of the deal." Somehow my client had managed to snatch defeat from the jaws of victory.

Word had gotten back to Tokai that my client was bragging to the world about how he had outgunned, outmaneuvered, and outfoxed the image-conscious bank.

Let everyone close with as good a feeling as possible. A good winner doesn't dance in the streets or shout from the rooftops. Hard bargains will be more readily acceded to if they include a face-saving *exit strategy*.

People Have Faces to Save

General William Westmoreland, former Commander of U.S. Forces in Vietnam, "formally announced the surprising withdrawal of his $120 million libel suit against CBS which aired a television show accusing him of conspiring to underestimate enemy troop strength . . . to paint a rosier picture of the Vietnam war." Both the General and CBS announced a victory, reported the *Los Angeles Times*.

After eighteen weeks of a losing but still unfinished trial, the General traded his lawsuit for a public statement from CBS that he was not "unpatriotic or disloyal in performing his duties as he saw them." CBS refused to apologize, however, for broadcasting the allegedly libelous program. The network's announcement was designed to allow Westmoreland to save face and retire in dignity.

Companies Have Faces to Save

Disney productions rented New York's Radio City Music Hall for the entire summer. The Music Hall's famed Rockettes were notified that for the first time in fifty-four years they would be out on the street during the Disney run. Disney management felt that the precision dancers were "inappropriate" in a show featuring Mickey Mouse and Donald Duck.

Disney was front-page news. But despite public appeals, demonstrations, and a thirty-thousand-signature petition, Disney continued to resist sharing its program with the high-kicking dancers.

Finally, a Disney spokesperson was allowed to gracefully backpedal. "It just took us a while to figure out how to fit in their numbers with what we had planned."

Nations Have Faces to Save

The late Senator George Aiken suggested in 1966: "The way to get out of Vietnam is to declare victory and leave."

Advancing to the winner's circle gives no assurance you will stay there. Victories are fragile. Handle them with care and they are yours to keep.

PART II

TROUBLE SHOOTING
Settling for More

9

FINESSING HOSTILITY, AGGRESSION, AND ANGER
Dancing in the Minefield

People who are hostile, argumentative, or angry are unreachable. Standing up to irrational people is the norm. Finessing people who insist on being right rather than reasonable is the art.

When You Are Under Attack

An attacker sets forth a position full throttle. The in-your-face approach is intended to run both you and your ideas into the ground. You're on the ropes and sliding. An agreement must be reached: you don't have the luxury of walking away. On the other hand, you can't deal with someone who won't let up until he *hears* the blood.

Although it's all talk, the other person is attacking with more than a big mouth. Their muscular, glandular, and nervous systems have all been summoned into the foray. Spot an ungentlemanly or unladylike gesture and you can add skeletal system to the list.

Telling the other person to "calm down" implies they have no reason to be upset. Their response will be to justify and defend their reaction to you.

Start converting the attacker into a pussycat early. It is much harder to deescalate an attack after you have launched an attack of your own: Personalities have come into play. Emotions are reaching their flash

55

point. Positions are becoming more polarized. Ideas are crystallizing from having been vigorously defended.

Persuading someone who is angry or hostile is like driving a car: you must come to a full stop before you can shift into reverse. Only when the other person has regained some composure and has reestablished equilibrium is it time to move in with your own strategy.

Operation: Containment

Here are four steps to bring an in-your-face attack to a screeching halt.

Step 1. Choose one of the following statements and deliver it firmly and calmly to your attacker:

> *You may be right in what you are saying.*

This *may be* statement is nonthreatening. It will not precipitate any additional emotional outburst.

> *You are probably right.*

If you are reasonably sure the attacker's statement is correct, then say so.

> *If I were in your shoes, I think I would feel the same way.*

This is a nonprovoking response if there is no possibility that the attacker may be right. It is a *confirmation* that the attacker's message has been understood and appreciated. Reinforce this statement by demonstrating that you understand *why* the opposing position has been taken. After all, if you were the mirror image—the exact alter ego—of the attacker, wouldn't you *have* to feel the same way? Don't confuse *confirming* that you understand what is being said with *agreeing with* what has been said.

Step 2. Do NOT attack the other person or the opposing positions.

Step 3. Do NOT defend yourself or your stated concerns and needs.

Step 4. Keep the dialogue going.

Remember the simple wisdom of bumper stickers that were popular a few years back: *What if someone gave a war and nobody showed up?* The philosophy behind these defusing tactics is equally simple: You can't play demolition derby if no one else is on the track. Mouth-to-mouth combat can't continue with someone who is saying the words that every arguer longs to hear: *You may be right.*

■ ■ ■

When emotions come into play, smart people do dumb things.

Dumb Thing No. 1: They Forget You Can Lead a Horse to Water but You Can't Make It Do the Backstroke

Get Real!

Count up the times you've heard someone say, "Oh, you are so right, you silver-tongued devil; I am now going to see things your way!"

Put on Your "Sensible Shoes"

You may be a Rambo of repartee who is able to outfox the other side with fancy footwork and quicksilver moves, but are you going to get what you want? No testimonial dinner is held and no record book, plaque, or trophy is awarded for excellence in debating or for getting in the last word. You are a winner only if you achieve your goal.

Turn negotiating dialogue into a confrontation or trial and you will lose. Even if your logic prevails, your prize will be a bitter, get-even opponent. And that is *if* you "win."

The Ego Has Landed

A group of us were dining at a small French café. Only our friend, Ron, was praising the Gerberesque pureed parsnips and insisting that the Barbie-size portion of veal was ample. At first I was surprised. To me, Ron is the personification of a hearty appetite. But Ron was behaving out of character for good reason. He had chosen the restaurant. Ron is no different from you and me, and nothing is as sacred as one's own judgment.

Arguments strain interpersonal linkage. In effect, their message is: the other person's judgment is not as good as yours.

People resist change because they are committed to the status quo . . . OR because in their mind there is a justification which supports their position . . . OR because they are attached to what is comfortable and familiar . . . OR because like Ron their "good judgment" is on the line.

As issues become more complex and outcomes less predictable we tend to become simplistic, relying on gut instincts and premonitions. It is always easier to take a stand than to understand. So too, it is easier to decide *against* than to decide *for*.

The persuasion progression is not about showing you are right. People do things for their own reasons, not for yours. The persuasion progression is about helping people see why it makes sense for them to do things your way.

Put someone on the defensive end of an argument, and they often end up saying only those things they can say well.

Put someone on the defensive end of an argument, and there is a good chance they may withhold information or distort the information they choose to give.

Put someone on the defensive end of an argument, and they will overgeneralize your differences: you *always* . . . , you *only* . . .

Put someone on the defensive end of an argument, and they will change from being stubbornly *right* to being adamantly *righteous*.

Put someone on the defensive end of an argument, and their most compelling thought will be to reciprocate all over you.

Dumb Thing No. 2: They Won't Admit Their Mistakes

"Professional investors generally agree on one bit of advice: Cut your losses and let your winnings run," reported *The Wall Street Journal*. However, most people will keep the stocks that are losers. "They don't want to tell themselves . . . that they made a mistake."

Your opinions and ideas are not undeniable truths to chisel in granite and pass down from generation unto generation. Better to 'fess up than to have your feet held to the fire and be proven wrong. There are those who will contend that an apology is an admission of weakness. Actually, an apology is a credibility booster. The impression you leave by not forthrightly dealing with a mistake can have a greater negative effect than the mistake itself.

When Coca-Cola reintroduced original Coke as Coke Classic, it admitted that it had misread consumer tastes in retiring the brand to begin with. The result, according to a top advertising executive, was that "Coke almost achieved a warmth and humanity out of having made a mistake."

Who knows, perhaps Richard Nixon's Watergate transgressions, if handled differently, could have been accepted by the American people. His coverup could not.

Laker star Magic Johnson, one of the most popular athletes of recent memory, found sympathy from a supportive and forgiving nation by calling a press conference and forthrightly telling us that even seemingly invincible heroes could become infected with the AIDS virus.

Democratic presidential contender Gary Hart's flimsy denial of monkey business on the boat *Monkey Business* threw a monkey wrench into a brilliant political career. By contrast, Democratic presidential contender Bill Clinton did not try to deny allegations of an extramarital affair. The result of owning up: 76 percent of those surveyed in a *Time* poll said the charges of marital infidelity would not keep them from voting for Clinton.

"I'm damn sorry it happened and you can bet that it won't ever happen again, and that's a promise." Lee Iacocca's note of apology, published in 23 newspapers, was able to turn around public opinion in a scandal that arose from a federal fraud indictment. Two Chrysler executives were linked to disengaged odometers in cars that were sold as new to the public.

Displaying an open mind and a spirit of joint cooperation while admitting that you have been wrong will reinforce linkage, encourage the other person to admit similar mistakes, and diffuse anger.

Dumb Thing No. 3: Instead of Zeroing in on How Something Is to Be Done, They Focus on Why It Wasn't Done That Way Before

Delivery trucks servicing neighboring businesses frequently block your driveway and cause your customers a great deal of inconvenience. This situation has been discussed with the owners of the businesses several times before.

When you next meet with your neighbors, do you:

- Ask why trucks continue to park in front of your driveway?

- Threaten to call your wife's cousin, Bubba, who owns a tow truck?

- Threaten to block their driveways in retaliation?

- Suggest solutions?

The first three choices will only make your neighbors angrier and more hostile.

Fix the problem, not the blame. Suggesting possible solutions is an *issue management* technique that moves the focus of discussions from having to justify your complaint to the proposed remedy. If you leave the resolution to your neighbors, they will give a higher priority to their own needs than to yours.

> **Standing up to emotional responses—anger, argument, irrational tirades—is not getting through to the other person. It is only "being impossible *back.*" Advancing the persuasion progression is not about a show of one-upmanship or a contest of wills. It is about winning.**

10

OVERCOMING REJECTION
Riding the Crest of a Slump

Rejection is a negative response. But a response by definition means the lines of communication are open. Rejection is managed by tactically presenting problems, surgical strike questioning, reframing your ideas, understanding how and when to use threats, and showing the other person how to retreat while saving face.

Hanging In Tough No. 1: Break Sore Spots into Component Parts

Deal with conflicts one bit at a time. Break big problems into smaller problems that can be reckoned with individually.

Separate monetary and nonmonetary segments, and discuss the nonmonetary first.

Hanging In Tough No. 2: A Problem Well Stated Is a Problem Half Solved

You have just moved into a neighborhood. The folks a few doors down own a large Doberman, Spike, who for years has been allowed to roam free.

61

Your kids have no place to play after school except on the sidewalk in front of your home. Although Spike is known and loved by the neighborhood, his very presence terrorizes your children, who refuse to go outdoors. Your children are just not ready to make friends with Spike. Calling Animal Regulation would make you the neighborhood villain.

You have no choice other than to visit Spike's owners.

■ ■ ■

Before you read any further, take a minute to jot down what you plan to say after you have introduced yourself.

■ ■ ■

Which of the following dialogues sounds most like what you wrote down?

A. We have a problem. After school, you should keep Spike locked in the yard or on a leash. [Explanation follows.]

B. We have a problem. Our children have no place to play. [Explanation follows.] Therefore, after school, you should keep Spike locked in the yard or on a leash.

If dialogue B sounds like what you wrote down, then give yourself a pat on the back. Your proposed solution (Spike must be confined) was disclosed only *after* the logic leading to that solution had been presented. The neighbor had to listen to your explanation in order to ascertain your request.

I can't always help it. When someone tells me a joke, as often as not I listen with only half an ear. My thought processes are too busy searching out and then mentally rehearsing a joke that I can share in return. In the same way, we all instinctively prepare mental counterarguments while the other person is verbalizing his or her thoughts.

In dialogue A, your logic was lost. Because you asserted your proposed solution *before* its supporting logic, your neighbor probably never heard the logic. Spike's owner was too busy preparing a rebuttal to the proposed solution. That's the nature of us humans.

Instead of leading with your proposed solution, use a one-two-three combination punch: (1) Lead with the facts. (2) Deliver your logic. (3) Follow through with your proposed solution.

Hanging In Tough No. 3: Surgical Strikes

There is nothing uglier than reason when it is not on your side.

Without being a *negaholic*, pursue new territory by asking questions that strike at the basis, principle, and logic behind the other person's position. Whether you already know the answers to those questions is not important.

People who feel they are being influenced or manipulated can't be influenced or manipulated. Statements lead to defensive retorts but questions will cause the other person to reexamine and justify an announced position. Only questions will separate reasons that only sound good from good, sound reasons. If a position is not realistic, the other person will soon discover its flaws.

Hanging In Tough No. 4: How to Be an Uncompromising Compromiser

Rejection does not exist in the abstract. By definition, rejection is reactive. Remove what is causing the other person to reject your idea and you have eliminated the problem.

The way something is framed is the difference between whether a glass is half empty or half full.

Two automobile manufacturers, one American and one Russian, agreed to a two-car race. The U.S. entry won hands down. A Russian news agency reframed the results: "In an international car race held yesterday, the Russian car came in second and the American entry came in next to last."

A rejected point or proposal can be presented again and again so long as it appears fresh and new enough for reconsideration.

Pick a Deal, Any Deal

Lower the price of the house you are selling and, to offset the price reduction, increase the simple interest rate on the note you are taking back. Reduce the price of the house if you are allowed to lease the house back rent-free for six months after title has changed hands. Lower your price provided that the buyer doesn't demand certain repairs be made as a condition of sale.

The nation was being blitzed with its lowest automobile financing rates ever. General Motors and Ford were down to 2.9 percent, Toyota was at 2.4 percent, and Nissan was at 1.9 percent. But a West Coast dealer won the interest rate war by offering 0 percent financing. According to newspaper accounts, dealers who previously were discounting price were "not coming down from sticker" but were merely *reframing* their discounts from price concessions to financing concessions.

In these examples, the net out-of-pocket cost to the seller is theoretically the same. Each new detriment is offset by a corresponding new benefit. The economic equation stays in balance. The concessions offered are more a reframing of an existing proposal than a substantive overhaul.

Hanging In Tough No. 5: How and When to Use a Threat

It worked for Gary Cooper in *High Noon.*

It also worked for Burt Lancaster and Kirk Douglas in *Gunfight at the O.K. Corral.*

But when Marsha told our office manager that she was quitting unless she got a 20 percent raise, the showdown tactic left her looking at the career opportunity ads.

Here are six showdown NEVER EVERs:

1. NEVER EVER lead with a threat. An ultimatum is a knockout punch to be used only after some initial rapport has been established. Threats are last, not first resorts.

2. NEVER EVER make a threat without first casting it as a warning, preferably a soft-touch warning. More about this below.

3. NEVER EVER make a threat you don't want to carry out. Don't threaten to quit your job or fire a valued employee if that is the last thing you would ever want to do.

4. NEVER EVER use a big threat in furtherance of a small gain. Tell your teenage daughter that if she comes home past her curfew "she will never go out on Saturday night again," and you will only look ridiculous. A threat has to be relative to its purpose and objective.

5. NEVER EVER make a threat that is inconsistent with the attitude you previously displayed. A threat requires perfect timing

and should appear as a natural and logical extension of demonstrated anger, thwarted expectations, or an unresolvable deadlock.

And now for the best Lyndon B. Johnson quote you may ever see. . . .

6. "NEVER EVER tell a man to go to Hell unless you can send him there."

Soft-Touch Warning

A *soft-touch* warning does not pull the dragon's tail because it is low-key, humanized, and nonconfrontational. It is a warning cast as the presentation of a mutual problem.

It was all still very hush-hush. The president of an NBA team had embezzled team funds. The stolen money was long gone, and the president had no apparent ability to make restitution. My Mission Impossible was to negotiate a face-saving exit, keep the president out of prison, and avoid any commitment for repayment that the president couldn't comfortably honor.

The tactic put into play was the unexpected: a soft-touch warning to the club owners.

The owners were warned that if the president was sent to prison, the team would receive nothing. And, obligating the president to restore *all* of the stolen funds would only encourage him to leave the country or hide future earnings.

Once a mutual problem is on the table, there is an opportunity to propose its solution. What would make sense, I explained, was for the president to make partial restitution by paying the team a "comfortable" percentage of his income for a negotiated period of time. That was the deal we settled on.

Hanging In Tough No. 6: Getting the Other Person to Bite the Bullet

Edging toward a conclusion that won't leave the other person smiling? Reexpress the problem, then ease the way to arrival at *your* conclusion, giving them credit for their contribution to the result.

Office Manager: Lisa, we have a super-high-priority job. I know of no one else in the office who works better under that kind of pressure than you. But I also know that you will only work late on Wednesday nights if it is a matter of life and death, because you have basketball tickets. Do you think anyone else around here can see the job through?

Lisa has been made a part of the decision-making process, which will help her reach the unhappy conclusion that she has no choice but to work late. The problem—an important rush job that no one else could perform as capably—is expressed before a conclusion is allowed to be reached.

Provide a way for the other person to gracefully retreat from an announced position. By introducing *new terms* or *revelations* into the discussions, you enable the other person to justify, to self and to others, your proposed changes.

Lisa has basketball tickets for Wednesday nights. Asking her to back down from her stated "no Wednesday night work" position is asking Lisa to compromise her stated principles. If Lisa's position is to be abandoned, there must be either *real* or *imagined* justification.

Office Manager: Lisa, I know you will be giving up an important game if you stay late. But I think our clients could be talked into giving up two seats in their box for Saturday's game, if you can see yourself clear on this one.

Lisa has been handed a *face-saving* crutch for breaking her Wednesday night work resolution. She hasn't backed down, she has simply traded in her principles for better seats.

> A winning mindset is a belief that stumbling blocks are overcome through persistence, a positive attitude, continuing interpersonal linkage, and maintenance of a resourceful, sincere, friendly, low-key negotiating climate so neither you nor your ideas are avoided.
>
> Marketplace bargaining is an event. Negotiating is a process. What is not happening for you *now* may happen for you *later.*

11

RUNNING THROUGH WALLS
The Trying Game

A stone wall mentality is much more difficult to manage than rejection. When you are stonewalled, the other person is refusing to have a meaningful dialogue—the lines of communication are shut down. If you pound on the wall with more of what wasn't working for you to begin with, you will only provoke more resistance. Don't smash down walls when you should be looking for a door.

Don't Give Up

My clients owed the May Co. a skosh under $3 million. For weeks, the department store folks refused to settle because "there was nothing to discuss." They were right. Hans Christian Andersen would have been hard put to fantasize a basis for denying my clients' liability.

Finally, I was told to "submit numbers." When they heard one they liked, they would let me know. It was an invitation to negotiate against myself.

Not wanting to start making what I knew would be the first in a long series of proposals, I balked at my clients' suggestion that I open with a "number" of $1 million.

I have been accused of beating dead horses by prolonging discussions that showed no vital signs. But because I have seen a lot of very experienced negotiators give up too easily and too soon, I keep going—not brashly or abrasively, but subtly and unobtrusively.

67

After numerous brief phone conversations in which no offers were made by either side, the May Co. offered to take a half-million dollars and call it quits.

Real effort is needed to jump-start a stale and weary dialogue. Even *creative nagging* is still nagging. Unless you keep forging on, you will have to consider discussions terminated. Without forging on, how will you discover motivator buttons or strengthen rapport? Negotiations haven't failed until—short of stapling the other person's coat sleeve to your desk—you have quit trying.

How to Unlock Sealed Lips and Closed Minds

If you ask questions that begin with *can, can't, is,* or *isn't,* chances are you will get a single-word response.

Single-word answers do not supply insight into the other person's desires, perceptions, and needs. They do not reveal reasons for resistance. Instead, they are positions that the person becomes emotionally committed to defend.

To make that rock talk, you need *probing questions* designed to flesh out the concerns and motivator buttons of people who are otherwise unwilling to open up. Design your questions so that they cannot be answered with a shake of the head or a single word such as *yes, no,* or *never.*

Practice imperative: To ensure that you neither prompt an argument nor appear confrontational, probing questions should be asked in a *sincere, unhurried, soft-touch* manner.

Defense lawyer Johnnie Cochran raised two tough questions "with a style that was very different from that used by his co-counsel [famed trial lawyer] F. Lee Bailey. Instead of beating up the witness, he established a rapport that led the prosecution witness to be freer in providing information."—Loyola University law professor, reporting on the O.J. Simpson trial in the *Los Angeles Times.*

Probing questions are the keys to revitalizing dialogue. You have five keys to choose from.

Key No. 1: Questions That Aren't Questions

Partially paraphrased "questions" are not questions at all. Information is elicited by paraphrasing the speaker.

Things are crazy down here and I won't be able to fill your order on Friday.

You won't be able to fill my order on Friday? (Paraphrased response.)

Well, we have this important job which takes priority.

Another job takes priority? (Paraphrased response.)

Your materials are in but there is a bonus if we get this other job out early. (A previously hidden agenda is revealed.)

To find out what had happened to the order, the listener partially paraphrased what the speaker had already said. This *soft-touch* technique is a favorite with psychiatrists. They know people will open up more readily when asked paraphrased questions that use their own words.

Tip: Try this technique in a social setting when it's hard to make small talk.

Key No. 2: "What" Not "Why"

Why elicits a general "because" response. *What* produces a more specific response that better reveals true needs and interests.

Why questions are intimidating and are usually associated with situations where we must be defensive:

That is my final decision.

Why?

Because I said so, that's why.

By contrast, *what* questions elicit fresh information on which new solutions may be based:

That is my final decision.

What *are the reasons it is your final decision?*

The reasons are . . . .

I can't really afford to buy it now.

*Under **what** circumstances would you be able to afford it?*

I can't do it now but maybe in a few weeks . . . .

*In **what** way will things be different in a few weeks?*

Key No. 3: "What If?"

What if questions pose *soft-touch* hypothetical possibilities. They are not offers to be accepted or rejected; they are questions to be answered. *What if* questions stimulate conversations while supplying new information and insight into the other person's interests and goals:

> *What if I were willing to wait until February to buy a new minivan from you?*
>
> *I notice you have four green minivans but only one blue one. What if I were to buy a green minivan from you instead of the blue one?*

Key No. 4: Statement Questions

Too many probing questions can make even the friendliest dialogue start to sound like an inquisition, prompting a *Hey, I am not on the witness stand* response.

Statement questions are probing questions disguised as statements. With some luck, the right lighting, and a little makeup, they will not be recognized for what they really are.

> *I was wondering what you thought of my proposal.* (Question: What did you think of the proposal?)
>
> *Although this makes a lot of sense to me, it may not seem like a good idea to you.* (Question: What do you think of this idea?)

Key No. 5: What Will It Take to Convince You?

"*What will it take to convince you* that now is the time to move [or, ours is the right company to do your job; or, my offer is both competitive and fair]?" is a good news/bad news question.

- *The good news:* The phrasing avoids prolonged questioning and second-guessing by eliciting a direct and unequivocal response.

- *The bad news:* The other person is encouraged to take a position. Because you may not like the answer this question evokes, it should be used only as a last-ditch or tight-move play.

For Every Problem, There Is Already a Solution—Whether You Know It or Not

Knowledge is important. But without imagination, knowledge has nowhere to go.

Dare to be creative! Novel and inventive approaches get people to change. You and the person you wish to influence are part of a *behavioral equation:* once you change, the other person will respond to give a new balance.

The greater your creativity level, the more alternatives, suggestions, solutions, and proposals you will be able to contribute to the persuasive process.

If you can overcome each new reason for resistance with a solution to overcome that resistance, then you have the flexibility and staying power necessary for finding a basis for agreement.

The response may be rejection. But even rejection is progress because it means you have discarded an unworkable alternative. Rejection is a positive vital sign that the lines of communication are open and alive. Withdrawal and resistance—the stone wall—are always more difficult to deal with than rejection because the lines of communication have slammed shut.

Brainstorming is the harmonious clash of ideas. Present your negotiating problem to a small group of your own colleagues and invite them to call out solutions "off the top half inch" with no constraints whatsoever.

Don't be timid. The chain-reaction phenomenon leading to critical mass is what is vital. Free and uninhibited exchange of ideas and thoughts encourages more ideas and thoughts. As often as not, a totally unworkable, unrealistic consideration will trigger the ideal solution.

In addition to your own brain, use all the brains you can borrow. For advice and counsel, look to others who have backgrounds different from your own. Friends and neighbors are ideal candidates. Borrow the thoughts of lawyers, accountants, and bankers who have broad experiential backgrounds. Each creative idea is a stepping stone toward another creative idea.

Spin Control: Manage Perceptions

Two unrelated labor problems that occurred during the recession of the 1980s demonstrate the incredible power of perception management.

The air traffic controllers' union, PATCO, struck. These highly skilled federal employees declared they would not return to work until they won a new contract calling for fewer hours and more pay. PATCO rejected offers of settlement, knowing that the safety of the airways and the well-being of the national economy depended on its members' unique abilities.

President Ronald Reagan took an equally strong stand. The strike was in contravention of the union's "no strike" government contract. If the strike were successful, it would encourage other federal employees to strike, fanning the fires of rampant inflation.

The PATCO members were critical to efficient management of the nation's airways. Yet, with enthusiastic popular support, President Reagan fired the strikers, who were *perceived* as self-serving, unfair, "greedy extortionists."

During this same trying period, Ford, General Motors, and Chrysler saw their losses escalate and their sales hit record low levels. To cut losses, plants would have to be closed and workers laid off—unless the United Auto Workers (UAW) agreed to relinquish previously negotiated major benefits. UAW members agreed that they would concede those benefits, which they had vigorously fought for and won.

The UAW membership did not perceive the Big Three as greedy or unreasonable but saw them as having no other viable alternative. The demanded concessions were perceived as part of a team effort to ride out the recession.

Managing Expectations

Frequently, a stone wall's foundation will be a *negative expectation* that results from a *pessimistic perception* or *pessimistic preconception*. Managing the other person's real or erroneous negative expectations is a vital part of the persuasion progression.

Managing negative expectations *begins* by telling listeners what they *expect, want,* and *need* to hear and, if possible, taking action that contradicts their negative expectations. This vital precept of *expectation management* has often been overlooked:

- Exxon's CEO did *not* fly to Alaska to observe the vast oil spill caused by the rupturing of its tanker, the *Exxon Valdez*.

- Union Carbide seemingly shrugged off responsibility for a disaster that killed thousands in Bhopal, India.

- A.H. Robins attempted to deny culpability for the medical problems suffered by thousands of its IUD users.

- Dow Corning failed to quickly disclose and assume responsibility for leaking silicone breast implants.

Managing negative expectations *continues* by forthrightly acknowledging the basis for those expectations while making a commitment to do things right:

- Prompt action was taken by Procter & Gamble to inform Rely tampon users of the danger of toxic shock.

- The deaths resulting from Tylenol tampering were immediately disclosed to the American public by Johnson & Johnson.

- Perrier did not hesitate in removing its bottled water from grocers' shelves and notifying the public of potential benzene contamination.

In its thirty-year heyday, Thom McAn was the best-selling shoe brand in the United States. But people just didn't want to shop there anymore, and the company was forced to close some two-thirds of its stores. The reason? Thom McAn customers *expected* to find "boring, ugly, and nerdy" shoes, a market survey revealed. Dispelling customers' negative expectations meant launching a bold and unusual advertising campaign: "Please excuse some of our shoe styles in the past. For years, our new and updated shoes were re-routed by a disgruntled postal worker and abandoned under a bridge near Chicago."

On a local level, expectation management meant my saying what a health club landlord needed to hear before negotiating a lease renewal: "I know my client has not been the best of tenants. However, he now has new management and the capital necessary to operate efficiently and to pay rent timely."

■ ■ ■

Sometimes, an overly *optimistic preconception* is the wall's foundation. It's not easy being an American icon. Harold Robbins is "America's Master Storyteller." It is much more difficult to negotiate for my client, Harold, than it is for my friend, Marty Safran, "America's Patio Furniture King." No one has overly optimistic expectations about any negotiated outcomes with Marty, but people who are in negotiations with the likes of Harold Robbins always expect more for themselves.

Representing wealthy Saudi Arabians in the mid-1980s, I soon discovered a similar *expectation* problem. Sellers, who had read fascinating newspaper accounts about newly oil-rich Arabs giving thousand-dollar tips to bellmen or gifting a favored waitress with a fine gem, were out to make a killing. Overly optimistic real estate sellers quickly jacked up their prices and then stonewalled us by refusing to negotiate.

Erroneous expectations had to be quickly dispelled. Anxious sellers were put on notice. There were no dancing girls. There were no harems. The price we were prepared to pay had to be competitive or there would be no deal.

Dire Traits: Instructions for the Care and Handling of Impossible People

Some stone walls are erected in response to what you are proposing. Other walls will have their foundation in the other person's negotiating personality.

Each of us has characteristics that cause us to react to a particular situation in a particular way. When confronted with what may appear to be a conflict situation, some people will slip into readily *readable* and identifiable resistance trait patterns.

The *persuasion progression* is not about *changing* the other person's conflict personality. It is about *managing* the other person's conflict personality. Here are some of the impossible types you may encounter.

Queen of Da Nile (Denial)

Her Highness, the Queen of Denial, makes herself oblivious to adversity and confrontation. A student of the ostrich school of problem solving, she is purposefully unmindful, unaware, and unconscious of conflict. She goes on as if there were no problems to solve. She remains in a state of orchestrated oblivion.

Don't let the queen deny what's happening. Face the issues head-on. The queen will respond if you are positive and not argumentative. Persistence is critical. "Even though you may not feel there is a potential problem, let's discuss these issues so I will be ready for any problem that may pop up. There is no harm in being prepared just in case . . . ."

Darth Evader

This "non-stick" negotiator is a sidetracker who will change the subject, pour a drink, remember an appointment, or do anything necessary to avoid a confrontation.

Calmly stay on track. Become angry or upset and your impatience will become the focus of Darth's attention—another way of evading the real issues. Resolve each issue before moving on to the next. Present proposals that require immediate responses.

The Mountain

The Mountain is a "flat-earth society" type whose life is a pattern of resistance. This dogged, mulish negotiator has managed to raise stubbornness to a new art form by refusing to budge to resolve a problem.

Don't become so position-oriented that you too become unmovable. Like Mohammed, go to the Mountain. Be both persistent and positive. Point out the benefits to be gained from negotiations.

Change to a Negotiator-Friendly Resistance Pattern

Each negotiating *level* has its own unique needs and roles.

Each level also has *people* who have their own personal needs for achievement, self-worth, and security; their different individual roles to play out; and their different constituencies to court.

When Thomas Watson, Jr. was IBM's chairman, he called a meeting of his top executives to remedy what he considered to be a pressing problem. A complaint had been received from an employee who had found just the right *level* for airing his grievance. He had written to Watson's mother.

Turning to different levels of authority—the store manager instead of the store clerk, the store owner instead of the store manager—will expose different *level interests* and different *people interests* and, therefore, different *patterns of resistance*.

An employer deadlocked with a local union might appeal to the rank-and-file membership in newspaper ads, hoping that the members themselves will pressure the local's management into adopting a pattern of resistance more consistent with the membership's needs than with the needs of the local's management.

At the top, you will always find the greatest flexibility. The top has the risk takers . . . the policy makers . . . the people who are so secure in their positions that they understand the exceptions as well as the rules.

At the bottom, you will find those who dare not deviate from established procedure. A Chicago bus driver made the national news by refusing to briefly leave his route to drive a passenger suffering a heart attack to a nearby hospital.

Rock On!

David Crosby had been told that his tax obligations were timely paid. But to his dismay, well over a million dollars was still owed to the IRS, which now had a stranglehold on all of his concert and royalty income. The IRS field officer assigned to the case wouldn't loosen that grip even as an ailing David Crosby waited for a liver transplant.

For reasons no one understood, the field officer was relentless in her efforts to collect from the legendary rock star. Month after month, she stonewalled negotiations by refusing to meet with David's representatives: "There will be no meeting because there is nothing to talk about."

A collection group manager, who felt it inappropriate to interfere, did prompt the otherwise intractable officer to open a dialogue with me. That dialogue was, however, an exercise in frustration and futility: "If David Crosby is really sincere in wanting to pay his taxes, he should start to raise cash by selling his guitars and clothes at a celebrity auction."

Dire situations sometimes require extraordinary action. Our strategy was to change negotiating levels by filing a Chapter 11 bankruptcy reorganization for the single purpose of moving David's file away from the field office's impossible people to the IRS office "downtown," where different decision makers and a different mentality prevailed. We planned to withdraw the Chapter 11 petition once we reached the sanctuary of a new and higher negotiating level.

The strategy was successful. The IRS officers downtown negotiated from a perspective where individual job performance was not measured in collection ratios.

Do What You Need to Do

Among the extraordinary actions that may be required to reach a new level of decision makers are: initiate a lawsuit, file a complaint with a regulatory agency, or bring media focus to the unresolved issue.

... And If You Still Haven't Gotten the Nod

Looking good when things aren't going your way takes a lot of style.

Monday mourning? If a result is not totally to your liking, instead of crying over spilled milk, be content it wasn't Jack Daniels. Your style will be remembered long after your disappointment is forgotten.

> **Finessing a stonewaller begins by "hanging in" and by knowing how to get the other person to talk and to keep talking. It is further advanced through the reshaping of the stonewaller's expectations and through knowing how to manage conflict personalities.**

12

FINESSING WORTH, VALUE, AND SHARE DIFFERENCES
Waging Peace

Many differences are quantitative *worth, value,* or *share* differences. Sometimes, they are best dealt with by negotiating *an approach* rather than *a position.*

Separated at Worth

A common mistake made by negotiators at all levels of experience is that they become committed to stated positions and allow these positions to become announced points of honor.

Positions elicit counterpositions. When defending positions becomes a matter of ego, personalities are wrongfully summoned into play. Positional bargaining without a strong fall-back option is a risky game.

Positional bargaining can be avoided by negotiating an *approach* rather than a dollar amount. One approach could be the use of *external criteria.*

The Abos Marine Blue Book contains the retail and wholesale value of boats. Kelley's Blue Book contains the value of cars. However, an external criterion does not necessarily have to be a published reference. Consultants are called on to settle executive salary disputes. Appraisals are often the external criteria used to resolve conflicts involving everything from antiques to business goodwill.

Mr. Superstar, an American heart throb whose face is often on the cover of *People* magazine, had fallen in love with a lakeside retreat—an older fixer-upper with a $3 million price tag. He was willing to pay whatever was truly fair, but in his mind the home's $3 million price tag was about $700,000 off the mark. Representing Mr. Superstar, we started negotiations.

"I do not haggle and $3 million is my price," was the seller's pre-offer proclamation. The seller's justification for the oversized ticket was in large part the home's history. The house was built and had been occupied by a real estate tycoon for whom a fair-sized California city is named—a fact that Mr. Superstar did not believe justified the price demanded. We wanted to talk dollars. The seller wanted to talk about throwing in towels and linens bearing the prior owner's monogram.

The M word (money) had to be sidestepped if we were to avoid a positional tug-of-war.

Our readily accepted solution was to negotiate an *externalization approach* rather than dollars. We suggested that a mutually agreeable appraiser set the price. If the appraised value was $3 million or less, Mr. Superstar was obligated to purchase. If it was $2 million or more, the seller was obligated to sell.

Randomizing, such as flipping a coin or drawing lots, is a simple externalization technique that I have seen used even by sophisticated businesspeople when traditional analytical approaches have failed.

At other times, a *formula solution* will mean the difference between resolving a dispute and going to the mats. You will need an arsenal of sure-fire, fast-acting deadlock busters. The six deadlock-busting formulamatic tactics that follow can be used in a variety of situations.

Deadlock Buster No. 1

I had negotiated the sale of Harold Robbins' hilltop mansion to Dino de Laurentis. However, during the pendency of the sale, a $1 million price reduction was suggested because the geological integrity of part of the grounds was put in issue. The parties' experts disagreed as to the seriousness of the problem. One thing was certain: Robbins wanted to sell and de Laurentis wanted to buy. What could be done to resolve this conflict?

An *approach* was suggested: The two disagreeing geologists would themselves choose a third geologist. The conclusion of this third geologist would be deemed controlling.

Deadlock Buster No. 2

To decorate their Turtle Creek mansion, clients "T" and "R" acquired four fine oil paintings of slightly varying value. Later, they decided to call it quits. What would be the best way to divide this art, realizing that each painting had a special value beyond its extrinsic worth?

It was agreed that one person would get the first and fourth choices of paintings, and the other, the second and third choices. If they couldn't agree on who would get which set of choices, a flip of the coin would decide.

Deadlock Buster No. 3

An actress and her production company employer were deadlocked over an appropriate salary for the fourth season of a very successful soap opera. How could this deadlock be overcome?

Both the actress and the company would write down their final position—how much they would pay or agree to accept. If the two figures were within 15 percent of each other, they would be averaged. If they were more than 15 percent apart, a neutral party would select the more realistic figure of the two submitted. ("Baseball" is the name often given to this deadlock buster.) This approach encourages both sides to be realistic and reasonable in the formulation of their final offers.

Deadlock Buster No. 4

As an alternative approach to the scenario in No. 3, the neutral party could write down what she or he believed was the fairest and most equitable salary. This figure would not be disclosed to either the actress or her production company, who would then write down their own final positions. The position closest to the neutral party's figure would be the salary for the coming season. (This deadlock buster is often called "golf.")

Deadlock Buster No. 5

"L" and "A" are in the midst of a divorce. Both worked for years building the family landscaping business. Each wants to buy the other's one-half interest in the business for as little as possible. They agree on only one thing: a stranger would not pay top dollar for the business. How can they break this impasse?

One spouse (the "deciding spouse") would decide what would be both a fair price and fair payment terms for a one-half interest. The other spouse would then get to choose whether to be the buyer or the seller of that one-half interest, using the deciding spouse's price and terms.

The deciding spouse, not knowing whether he or she would be the buyer or seller, would set parameters that would be realistic and fair to either side. If the role of the deciding spouse can't be agreed on, then a flip of a coin would be determinative.

Deadlock Buster No. 6

Jane owned a champion female Irish Wolfhound. Jane knew little about dog breeding, the care of a pregnant bitch, or what to do with a newborn litter. Paul, an experienced breeder and a new acquaintance, owned a champion male. It was agreed that the litter would be shared equally.

The problem standing in the way of true romance was Jane's concern that Paul, with his superior expertise, would choose the best puppies for himself, leaving Jane with the less desirable offspring. No one else in the state knew as much about Irish Wolfhounds as Paul. How could Jane avoid being at Paul's mercy?

Paul would select two pups at a time. Jane would then select for herself one of the two pups chosen by Paul. Not knowing which pup Jane would select, with each draw Paul would pick out two pups with the greatest championship potential.

> **Hammering away with a go-nowhere *position* produces three things: (1) irritability, (2) lessened rapport, and (3) stronger commitment to the positions being defended. If the other person acknowledges a true interest in making a deal, then suggest an externalization or formulamatic approach. If that suggestion is refused, then call the game "hardball."**

13

FINESSING PEOPLE WHO WOULD RATHER BE RIGHT THAN REASONABLE
Slow Squeezing

They seem to be everywhere: people who would rather be right than reasonable. Often, the disagreement with these impossible people is not so much about money as it is about fairness. The most effective way to deal with such people is through the steady, patient, unemotional application of all the techniques you've learned in Part II of this book. I call this *slow squeezing.*

Let me tell you about my worst vacation day ever.

My wife and I arrived in Zagreb, in the former Yugoslavia, on a Saturday night in November. In our room at the Intercontinental Hotel was a brochure extolling the beauty of Plitvice Lakes, sixteen small lakes connected by waterfalls in a beautiful mountain setting.

A Sunday visit to Plitvice Lakes sounded wonderful. According to the concierge, Plitvice Lakes tour buses did not operate off-season, but public buses ran in each direction on the hour. It was a two-and-a-half-hour journey for $2.50—a true bargain. We were concerned about the weather, but the concierge assured us that the tram that circled the lakes every forty-five minutes was enclosed, and that a "visit to the lakes was an absolute must."

We arrived at the lake at 1:00 P.M. only to discover that every restaurant and shop was locked until summer. The tram ran only every three hours in the off-season, and the next tram was two hours later. Suddenly, it began raining. I'm not talking drizzle, I'm talking buckets. With no place to go, we raced back to the main highway to catch the 2:00 P.M. return bus.

It gets worse.

There was no 2:00 P.M. bus. The 3:00 P.M. bus and the 4:00 P.M. bus passed us by. They were too filled with villagers returning to their jobs in Zagreb after a weekend at home. By 4:30 P.M., we were very concerned, anxious, and wet.

There were no taxis, there were no buses, there were no restaurants. There was coldness, there was rain, there was darkness.

Sloshing down the highway, we came across a local man who offered to drive us back to the hotel for $85. I was too wet and cold to think about negotiating, and I gladly accepted without a whimper.

Before going up to my hotel room, I stopped at the assistant manager's desk, feeling some sense of drama as I stood before him soaking wet. Certainly he would be sympathetic to the plight of a shivering guest.

I was wrong. He was unprepared to reimburse me the $85 or offer even a hot bowl of soup. He did agree to explain the situation to Mr. Bratas, the manager, when he arrived in the morning.

Here's the next morning's dialogue between me and Mr. Bratas.

Manager: I have received a memo from the assistant manager explaining in detail what happened.

We regret the inconvenience. The hotel, however, does not take any responsibility for what happened.

Bob: Mr. Bratas, you may be right in what you are saying.

Acknowledging that Bratas *may be right* was both a defusing tactic and a modulating device, setting a tone for calm, nonpositional dialogue. It was also demonstrative of my having an open mind. Criticizing or yelling would only have caused Bratas to become more defensive.

Addressing Bratas by name, I was both *personalizing the negotiations* and reminding Bratas that *he* was an *active participant* in the problem resolution process. I did not want him to sit in silent judgment while I spun my tale of woe.

Bob: Perhaps I am totally wrong in asking the Intercontinental to reimburse me. The hotel brochure in my room encourages visits to Plitvice Lakes. Your concierge told us that it would be a wonderful, relaxing way to spend our Sunday. Am I wrong in believing that the hotel was recommending a visit to the Lakes?

Bratas had been invited to be both candid and objective with me. I needed Bratas to become *involved*, to evaluate the situation *with* me as part of a *collaborative*, nonadversarial effort. To accomplish this collaborative involvement, I sincerely solicited Bratas's criticism of both my facts and my analysis of those facts. A position-oriented approach was painstakingly avoided.

Wanting Bratas to reciprocate, I was allowing my conclusions to be tested by his sense of what was fair and reasonable.

Bob: I appreciate the time that was taken by your staff in explaining how to take the bus to the lakes and back. Their interest and desire to be helpful is not in question.

Staff personalities had been separated from the dispute. By telling Bratas that his staff tried to be cooperative and helpful, I was setting a hotel *pattern of conduct* and hospitality that I expected him to abide by. If brought into our discussions, the concierge would not consider my attack to be against him personally.

Bob: Hopefully you and the Intercontinental will want to be fair with me. I do not want to appear greedy and I know you too want to resolve this situation in a manner that is both sensible and fair.

Fairness, not money, was my primary stated concern. Bratas could not fault such an approach. Not wanting to sound self-righteous, I did not say: "Sure, the money is important, but even more important to me is whether I am being fairly treated."

Bob: Perhaps I should really be discussing my feelings with the Intercontinental's management in the United States. To whom do you recommend that I write? Do you think if my travel agent also wrote that it would help?

This *veiled ultimatum* reminded Bratas that I was serious about this situation and that the problem would not end with our discussions. I was not "reporting" him to management, but I did want to discuss my *feelings* with management. Bratas was on notice that he would have to continue to deal with the problem.

> **Bob:** Mr. Bratas, I understand that your position is that you have no obligation to reimburse me the $85 I spent.

By acknowledging that I fully comprehended Bratas's position, I was *confirming* that I understood what he had said without *agreeing* to what he had said. By not having to reassert his position of nonresponsibility, he would perhaps be less defensive.

The words *you* and *your* (rather than *hotel*) were being used. Even though personalities were purposely being kept out of the picture, it was still very much a person-to-person dilemma.

> **Bob:** I am curious. What is the reason you do not want to reimburse me?

My question generously presupposed that Bratas had a rationale for his stated position. This may or may not have been true, but the approach would compel him to show his cards and produce the logic behind his stated position.

> **Bob:** Let me ask a few questions to make absolutely sure I understand the facts:
> —Is the brochure in every room because the hotel recommends visits to Plitvice Lakes?
> —Is it the duty of your concierge to assist guests with local touring?
> —Should the concierge have dissuaded rather than encouraged us from going to the Lakes?

These pointed questions were designed to elicit answers that I knew already. The questions prompted Bratas to rethink the fairness and logic behind his stated position. If Bratas was to change his mind, it would be because of *questions asked* rather than *statements made*.

> **Bob:** I think I understand what you are saying. The hotel has no responsibility to me because it has no control over whether

buses are filled or Plitvice Lake facilities are closed. If my understanding is wrong, please tell me.

Again, I had confirmed in positive, unsarcastic terms that I understood what Bratas had told me. He had now been invited to tell me whether my perceptions were wrong—a reminder that I wanted our communications to be open and clear. More importantly, the logic and rationale behind Bratas's position had been identified and contained. This "logic" could now be openly dealt with by both of us.

Questions rather than *statements* were posed to Bratas, causing him to respond with answers rather than defensive retorts. Questions also caused Bratas to remain an involved participant in the persuasive progression.

Bob: I know that you are trying to be fair with me.

By reminding Bratas that fairness was the standard of a mutually agreeable solution, I wanted him to continue to be worthy of my appreciation of what he, as a person, was trying to accomplish.

Bob: The suggestion to go to the Lakes was the hotel's suggestion which was reinforced by your concierge. The concierge also knew it was off-season, so the regular tour buses would not be operating again until summer.

Do you think it is reasonable for me to expect that he would have known that Plitvice Lakes had become a desolate, off-season area?

You are right that a concierge has the job to assist hotel guests with their travel plans. I agree with you that he probably didn't know that on Sunday returning buses would be too full to stop at the Lakes for passengers. *What*, however, is the reason for the concierge not knowing the status of a hotel-recommended attraction?

I had to deal with a behavioral truth: It is more important for people to be right than to be reasonable. I had reaffirmed that what Bratas had told me earlier was "right." Bratas was not being cross-examined in front of a judge or jury. He alone would decide whether I would be a winner. If Bratas was going to change his mind, it would be for his own reasons, not mine. My job was to cause him to generate his own reasons for wanting to change.

Using the word *what* rather than *why* kept an important question from having an accusatory quality.

> **Bob:** One fair method of resolving this situation would be for the hotel to reimburse us the $85 we spent, less the cost of two return bus trips and the cost of taxi fare from the bus station back to the hotel. Do you think that makes sense?

A settlement possibility had been presented for Bratas's evaluation. The proposed solution was not tendered as being mine or his. Instead, it *evolved* from our general dialogue without any claim of authorship. If it was rejected, it was not *my* proposal being refused, which would make it easier for me to try other possibilities.

The settlement was proposed only *after* the reasoning supporting the proposal had been communicated.

> **Bob:** If we are able to agree, then you can adjust my hotel bill. If we are unable to reach a satisfactory resolution to this situation, then I would like to discuss the matter further with whomever you believe to be the appropriate person in the United States.

I had reiterated that a "no" answer would not be conclusive. Although I didn't want to sound threatening, I did want Bratas to know where he stood with me. A harsh threat or clear warning, however, would only have destroyed the tone of objectivity I had created.

Wanting to make a positive answer as easy as possible for Bratas, I had suggested crediting my bill rather than writing a check or reimbursing me in cash. *Adjust* is a word associated with fairness and reason.

After Bratas consented to adjust the bill, I suggested it would be both a nice goodwill gesture and appropriate hospitality if we were guests in the hotel dining room that evening. Bratas agreed, and it is with fondness that I still remember the cherry strudel.

The art of finesse is influencing and controlling outcomes with a soft touch but a firm goal.

PART III

HARD BARGAIN
Winning When the Score Is Kept in Dollars

14

ANALYTICS
Choice Points

The persuasion progression is about bringing the other person around to see things your way. It is now time to ask: What do you want to persuade the other person to do? *Analytics* are the dynamics you must consider when you determine your negotiating objective.

How hard a bargain will you drive? Will you be opportunistic? Tough? Moderate?

Your answer is not a constant. In each situation, you will need to ask:

- *What is a winning result?*

- *What is my negotiating goal?*

At this point in my seminars and workshops, more hands are raised than at any other time. Invariably, the question asked is: "How can anxiety-provoking *hard-bargain* tactics be used with soft-touch tactics, which are tender with egos?"

The negotiating game's most common error lies in a belief that there must be a symmetry between personal conduct and negotiation goals: tough demands = tough persona; soft demands = kinder, gentler persona.

91

How you do something and *what* you do are not the same. Iron fists *do* fit in velvet gloves.

Doing business with a hard nose is one thing. Doing business with an unfriendly, unlikable hard nose is something else. Stiff terms don't have to be accompanied by a stiff persona.

Having a soft-touch negotiating personality and being easy are not the same. Easy or *soft-touch/soft-bargain* negotiators will lose in a positional hard-bargaining game. *Soft-touch/hard-bargain* negotiators will invariably do better than *hard-touch/hard-bargain* negotiators. Why? Because a nice-guy persona makes not-so-nice deals go down easier.

Excuse Me for Interrupting Your Reading, but Would You Be So Kind as to Hand Me Your Watch and Wallet?

After one hundred armed robberies of hotel guests, Lon Perry, the infamous "Gentleman Bandit," surrendered to Houston police. Some of his victims regretted that he had given himself up. Others from whom he had stolen cash and jewelry couldn't say enough nice things about him: "unfailing graciousness," "really very nice," "caring," "apologetic," "friendly manner." "He held a gun on me with one hand and returned wallet pictures of my grandchildren with the other," reported one grateful grandpa, who went on to say, "I liked him."

Lon Perry's demands were not only unconscionable, they were criminal. But he made them with finesse, grace, and a *soft-touch* style that created no animosity toward him as a person.

Coopetition?

Those who first came to America bargained tough. Winning was measured by what they had achieved when the papers were signed, the hands were shaken, and the dust settled. Negotiated outcomes had clear winners and clear losers. It made no difference whether they were Asian or European or Latin. They had come from towns and villages where a *marketplace mentality* was an inherent part of their cultural and ethnic identity. The doctrine of caveat emptor—*let the buyer beware*—was very much a part of yesteryear's less protective notion of American jurisprudence.

Today, students are learning that winning is not always a matter of getting as much as you can for as little as possible. They are learning that the real "other side" may not be local subcontractors and suppliers but foreign competitors bent on getting a larger share of the U.S. market. Traditional domestic "opponents" such as labor, materials vendors, and components manufacturers can sometimes be viewed as potential allies.

They are being taught that in today's world, many situations offer an incentive for *bargaining moderation* as well as an incentive for bombs-away competitiveness.

They are being told that sometimes a moderate stance yields a greater return than hard-bargain competition, and the line between winning and losing is at times too thin to perceive.

Hard bargaining doesn't mean closing your mind to the potential benefits of moderation in bargaining. Only an unskilled negotiator will summarily reject mutual gain possibilities without giving them any consideration or thought. That consideration, that thought, that flexibility of determination is the mark of a pro.

There will be times to be a flat-out opportunist.

There will be times when you will be dealing with customers of long standing, business associates, family, or key employees, and the importance of the relationship will overshadow the substantive result.

There will be other times when you will be so firm on certain issues that you may even refuse to negotiate. Neither Sears salespeople nor the clerks at your local Blockbuster negotiate, and there is no reason why you have to either. Some things are just not negotiable, and that is OK.

In many situations, there will be both a strategic motivation to be moderate and a strategic motivation to be exploitive. In those situations, you will find yourself blending tactics to achieve a result that will be to your distinct advantage but will ensure a stable and harmonious conclusion.

Have a Game Player's Mindset

Life is not monochromatic. Negotiating opportunities are not uniform. There are no McDeals so there can be no scripts or formulas to see you through.

The *positive-result delivery system* of this book is easy to understand and easy to use, and it will dramatically increase your ability to influence negotiating outcomes. Only one barrier stands between its methodology and its application: your lifetime of habits.

Recognizing a student as someone who had attended my negotiating seminar about a year before, I asked why she was again enrolled. "So I will remember to use what I already know," she replied.

If you discover the good, sound, workable possibilities in this book and then don't use them, you might as well not have read this book at all. By viewing life's negotiating situations as a game, you will overcome old habits and better remember to use what you now "already know."

With a game player's mindset, you will view your negotiating opponent as a challenge rather than an enemy or adversary.

As a game player, you will set and revise goals. You will seek perspective. Without perspective, you will see leaves instead of trees, trees instead of forests.

And without perspective you will never see the *butterflies*—those small, simple, but profoundly important possibilities of the persuasion progression.

Explaining his theory of how a major occurrence could be produced by a minor one, meteorologist Edward Lorenz, discoverer of the *butterfly effect*, wrote in *Newsweek*, "If a butterfly flapped its wings in Brazil, it might produce a tornado in Texas. Unlikely as it seems, the tiny air currents that a butterfly creates travel across thousands of miles, jostling other breezes as they go and eventually changing the weather."

As a game player, you will analyze and appreciate relationships and sequences of events; you will identify your negotiating problems so you can correct them next time; you will be less behavioral and more analytical; and you will develop a defensive awareness to the other side's use of tactics, becoming more sensitized to your own tactical and strategic opportunities.

Everyone who has been told to exercise more or to start eating sensibly knows that it is as hard to get into a good habit as it is to break a bad one.

A book on dancing won't make you light on your feet, a book on sex won't make you a great lover, and a diet book won't make you thin. To convert the methodology of this book into a skillful resource takes time, thought, and practice.

In every instance, you will achieve more and will face less resistance if your hard bargain is delivered with a soft touch. Whether your hard-bargain strategy will be overreaching or moderate, or whether the tactics you choose to implement that

strategy will be rigid or accommodating, will be a function of your personal style, how you define "winning," industry custom, a myriad of external factors, and your own flexibility in being able to balance all of these along with the critical analytics that are discussed in the next two chapters: *relationships* and *power.*

15

RELATIONSHIPS
Walking Between the Raindrops

Relationships are a *choice point* analytic. They provide insight through precedence, create special obligations, and bring dimension to how winning is defined.

So you want to sell your car. You won't deal the same way with your favorite nephew as you will with the guy wearing three gold chains and mock ostrich loafers down at the used car lot.

Because no two relationships are ever quite the same, no two negotiating situations will ever be quite the same. In a relationship with a person who, you believe, will be extremely demanding, you too will be extreme. In a relationship with someone who, you believe, will be fair, you may be more moderate in your demands.

But if there is no relationship at all, what do you do?

Will you be moderate in your demands, assuming the other person will in turn be fair with you? Will casting your proposal in moderate terms leave you without negotiating slack if your reading proves untrue?

The Place Not to Be Scene

Think of a person you know, someone outside your household. Perhaps a cousin. Or the person with whom you had lunch yesterday. Maybe it's

96

the last person you negotiated with. It may even be your next-door neighbor. Let's call that person "Bill."

Now let's use a classic scenario to highlight how relationships impact and modulate your bargaining course of conduct.

The set: A jail cell.

As the scene opens, you are placed in the cell. You have been justifiably arrested for armed robbery. You are told that your accomplice, Bill, is in a separate cell off-stage.

A prosecutor enters the scene. She tells you that she does not have an open-and-shut case and is therefore making the following offer *separately* to you and to Bill:

If	Your Years in Prison	Bill's Years in Prison
Each of you confess	10	10
You confess and Bill is silent	0	20
Each of you remain silent	3	3
You are silent but Bill confesses	20	0

The Prisoner's Predicament

Will you:

- Remain silent, assuming Bill will do the same (an optimization strategy yielding just three years in jail for each of you)?

- Confess, hoping Bill will remain silent (an opportunistic strategy whereby you would walk)?

Your decision will rest entirely on how you *read* Bill's character, personality traits, and needs. This reading will only be possible because of a preexisting relationship. If the relationship has been casual, the reading will be cursory—and could be wrong. If your relationship with Bill has been one of long duration, you'll be able to read Bill with greater certainty.

The next time you spend time with the person you have designated as "Bill," propose the scenario, write down your secret-ballot decisions, and see how well you really know each other.

Family and Friends

She Got the Gold Mine, I Got the Shaft*

My law partner, Fred Glassman, is a brilliant divorce lawyer. His talent enables him to score one resounding "victory" after another. In a straight numbers game, Fred knows how to win big.

He is sought out by clients who want to pay the least possible amount of alimony, have rock-bottom child support obligations, or extract the last dime in a community property division contest.

But Fred no longer has a pure "rack up the points" approach to his cases. He will tell you that, as a result of becoming more *relationship sensitive,* he has a new effectiveness. Clients are happier, and Fred receives far fewer calls from clients that begin with *I have a problem* and continue with *My kids don't want to see me anymore* or *I don't get invited to family functions anymore* or *My family has disowned me.*

One man who has been divorced almost ten years still refers to his "ex" as "the Plaintiff." Parties in a divorce often feel retaliatory, but Fred knows that custody of a dining-room set is not as important as a family relationship, and that there is much more to be achieved in dismantling a marriage than calculatingly dividing up appliances, furniture, cars, and offspring.

Fred has learned that *winning* can be defined many different ways. He now realizes that a spouse is a spouse for as long as the marriage lasts, but an ex-spouse is forever. He also knows that the relationship of the parties—whether friends, partners, family, or almost ex-family—may be worthy of special negotiating consideration.

Pollyanna gobbledygook?

The day the Muhammad Ali divorce settlement papers were signed in our offices, the Greatest drew sketches for our staff as his way of saying, "Thanks for being nice." The next day, our client, Veronica Ali, appeared on *Good Morning America* telling a national television audience about her "dream divorce."

* Title of song recorded by Jerry Reed.

The Contractor's Trilogy

In some situations, there may not be a *preexisting* relationship. But will the deal itself give rise to a *new* ongoing relationship?

First Script

You want to build a new home. The contractor with whom you are dealing has fallen on hard times. He is prepared to take your job even though he will lose money; he has to keep his crew working. You are wondering why "Our Lady of the Upper Hand" has smiled on you with such great favor.

As the prospective home builder, will your terms be predatory? Hard? Moderate? I suggest they be moderate.

Second Script

You want to buy construction equipment. The contractor with whom you are dealing has fallen on hard times and must immediately sell some of his equipment to raise critically needed cash.

As an equipment buyer, you have no reason to be moderate, and an opportunistic bargain may be the best bargain.

■ ■ ■

The difference between the first script and the second is whether the negotiations will give rise to a new ongoing relationship.

Ask anyone who has ever built a house. The most difficult negotiations often occur *after* the deal is signed: postcontract changes, modifications, delays, call-back work—all traditional opportunities for retaliation. In the first script, a new ongoing relationship must be reckoned with.

There is not and will never be an ongoing relationship when you bargain to buy used equipment, or you bargain at swap meets, or you bargain to buy firewood, or you bargain with street vendors in Puerto Vallarta. These are all examples of what is referred to in street lingo as *popcorn deals*—marketplace transactions of limited scope. With no lasting relationship to consider, a good bargaining result can be as one-sided as a flood.

Who is the real winner—the person who is told *You have a deal. It is a pleasure doing business with you* or the one who is told *You have a deal. Of all the low-down cheap propositions, yours is the best?*

The answer will depend on whether there is or will be a relationship to pamper.

Third Script

You want to buy a home. The contractor with whom you are dealing has fallen on hard times and must immediately sell the home he built several years ago for his family. It will take two months for the sale to close and title to transfer.

As the home buyer, how hard a bargain will you drive?

You may want to take a bargaining stance somewhere between the moderation shown in the first script (building a house) and the opportunistic bargain driven in the second script (buying used equipment).

There will be times when the alienation of the other side will not be as important as the victory of the moment, when winning will be quantifiably measured by what is in hand right now.

In the third script, if you buy the family home too cheaply, will the seller try to break the contract if a more attractive opportunity presents itself? Possibly so. As a member of the great loophole industry, I can attest that there is no such thing as a contract that can be guaranteed as absolutely unbreakable.

In some bargaining situations, both sides should walk away from the haggling with something more than scars and bruises for their efforts. At times, it will make good sense to leave something on the bargaining table to lessen the chance that the deal will sour. That something will be the difference between walking away with a great deal and an exploitative one.

You do not deal with everybody in the same way. Old and newly created relationships are an analytic in determining your negotiating objective.

16

POWER
The Insurmountable Opportunities Factor

Negotiating power is a *choice point* analytic. Power is an enigma—it can be very real or only a state of mind. Understanding power is understanding how it is lost and how it is created.

Sam has been interviewing for a job in his hometown for three weeks. So far, not even a nibble. Like his car, Sam is fully detailed: salon-perfect nails, shirt creased, hair styled. His Florsheims still have shiny soles and he is wearing a new suit that his salesman guaranteed him would boost his self-esteem. Sam's resume is on high-quality bond paper.

Sam is now walking into job interview no. 6.

Hal has been interviewing for a job in his hometown for three weeks. Even though Hal is no more capable or personable than Sam, somehow he has managed to bag two interesting offers and the prospect of a third. He is wearing a suit he bought a few years ago, but only someone with an extraordinarily keen sense of fashion would know it was yesterday's news. Hal's resume appears shop-worn. It was on the back seat when his dog jumped into the car.

Hal is now walking into job interview no. 6.

Who has the superior negotiating power, Hal or Sam?

101

Hal.

Hal has something Sam doesn't have. He has options. His options give him the ability to take risks.

Hal is not committed to negotiating a deal. Other job opportunities are available to him. They are the *fall-back opportunities* that give Hal the *ability to set limits and to take risks.*

Sam, the job applicant who has not received a job offer, won't be able to as successfully discuss salary, benefits, and vacations.

Recall your last south-of-the-border *vaya con Kaopectate* vacation? You made a final offer to a street merchant and sauntered away. How he followed, somehow walking backward in front of you with the grace of someone with eyes in the back of his head. How he met *your* price precisely at the moment your foot hit the first step of the tour bus.

Give it some thought. Haven't your most successful negotiations almost always been conducted at times when you really didn't care whether you made the deal or not?

In not caring too much about the outcome, you allowed yourself to take bigger risks. You were free from the pressure and anxiety of having to enter into an agreement or make a commitment. This freedom to say *I pass* is the primary source of negotiating power and should be a determinant of how cooperative or exploitative you will be in setting your terms.

The One That Got Away

Last year, good friends came to me for advice.

For over a year, my friends had been looking for "just the right" 1953 Corvette. At long last, a wonderful '53 was put up for sale. The price was on the high side. My friends understood on good authority that two other 'vette buffs had already submitted offers.

My friends needed to know whether they should:

- Propose an extremely low price.

- Propose a price close enough to the asking price that it would be accepted without further negotiations.

- Propose a price somewhere in between.

When you are bargaining for something unique—a custom cabin, a classic Corvette, an antique clock—it is important to understand *what* you are bargaining for. What is your primary objective: to get the best possible *price* or the strongest possible *commitment*?

When you don't have fall-back options, a commitment may be more important than price. In these situations, what you think you are overpaying is the premium for not losing the deal.

After I explained this to my car-buff friends, they proposed a price that was close to the asking price. Their offer was accepted without further negotiation.

Power Moves

Like the Abominable Snowman, Big Foot, and the Loch Ness Monster, negotiating power is as much illusion as it is reality.

Power shifts. After 444 days in captivity, fifty-three American hostages being held captive in Iran were released. During the preceding fifteen months, the Carter Administration had never stopped negotiating for their release. Why were the hostages on their way to the Teheran airport on the very day Ronald Reagan was being administered his oath of office? The incoming administration had already voiced a hard-line approach. The Iranians knew that their negotiating risks were going to change dramatically.

Power vanishes.

It builds.

It reappears.

Power is a state of mind. A Penn Central Railroad-owned company was selling one of the last large pieces of undeveloped land in Orange County, California. Everything came to a jarring halt after two days of grueling negotiations. Someone had learned that the buyer, who was "all hat and no cattle" had come into town on the Greyhound bus! If you believe you have negotiating power, then to some extent, you do.

Power is always relative. 1981 is not remembered as the incredible rookie season of Fernando Valenzuela. Nor is it remembered for the Los Angeles Dodgers' comeback in postseason competition, culminating in a World Series victory over the New York Yankees.

It is remembered as the season of a player strike that eliminated a third of the schedule and created the first split season.

The dispute between the players and club owners was over the compensation to be paid to free-agent players. The players figured that their strike would force the owners to negotiate. Empty stadiums would mean that profits from ticket sales, advertising, concessions, television, and radio would all be out the window.

So far so good. But the players lacked one critical piece of information. The owners, anticipating a strike, had assessed their own lack of leverage and purchased $50 million in strike insurance. Hefty insurance payments replaced a good portion of the owners' lost revenue. The owners let it be known they were in no hurry to settle with the striking players.

The players lost $28 million in salaries because they were unable to negotiate an acceptable deal until after the owners' strike insurance ran out. Seven weeks after the strike began, it ended.

The players' power was *relative* to the owners' power. *Reading* the other side means reading its commitments, objectives (the owners were not prepared to quickly concede), strengths (the players didn't know about the strike insurance), and weaknesses. Power does shift, and most of today's students of baseball history would say the players won by striking.

More Power to You

At a seminar-workshop, "Art," an architect, told the class that he was never sure whether to bid high or low on prospective jobs. Here is how my class addressed Art's dilemma.

Art, who is negotiating a major design project, knows that the lower his bid, the less risk he has of losing the job. The higher his bid, the greater his risk of falling out of negotiations. Times have been tough lately for the building industry in general.

In setting his bid parameters, Art will weigh his options and evaluate his fall-back positions by assessing what other work may be coming in to pay the rent and the staff and put milk on the table.

Reality Check

Art would be lulling himself into an illusory sense of well-being if his fall-back possibilities were only so-so alternatives: writing an architecture book, enrolling for postgraduate study, or guiding visiting Americans on a tour of the classical architecture of Greece. In combination, his list seems viable, but the choices have to be looked at individually. Unfortunately, Art doesn't have a dependable, bankable option in the bunch.

All is not lost, however. Art can create options where none existed before, but first he must consider realistic alternatives:

- Moving to an area that isn't as economically depressed as his hometown.

- Promoting the remodeling aspect of his business, knowing that people will often remodel when new construction becomes prohibitively expensive.

- Working for the city in its building permit department.

- Going "in house" for a major franchiser or chain retailer that has expansion plans and needs an architect.

From realistic alternatives come true options. Art likes the alternative of going in house and the security of a salary. In psyching himself for the job interview, Art knows he has an option (the ability to bid low to win the design project back home), which gives him both leverage and confidence.

If offered the job, Art has the ability to risk bidding high on the design project: he knows that the job offer is a fall-back option. Art's leverage positions are strengthened even more as he creates and adds other contingency plans to his list of options.

In negotiating the design project or in negotiating the job, Art now has the power of options—the power to pass, the power to walk. He has the essential elements of control. Art has, in fact, created negotiating power.

The Infomaniac's Edge

The Sheik, a member of the Saudi Arabian royal family, had retained our law firm to negotiate the purchase of a major piece of Carefree, Arizona, real estate. Its owner was singer Wayne Newton.

Everything I needed to know about Wayne Newton's alternatives to negotiating an agreement with us was front-page news. He needed to raise instant cash to purchase the Aladdin hotel and casino in Las Vegas. For the price of a Las Vegas newspaper, we were able to track and quantify his needs. Newton had to sell the Arizona property *now* or lose his lifetime dream of owning a casino hotel.

The Sheik was the perfect potential buyer. Not being accountable to any board or committee, he wouldn't be bogged down in red tape as would others. Our belief that the negotiating power was on the Sheik's side was continually renewed in newspaper stories. We knew we had landed a super deal when, a few months later, Wayne Newton offered the Sheik a handsome profit to repurchase the property.

Valuable information is all around you. Sometimes it is as obvious as a Las Vegas newspaper story. It is often so obvious that it is overlooked.

Tapping into *scuttlebutt power* means knowing how to plug into the grapevine. Secretaries, maintenance workers, clerks, salespeople, and receptionists all have inside information.

Here are some other sourcing tips:

- *Real property title reports* contain telltale signs of financial pressure. Look for recent borrowing collateralized by real estate, creditors' liens, unpaid property taxes, and pending foreclosure actions.

- *Personal property lien indexes* may disclose signs of financial pressure. Note any mortgaging of equipment, fixtures, and accounts receivable.

- *Private credit reporting companies* like Dun & Bradstreet and TRW make their information available only to subscribers. A friendly subscriber, such as your banker or a business friend, may be willing to bend the rules and order a report for you to see.

- *Credit investigating services* are available to the public and can supply comprehensive financial profiles. If the deal is big or important enough, a service's fee may be your best investment of the year.

- *Litigation records* and court files will reveal the other side's problems and motivations.

In one recent instance, our firm found that an investment property was being sold because of a "secret" divorce.

On another occasion, we found that a substantial manufacturing business was being sold because its two owners were in litigation with each other. The court, with the wisdom of Solomon, had ordered the business sold. In this instance, the parameters of an acceptable deal were part of the public record.

Practice tip: When do you start to gather information? Early! Once negotiations start, friendly, folksy, seemingly innocent small talk suddenly takes on the character of highly confidential information and critical facts become much harder to pry loose.

How much effort you put into information gathering is simply a function of what is at stake. Calling every plumber in town to save a few bucks on fixing a stopped-up drain doesn't make sense. Calling every Mercedes Benz dealer in the county to get quotes on that new sedan you admire does. As long as you will realize a reasonable return on your effort, it makes sense to spend the time and money gathering information.

> **Power is the ability to say "I pass." Power can be measurably real and absolute. Power can also be a state of mind. Power does not exist in the abstract; it is always relative.**

17

BASIC TRAINING
Bombs-Away Bargaining and White-Knuckle Horse Trading

You have established a negotiating goal by defining "winning." Now is the time to implement hard-bargain tactics to achieve that goal.

I've never been into collecting antiques, stamps, or miniature elephants. I collect negotiating tricks.

I have gathered these tricks the world over, in places as near as LA board rooms filled with sophisticated strategists cutting mega deals and as far away as Third World marketplaces where streetwise kids haggle for squawking stewing hens as if their family's next dinner depends entirely on their savvy.

In the remaining chapters of this book, I am able to share with you part of my collection: the best of the best tricks.

The Winner's Curse

You have decided to sell your camper. It would be your lucky day if you got $9,000 for it. You are approached by a buyer who offers to bring you $11,000 by the end of the day.

What would your best bet be?

- Counter.

- Accept the offer without another word.

- Tell the buyer you will consider the offer.

Lessen the chance of what Madison Avenue calls "postpurchase evaluation" and others call "buyer's remorse" by countering, even if the counter is an unimportant condition.

In the camper situation, your counter might be "You have a deal providing I can remove the bookshelves."

M.K. is a certified public accountant who does a pretty fair job of budgeting for everybody but himself. The offer I made M.K.'s banker to restructure his long-past-due loan was borderline reasonable. It was, I figured, a place to start. To my surprise, the banker accepted the proposal without hesitation.

Instead of feeling like a winner, I felt a sense of disappointment and frustration. I wondered how much better I could have done. For days, I had nagging thoughts about reopening the negotiations.

If you are ever offered eternal youth in exchange for your promise never to eat lasagna again, there is only one thing you can possibly do. Counter.

People aren't happy with a deal they haven't worked to get. Accepting a proposal, no matter how perfect, without some haggling is dangerous. Negotiators *need* to negotiate. They need a sense of mastery. When a deal is too easy, they assume that something is wrong.

Practice tip: Use long pauses to avoid an impression of eagerness. Quick responses are not demonstrative of a hard-driven bargain.

Head First? Feet First?

Melissa owns a small vacant lot at Vista del Condo. You want to buy it. The lot is not formally on the market, but you have heard from friends that Melissa is thinking about selling.

Lots in the neighborhood vary a great deal in size, distance from the lake, and view. There are no accurate comparables to determine price.

Rather than proposing a price, Melissa has suggested that you "make an offer" to purchase.

Should you:

1. Encourage Melissa to first propose a price?

2. Make the initial offer?

Who should make the opening move? Consult your intuition.

1. *The case for encouraging Melissa to first propose a price.* Why lose this one-time opportunity to ascertain Melissa's limits without having to disclose your own? Once Melissa has announced her price, you know her ceiling. Her upper limit has been crystallized. Can you recall ever being prepared to give up much more than what was demanded by the other person? Melissa's opening move establishes her parameters without any cost to you.

2. *The case for your making the initial offer.* If you let Melissa make the opening move, you are asking her to establish a position. People overzealously defend stated positions, retreating only begrudgingly.

Anchors Aweigh: Group 1 real estate agents were taken to a house where they were given a talk on neighborhood values and were told that the asking price of the house was $65,900. Group 2 real estate agents were taken to the same house and heard the same pitch with one exception—the asking price was bumped to $83,900.

Both groups were independently asked to make their own estimates of the value of the house. Group 2 agents set the home's value more than $6,000 (almost 10 percent) higher than the Group 1 agents' estimate.

Supply people with data—any data—and they tend to use it. This behavioral propensity is known as *anchoring*. The first price thrown out by either party can become a bargaining anchor even though that initial price may be unreasonably inflated or deflated.

Still not sure who should make the opening move? Then first consider *testing, testing, testing*.

"Melissa, this *is* an unusual lot, but a somewhat comparable lot sold last summer for $9,000." This nonpositional opening allows you to read Melissa's reaction while mentally preparing her for your low offer. If Melissa wants to test the waters, she will now tell you about high-priced lots that *she* considers "comparable."

Practice tip: Grab a price break before making your opening move: "What is the most this store has discounted this big-screen TV?" You may not bag a true answer, but some price reduction may be offered for having tested the waters.

The Spanish Rice Principle

In public junior high, my friends and I lived and died by the school cafeteria's daily entrées, which were posted a week in advance. Because "Children are starving in China," a clean plate was mandated by the school. (It wasn't until I visited Beijing that I learned kids in China don't eat tuna noodle casserole, meat loaf, or tamale pie.)

On meatless Fridays, spaghetti was everyone's big favorite. Spanish rice, although always the most colorful, was barely tolerated. Fish (*gag!*) was the worst of all possible fates.

Imagine our despair one week when news of a mistake leaked out: the menu was in error. For the coming Friday, fish would be replacing spaghetti. An announcement that a six-day school week was just around the corner would have been less of a blow.

Imagine our sense of elation and relief when a few days later it was revealed that the fish rumor was totally false. Spaghetti was being replaced not by fish but by Spanish rice.

Why was everybody suddenly happy about so-so Spanish rice replacing wonderful spaghetti? Because, when compared to fish, Spanish rice looked terrific.

A person who expects less and receives less will be more satisfied than a person who expects more and receives less. Happiness is relative to expectations. You can make the other person happy by first disappointing him.

Want kids to be happy with Spanish rice? First tell them you will be serving fish.

■ ■ ■

I love telling my crisis management clients and students the following story. Is it true? I have never really known for sure.

A bookkeeper was hysterical as he confessed to his friend that earlier in the day he had stolen $10,000 from his employer's safe. Prison, it seemed, was a more attractive alternative than what his bookie had threatened.

When the friend asked how much cash was left in the safe, the bookkeeper said, "About $90,000."

"Bring me the rest of the cash," the friend instructed. "I have an idea that may keep you from going to prison."

An hour later, the bookkeeper dutifully reported back to his friend with the remaining money. The streetwise friend, knowing that happiness is relative to expectations, telephoned the company president: "Your bookkeeper has just stolen $100,000 from you. You will be happy to know that he will agree to return $90,000 if you agree not to press criminal charges and further agree to release him from any liability."

The president said a prayer of thanks for being able to recover 90 percent of what he had lost.

■ ■ ■

You were in a fender bender. Both you and the other driver were partially at fault. Everything is fine now, but you have had your share of aches and pains. Hoping for a $5,000 insurance settlement, you daydream of a dozen ways to spend the money.

When the insurance adjuster finally makes you an offer, it is for a heart-clutching $1,200. (You have just been told that the insurance company is serving fish.)

- With a $1,200 offer, are you still going to expect to get $5,000?

- Which initial insurance company offer would have maintained your level of expectation close to $5,000: $2,800? $3,300? $4,200?

Offers impact expectations. Expectations impact goals. With a $1,200 offer, you will now be content to get a decent settlement, even one much less than $5,000. (Spanish rice is starting to look good.)

Since birth, most of us have been conditioned to be moderate in our demands. We are taught that nice people are always reasonable in their wants. But extreme demands yield the best bargaining results. Agreed: your chances of discouraging the other side from doing business are greater with extreme demands. But over a period of time the increased rewards will far outweigh the lost deals. The realities are: Most people set their bargaining goals too low, and people who want more get more.

When I suggest you open extremely high if you are a seller or extremely low if you are a buyer, I'm not giving you a license to be totally unreasonable. A crazy position will not create interest and will not be a bargaining anchor. It will be taken for exactly what it is. Crazy.

Wolfgang Puck is considered the father of the gourmet "designer pizza." Wolfgang's counter to my request for a $25,000 retainer fee was, "Fine, as long as it is in Spago food credits." Factoring in the extra hours at the gym working off the duck sausage pizza, the proposal seemed crazy. When I read a newspaper story about a lawyer Wolfgang *did* hire for food credit, I realized that what is crazy is in the eyes of the gastronome.

May the Force Be with You

After several offers and counteroffers, you have finally offered Melissa $9,800 for her lakeshore lot. Her counteroffer is $10,600. At what price will an agreement probably be struck?

- $10,000.

- $10,200.

- Some other amount.

Keep these behavioral propensities in mind:

- When coins are flipped, the great majority of people (90 percent in one test group!) will choose heads rather than tails.

- "Head for the line on the left, since most visitors automatically head for the one on the right" suggests the *Official Guide to Walt Disney World*.

- The chance of reaching agreement at a "let's-round-off" number ($10,000, in the Melissa illustration) is second only to the probability of reaching a numerical "let's-split-the-difference" compromise, $10,200.

Play to the force of *magnetic numbers* by tactically putting yourself in a position where *propensity power* is working to your advantage. Plan several moves ahead, making offers and counteroffers that will "naturally" lead to your precalculated compromise proposal to "split the difference" or "round off."

Practice tip: A more extreme opening offer provides you the space to edge towards a winning "let's split-the-difference" compromise proposal.

The Terms and Conditions Game

At long last, you and Melissa have agreed on a price. You are now ready to discuss financing terms, a closing date, who will pay the title insurance premium, and other essential issues.

Should you bring up these issues:

- Collectively, so that they can be considered by Melissa in the aggregate?

- Individually, starting with those least important to you?

- Individually, starting with those most important to you?

Introduce your terms and conditions incrementally—an issue at a time, starting with those that are most important to you. Be extreme in your terms. Ask for more than you should reasonably expect.

There may be some rejections, but presenting Melissa with some items she can say "no" to will give her a needed sense of bargaining mastery. Terms and conditions not accepted by Melissa should be set aside and dealt with only after you have gotten as many "yeses" as possible.

(Melissa will do better if she does not allow you to present your terms in piecemeal fashion, reserves her response until all issues are on the table, and then evaluates the picture as a whole.)

Those Winning Odds

With some sense of bewilderment, I observed that prospective auto body shop customers just weren't bargaining. Customers were happily accepting estimates as if they had been handed down from Mount Sinai on tablets of stone. Two facts became readily apparent: (1) this marketplace phenomenon had nothing to do with insurance coverage, and (2) the sacrosanct bids were very odd and very precise amounts: $2,127.48, $1,617.63, and so on.

Think about it. If the bids had been round estimates like $2,100 or $1,700, the customers' normal reflex reaction would have been to roll up their shirt sleeves, plant their feet in a batter's stance, and go for the discount.

People bargain when the quoted amounts are round and easy. Round numbers come with a built-in invitation to haggle. They don't sound real or firm. They sound like what they probably are—ballparkish and high.

Because odd amounts sound less susceptible, more real, and more like the result of considered deliberation, people are less inclined to negotiate any changes.

When they do negotiate an odd amount, people expect less of a concession than they would with a rounded amount. Enough said.

Next time numbers are in play:

- Punch some keys on your calculator.

- Pensively leaf through a catalog.

- Repunch the calculator.

- Pick up a list of numbers and run your finger down the page, stopping somewhere in the middle.

It doesn't matter if your odd number is truly a deliberated figure, as long as it appears to be well thought out.

Bad Breadth

I have a better proposal from your competition.—*Every buyer since the dawn of humanity.*

Prices will be increased momentarily. My inventory is dangerously depleting.—*Every seller since the down of humanity.*

Michael confided that he was depressed. On a recent sales trip, all he'd heard was that his prices were "too high," that he was "ridiculously expensive," that "last year's prices were much more reasonable," and that "the competition's prices are much more attractive." The motivator buttons had been punched, and Michael was torn between lowering his prices to recapture lost business and holding the price line.

Gail, one of Michael's customers, finds Michael doggedly inflexible when it comes to price.

The Persuasion Equation

Gail and Michael are barreling toward each other on *price*, a narrow, one-lane bargaining route.

A collision is inevitable. There is no room to maneuver on a one-lane route. Both Gail and Michael need to widen the route by creating new lanes.

Buyers do not buy *things*. They buy *deals*. Price is only half the equation. The other half is the deal. Price = deal.

A deal is made up of terms or components, each of which, like *price*, is a bargaining lane. These are the bargaining lanes of a deal:

- *Finance lane*. Cash or credit, interest rates, terms, discounts for early payment, quantity discounts, prices of extras and add-ons, collateral or security.

- *Risks lane*. Warranties, guarantees, inspection procedures, repairs, downtime.

- *Delivery lane*. When, where, and how deliveries are made; who pays the carrier; who is responsible for damage; late penalties; packaging.

- *Relationship lane*. Exclusive selling rights, advertising allowances, sole supplier rights, guaranteed minimum purchases, training, ongoing support, duration of contract.

- *Specifications lane*. Allowable variations, quality tolerances.

Michael can add bargaining lanes by restructuring the equation: *lesser price = lesser deal*. "Yes, I can lower the price *if* I don't have to individually package the units and *if* you will pay on delivery."

Gail can create lanes by agreeing to Michael's price *if* Michael expands the deal: *same price = expanded deal*. Anything that would cost Gail money is worth money.

Gail may also request *concessions* she doesn't really care much about. Why? Because if Michael can't or won't agree to Gail's requests, there is a good chance that Michael may reduce his price. In this instance, Gail's nonconfrontational maneuver is in effect an oblique run at Michael's price position.

Gail's tactical *give-and-get* word is *if*: "I will accept your price *if* you will deliver and *if* I can pay in ninety days."

The Take on Give and Take

Call them give-and-get or give-and-take, or bargaining back and forth moves. *Concessions* are an essential element of deal-making. Here are four things you must know about making concessions.

1. No One Can Take Just One Concession

No one can eat only one peanut, or take only one potato chip, or ask for just one concession.

If you are tough in doling out concessions, you will dampen the other person's bargaining aspirations. Granting quickie concessions is a sign of insecurity and weakness. The other person will gain self-confidence and will become tougher and more demanding.

Khrushchev "seriously underestimated Kennedy." The young U.S. President, wanting to display "candor and reasonableness, responded to Khrushchev's complaints about U.S. actions around the world by conceding several times that Washington had made mistakes. . . .

"Khrushchev, unfortunately, took it as a sign of weakness. Emboldened, the Soviet leader built the Berlin Wall and installed nuclear missiles on the U.S. doorstep."—*Los Angeles Times.*

When the latter situation developed into the Cuban Missile Crisis, Khrushchev blinked, and the silos were dismantled and shipped back to the U.S.S.R.

2. We Aren't Talking Checkers

Many folks think it is unfair or rude not to meet a concession with a reciprocal concession. All our lives, we have heard popular platitudes that reinforce this notion: "One good turn deserves another"; "You scratch my back and I will scratch yours." These are myths!

Bargaining is *not* a game of checkers. There is nothing organized about bargaining, and there are no rules mandating that my move is followed by your move followed by my move.

3. Nothing Is for Nothing

Everything has an exchange value.

Bargaining is about trading. Bogus issues can be introduced for no purpose other than conceding them in exchange for something else. A trader will convert molehills into mountains simply to inflate the importance of *throw-away points* and use them for extracting concessions.

Suppose the other person insists on delivery in two weeks. Delivery is viewed as a *primary point.*

Your company could easily deliver in *one* week. Delivery to you is a *throw-away point.* A boastful *no problem* would normally be your unhesitating response. But why toss out your *throw-away point* when, with some puffing, it can appear to have *primary point* status? *If you want delivery in that short a time, the cost will be 10 percent more.*

Keep the quid pro quo myth alive. Remind the other person that being well-bred means courtesy, diplomacy, and, above all, concession reciprocity.

Soft Touching: Grant a minor goodwill concession now and then, *without* asking anything in return.

4. Small Fish Look Bigger in a Teacup Than They Do in a Pond

Competing within blocks of each other, A-1 Electronics and Hitech Electronics are equally reputable retailers of consumer electronics.

You are in the A-1 store, getting ready to purchase a Panasonic telephone answering machine for $54. A friend who happens to be in the store tells you that the Hitech store a few blocks away has a special promotion on that very machine and is selling it for $27.

Are you going to: buy from A-1 for $54 or buy from Hitech and save $27?

You are in the A-1 store, getting ready to purchase a Sony television for $1,350. A friend who happens to be in the store tells you that the Hitech store a few blocks away has a special promotion on that very television and is selling it for $1,323, a discount of $27.

Are you going to: buy from A-1 for $1,350 or buy from Hitech and save $27.

You are like most of us if you would go to Hitech to save $27 on the answering machine but not to save $27 on the television set.

The physical effort to get to Hitech and the $27 savings are identical in both instances. The only variable is the percentage of savings. There is a 50 percent savings with the answering machine, but only a 2 percent savings with the television. Perceiving the concessions relatively (as a percentage) rather than absolutely ($27 cash savings) explains your willingness to change stores only for the answering machine.

How you couch a concession may make all the difference between whether your deal locks in or goes off the screen.

You are a new car dealer who has quoted a potential buyer a $20,000 purchase price plus a $1,000 extended warranty fee. Having already made a concession from sticker price, you are prepared to make an additional $500 concession to sew up the deal. Your tactical choices as to how to cast the $500 concession are: reduce the extended warranty fee by 50 percent or reduce the purchase price fee by 2.5 percent.

Reducing the warranty fee by $500 has the impact of "slashing" the fee in half. Reduce the purchase price, and you are not slashing anything. You are only nibbling. Your concession will be perceived as being greater if it is offered as a percentage discount off the smallest fee item: *If you are prepared to buy now, I will reduce the warranty fee by half.*

This time-honored principle of *perception management* is best remembered by passing on some advice from Jack Lalanne.

On the eve of his seventieth birthday, the fitness guru stated that his reasons for wanting to stay thin and fit were based on a simple formula:

"Every two inches you take off up here . . . makes your business down there look an inch longer. Isn't everything relative? If you have a . . . 50-inch waistline, the thing doesn't look very big, does it?"

Hard-bargain "basic training" comes with a reminder: A soft touch will prevent resistance while yielding a better and more stable result. Hard-bargain deals are easier to close when egos have been coddled along the way.

18

MIND TRICKS
The Squish Factor

Manage how other people feel about themselves and you manage how effectively they will negotiate against you.

Technique is what makes a soft-touch style compatible with a hard-bargain stance.

Technique is the *art of performance*. Adopt a soft-touch style and your hard-bargain plays will not appear calculating or manipulative. Hard-bargain plays should come across as unplanned and spontaneous.

The soft touch of the persuasion progression is advanced throughout the hard-bargaining process. Personalization, rapport, involvement, and identification—the hallmarks of "Gentleman Bandit" Lon Perry's likable way—must continue as an integral part of the persuasive process.

Technique is also the *art of application*. The same paint can be applied with a fine brush or an industrial roller, depending on what is to be accomplished.

Soar Like a Turkey

I was feeling like an eagle. And why not? Later in the day, I was scheduled to meet with the board of a national health care outfit interested in retaining the services of our law firm. Was I ready! A freshly pressed favorite suit was set off by a new, thoughtfully selected Polo tie. My car, which always seems to perform best when it sparkles on the outside, was freshly waxed. Most often, small things have the greatest impact and modulate how we feel about ourselves.

For me, the metamorphosis from eagle to turkey was an easy one. A few drops of Chin Chin's Szechwan dumpling sauce splattering on my tie during lunch is all it took.

From the moment the sauce found its mark, I was mentally no longer at the top of my game. To the outside world, those spots were probably barely noticeable. For me, they were the consuming focal point of my entire being, and I felt self-conscious and uneasy.

If it's not one thing, it's two: If you have ever been nudged off-balance by a spotted tie, a dangling coat button, a bad hair day, mismatched socks, or a hurtful remark, then you have experienced what this chapter is all about: those "small things" that clip people's wings so they will soar like turkeys.

The Bleeding Edge

Maybe you've felt it before. I have.

That *zingular sensation*. A roller-coaster drop in your negotiating expectations when the other person:

- Constantly reschedules your appointment.

- Keeps you waiting in a reception room.

- Tells a secretary to hold calls *for about five minutes*, or, even worse, lets your meeting be interrupted by a stream of incoming phone calls.

- Uses an esoteric vocabulary.

- Makes adverse comments about you, your company, or your products.

- Looks and acts with total indifference toward your proposal, looks more at the clock than at you, and gazes around the room.

- Conducts business with you and a staff at the same time.

- Forgets or mispronounces your name.

- Reels off a list of his or her company's international branch offices.

- Asks about people, places, and things you know nothing about (*Can you recommend a restaurant in Sydney?*).

- Praises the competition.

- Asks for your bank references.

- Hits you with rapid-fire percentages, big numbers, and so on.

Torpedoes du jour: When I was in the service of God and country aboard a navy cruiser, I witnessed how a fellow officer emotionally devastated and demoralized a goodly part of the ship's junior-officer complement with a well-thought-out "Gotcha!" Jim spent the morning walking the passageways and whispering caringly to his shipmates, "I don't care what anybody else says, I think you are doing a good job."

Wanton Soup

Sometimes it happens at a family Thanksgiving get-together. Or perhaps at a friend's home. You just know that every once in a while you are going to be the one who ends up sitting on a folding chair at a dining table. Being seated an inch or so lower than other guests leaves most of us feeling uneasy, less talkative, and out of it.

In the game of psychological one-upmanship, points are scored when the other seating in the room is shorter than the "power chair" at the head of the table. There is a correlation between table shapes and chair heights and the ability to convince and influence others.

Sound like musical chairs nonsense?

Maybe so, but while the Vietnam war raged on, negotiations at the first Paris truce talks could not get underway for days because peace-loving emissaries could not agree on the shape of the negotiating table.

Sitting at the head of a rectangular table can transform your aura from "I'm here" to "I am in charge." Why else is the head of the table always blessed with the wine list and cursed with the check?

In Admiral Hyman Rickover's obituary, *Time* reported: "Winning a spot in Rickover's navy was not easy: prospective submariners often had to sit before the old curmudgeon on an unbalanced chair whose front legs had been sawed off by several inches . . . ."

Having negotiated his lease, I looked forward to viewing *Hustler* magazine czar Larry Flynt's newly built-out, full-floor Century City offices. Larry's personal office was the longest I have ever seen. "Early Rickover" could best describe the decorating effect, and it was perfect. Walking to Larry's desk seemed like a journey. Feeling that my visit was suddenly taking on the aura of a pilgrimage, I wasn't sure whether I was there to see Larry or to have an audience with him.

Too much creature comfort can sometimes be as devastating as too few amenities. If the other person is not used to opulent surroundings, the experience can be terrifying.

When a big case for Inga was settled, I invited her and her husband to a victory celebration at L'Orangerie, Los Angeles's premiere gourmet restaurant and a client of mine from day one. For Inga, whose most revered recipes start with a can of soup, my gastronomical offer soon became a stressful and disquieting experience as she and Sid stared in puzzlement at the four forks, two spoons, and four knives before them.

In the land-boom mid-1980s, I represented a middle eastern consortium buying $8 million worth of land near the Dallas Galleria. The land had been in the sellers' family for three generations—long before anyone foresaw that this would become one of the most fashionable sections of the city.

To my surprise, the lawyer representing the sellers—an elderly African American couple—insisted that the final papers be reviewed and signed in the family home. Three lawyers, two title officers, a banker, a mother, father, aunt, daughter, and grandson all crowded into a spartan living room for the passing of title, money, and legal documents.

Why wasn't the closing held ten minutes away in a law suite that housed all of the staff, equipment, and facilities needed to efficiently conclude the transaction? The sellers' lawyer confided that his elderly clients felt intimidated by his firm's luxurious downtown offices. The fact that they were about to become multimillionaires wasn't enough to ease their feelings of discomfort.

The persuasive fact of life is that people who are physically or psychologically uncomfortable want their negotiations to be short—so short that a concession or two to expedite the conclusion to a bed-of-nails situation may not be too high a price to pay.

Feeling psyched out? Anxious? Submissive? If you swoon over their decor—*Love the mid-calf high-pile carpets and the dancing water display in the reception room*—you play to your own insecurities. Feeding the other person's ego seldom helps and usually only makes matters worse.

Go Figure

Platinum blonde hair, blue eyes, classic features, an incredible figure—a fifteen on a scale of ten—my former next-door neighbor was a first runner-up in the Miss America beauty pageant. But nobody is perfect, and she had this devastating social problem: Men were so intimidated by her beauty that they couldn't carry on a conversation with her, much less ask her for a date. A man negotiating with her might accelerate the negotiations rather than subject himself to the tongue-tying uneasiness prompted by her presence. Other women who are considered classic beauties tell me that they too share this same paradoxical dilemma.

Short of suggesting plastic surgery, what does this discussion about beauty queens mean to you?

Overt psychological intimidation can be accomplished by even the most ordinary among us.

There are times when you will painstakingly take on an image of warmth and approachability. At other times, you will opt for an aura of authoritative command. Sometimes, however, you may want to take your choreography one step further by wearing, carrying, or arriving in power boosters that lessen the other person's resistance.

If a person's *power props*—whether jewelry that would be the envy of Elizabeth Taylor, an alligator briefcase, or a limousine curbside—make you feel like the third cousin to a second-class citizen, then you are being taken on a *gilt trip!* Your best defense is to understand that power props are only effective if you allow yourself to be intimidated by them.

The Old Bawl Game

Bill Cosby has this advice for grabbing the winning edge on the home front: "When discussions get heated, be the first to dash into the bathroom, lock the door, and cry."

Anyone who has ever had to deal with a teary-eyed spouse knows that tears can be so disarming that rationality and logic are washed away.

Crying is an emotional tactic effectively used by both women and men.

The Force of Logic/The Logic of Force

A Cal Berkeley speech course professor taught us that sometimes lions are better off not roaring. If what we have to say really makes good sense, then the overamplification of our voice will only detract from the message of our words.

Yet, though yelling is a boorish tactic, there may be times when raising your voice will get results. A loud voice can be effectively intimidating.

Best scream play: If you know the other person is a screamer, hold the meeting at a nice restaurant. A screamer who can't scream is a fish out of water.

More sound advice: Keep the negotiations so structured and formal that the likelihood of the other person's yelling is minimized.

Ham on Wry

I have been present when clients have said, as calmly and calculatingly as if they were old-time method actors, "I am going back into the negotiating room and I will be mad as hell. I might even throw a temper tantrum!"

For some would-be thespians, the head game is theatrics. Indignation and righteous anger are contrived, premeditated, and acted out as a tactic to prompt a concession by way of an apology or act of appeasement.

Never allow yourself to be goaded or lured into an emotional outburst. If you know you are ready to explode, take a break. Speak when you are angry or upset and you will give the best speech you will ever regret.

Gullible's Travels

A client's palatial home was devastated by the Northridge earthquake. The insurance carrier contended that much of the damage resulted from improper soil compaction when the lot was originally cut from the hillside.

After months of negotiations, the insurance adjuster told me that she would soon be taken off the claim. She cautioned that unless her totally unacceptable settlement offer was accepted, I would be forced to negotiate with the carrier's most difficult claims supervisor. Although my client had become anxious and had thought about capitulating by accepting the departing adjuster's offer, she instructed me to continue negotiating. Within a few weeks, the supervisor agreed to a figure close to my settlement demand.

Merchant of fear tactic: Putting the other person on notice that what they think is light at the end of the tunnel is really a fast-moving freight train. Letting them know that unless a proposal is accepted, troubles will mount, costs will go through the ceiling, or in my case, I would "hit the wall" when my client's file was turned over to a supposedly inflexible supervisor.

Defensive tip: Don't become desperate just because you are being told that it's always darkest before it's totally black. Give the situation some thought. Ask yourself whether there is a genuine reason to feel pessimistic. Despite Chicken Little's prophecy, the sky has never fallen.

Soul Erosion

The best-selling book, *The One Minute Manager,* is based on a simple truism: People who feel good about themselves produce good results.

Conversely, another best-selling book, *Winning Through Intimidation,* is also based on a simple truism: "The results a person obtains are inversely proportionate to the degree to which that person is intimidated."

Two best sellers, one lesson: Manage how the other person feels about themself and you manage how effectively that person will negotiate against you.

Some mind tricks are geared to gnaw away at the other person's perception of their negotiating power. To negatively charge their expectations. Other mind tricks have the specific purpose of causing the other person to become conciliatory, confused, or irrational.

There are also mind tricks that are a play on the power of *because I said so.* But then, according to Peter Ueberroth, "authority is 20 percent given and 80 percent taken."

> **People who are uneasy are not at their negotiating best and will grant concessions to extricate themselves from an uncomfortable situation. In making these concessions, they will be guided by their emotions rather than by their sense of reason.**

19

SLIDERS AND CURVES
Hold-On-to-the-Roll-Bar Negotiating

The fact that a hard-bargain tactic produces anxiety, tension, discomfort, stress, or pressure does not mean that it can't be applied with a soft touch. Nor does it make it an unconscionable device. Some tactics just aren't as pretty as others.

Many of the tactics described in this chapter are mutually exclusive. Others can be used in combination. No one tactic is so universal a tool that it will work in every situation. Be intuitive. Pick and choose.

Soft touching: Don't overkill. Too many is too much. You wouldn't plead insanity to a parking ticket offense nor would you charter a Boeing 747 to go to Wal-Mart.

Practice tip: Most power plays are no stronger than your own credibility. Your persuasiveness quotient will always increase when you substantiate critical facts *and* the source of those facts.

Numb and Number

Today's the day of the Big Game. The World Series of Bargaining.

It all takes place just after lunch at Big Ed's Discount Appliances, home of the "Big Deal." You and your wife have decided that you will lead off for the All Stars. You will go it alone. Because you know exactly

127

what you want to buy, it is now just a matter of getting the best price possible. And, of course, it is a matter of personal honor.

Immediately upon entering, you recognize Big Ed from his TV commercials, which air between 3:00 A.M. and 6:00 A.M., during the "Early Early Movies," a favorite of yours because you are a big Edmund O'Brien fan.

You know exactly what you are looking for in the way of a washer and dryer. It's a combination with control panels whose beauty is made possible through the miracle of simulated walnut. Quickly you find it halfway down the main isle. The ticketed price is $1,200. Big Ed himself approaches and you ask if he will accept $1,000. "No!" is his unequivocal response.

It does not take a keen sense of perception to know that this fellow is in no mood to bargain. Needless to say, you are disappointed. For all of your adult life, you genuinely thought that *bargain* and *independent local retailer* were synonymous. Besides, where is the "Big Deal"? You struck out, and it is apparent that you have hit your slump.

It's a new day. This time, your wife will go it alone at Big Ed's. She is your team's last chance to pull the game out of the fire.

Unlike you, she takes an hour and a half of Big Ed's time comparing brands, debating the merits of gas versus electric, scrutinizing color charts, taking physical measurements, reviewing warranties, studying upgrades, evaluating features, and having Big Ed write down vital product data. She "selects" the same $1,200 washer-dryer combination and offers $1,000.

With about 20 percent of his working day invested in her, will Big Ed want to start over with someone in whom he has no time invested? Someone who may not be as "real" a buyer as your wife? Big Ed remembers from his high school Modern Business class that, by definition, investments are supposed to pay off. Your wife's offer is accepted. She has become a bargaining superstar by causing Big Ed to invest in her.

What if your wife were still bargaining at 6:00 P.M. on Saturday? Would Big Ed chance losing his investment of valuable time by asking her to come back Monday morning to continue the dialogue?

Years ago, I was in Las Vegas with a handful of college friends. We spent half our time gambling and the other half looking for each other in the cavernous hotel casinos. Goldberg, however, was easy to find. He had become a fixture at a crap table where he was losing his tuition, food, and book money.

"Goldy, why are you spending all your time at this same obviously unlucky, very cold crap table?" we asked.

"I have an investment in the table," he replied.

The Goldberg Effect

The greater the other person's investment in time, preparation, or money, whether it be at a crap table, on a retail showroom floor, preparing a bid proposal, or obtaining relevant information as to your needs, the greater that person's propensity to grant concessions.

Buy, Buy

Confession of a reformed shopper: There was a time I really didn't like about one-fourth of the clothes in my closet.

Maybe it's because the fit wasn't really that good, or the colors and style were not really me. In a way, each of these sweaters, coats, and ties was a trophy. A trophy for having waited patiently in the cold for a 50-percent-off sale to start. A trophy for being fleeter of foot and stronger of arm than those other shoppers who left the starting gate with me. So what if I never wore those sale items more than a few times. A bargain is a bargain. The price was right.

Barbara, a legal secretary, saved for three years to treat herself to a Mediterranean cruise. One of the ports of call was Barcelona. The way Barbara tells it, she was walking down the Ramblas in the direction of the ship when she was greeted by a street vendor with a nonstop grin. Until that moment in time, Barbara had never given any thought to owning a black velvet painting of Barcelona. Years later, Barbara is still not sure what happened.

"Señorita, will you buy a souvenir painting for $60?"

"No, thank you."

"How much will you pay?"

In a devil-may-care manner, Barbara, without thinking, said "$10." After some emotionally charged bartering, she paid a "for-you-lady special price of $43."

Had Barbara suddenly changed her mind, realizing that until this moment she had been denying herself one of life's aesthetic pleasures? No. Barbara had been so sucked into the back-and-forth of haggling that hacking out a deal took precedence over her desire to not own a puce Barcelona bathed in iridescent gold and persimmon moonlight.

Suppose this vendor, this master of sidewalk psychology, had asked tourists, "Do you want to buy a souvenir painting?" He would have been out of the painting business.

The Barbara Effect

When you let the bargain, not the item, become the objective of the bartering, the process becomes the product.

Planes, Trains, and Old Refrains

WARNING: Answering the following questions may be hazardous to your deal:

- *Don't you believe me?*

- *Don't you trust me?*

The preceding public service reminder was brought to you by a guy who, while bargaining over custom-built wall cabinets with "Sam the Innocent," a finish carpenter, was told, "I can't go any lower . . . you are now getting a price which is my cost plus 10 percent." Silly me. I pressed on. Sam, with sad eyes and Lincolnesque sincerity, responded, "Don't you believe me?" I accepted Sam's *down-to-the-bare-bones* proposal.

Less than two weeks later, Sam agreed to build the identical cabinets for our neighboring tenants for 20 percent less than our "rock bottom price."

Anyone who is forced to declare that they believe or disbelieve the other person is leaving the safety of high ground and heading into a no-win trap.

- Telling Sam that *I believed* his price was close to his cost prohibited me from further negotiating.

- Telling Sam that I *didn't believe* him would have destroyed linkage with a person with whom I was about to have a working relationship.

Defensive tip: Few of us are visionaries. On the old television show *To Tell the Truth*, the pretenders were chosen more often than the real McCoys. Let the other person know that "It is not a question of whether or not I believe you or trust you. . . . The price you are quoting is just not acceptable."

Auction Negotiating

Auctioneers tell me they can often agitate bidders into such a competitive frenzy that when the hammer falls, the price will be far greater than the amount that would have been paid for the same item in a gallery or store. In an auction, emotions come into play, and decisions are sometimes foolishly made.

A federal judge ordered jet-set palimony attorney Marvin Mitchelson to pay $1.2 million to Sotheby's for jewelry he had bought at an auction months before.

"The lawyer just does not have the money to pay for it. He bought [the jewelry] at an auction where there was a lot of emotion going on. You get caught up in the excitement and it becomes a game to outbid the other guy. But the next thing you know you've bought something."— Mitchelson's attorney, Los Angeles *Daily News*.

The Mitchelson Effect

Working or appearing to work with several competitors at the same time creates an auction climate. The need to win races is sometimes fueled more by emotion than by logic. When emotions are summoned into play, irrational concessions are granted as part of the price of victory.

Defensive tip: If you find yourself in an auction, stop and grasp the realities of the situation. Your goal is to land a favorable agreement, not win a race. Any time your goal becomes beating your competition, you will only be negotiating against yourself.

Fast Food for Thought

I asked my client what in the world motivated him to buy his now very defunct turkey pot pie franchise business.

"I was so busy qualifying myself as a hard-working, stable, sincere, energetic, God-fearing, peace-loving, financially capable franchisee that I never really stopped to think about whether or not it was that good an investment," was his reply. Franchise sellers are masters of *Don't sell them—have them sell you* hard-bargain table-turning.

College fraternities are often masters of negative selling. Rush chairmen recruiting new members will ask: *What school offices did you hold? What sports did you letter in? What contests did you win?* The rush candidate feels less and less worthy of membership with each new question designed to elicit a *None* response, and his desire to join the fraternity increases proportionately.

Circling the Wagons

Does the name George Armstrong Custer ring a bell?

A major U.S. computer manufacturer supposedly increased its sales volume dramatically when it adopted the *circling-the-wagons* tactic. By surrounding a potential buyer with a *wall of flesh*—experts from engineering, sales, and programming—the outflanked buyer is literally overwhelmed into making the on-the-spot purchase.

(One of my seminar students has suggested that, in historical retrospect, it would have been wiser for our early settlers to move their covered wagons into a defensive square rather than a circle. Her reasoning was that the attacking war parties could never have made all those sharp corners.)

Defensive tip: If the other person shows up with a team of gray-flannel commandos, grab one other person from your camp for emotional support. Two can take on ten, providing they have the necessary facts and knowledge.

Every Book in the Trick

Not too long ago and before they were regulated by law, book clubs would send their monthly selection to anybody and everybody. It didn't matter that you weren't a member of the club and didn't want the book. If the unsolicited book wasn't returned within the specified time period, you were obligated to pay for it. It was that simple and it was *fait accompli* marketing's finest hour.

A leasing agent sent me a completed form lease with a request to sign it and return it with a rent deposit. Without saying a word to the agent, I crossed off several bothersome provisions, signed the lease, and mailed it.

The gambit is played out by acting as if a point has been agreed on, a concession given, or an issue decided, even though no agreement has been reached. By acting as if a matter is *fait accompli,* it becomes *fait accompli.*

Defensive tip: Negotiations are over only when *you* believe or want them to be over. Don't accept other people's terms just because they have folded up the negotiating table and are starting to put it in the back of their van.

Anne of a Thousand Nays

Take No. 1

With a lump in your throat and a tear in your eye, you are selling your old oak rolltop desk. The weekend-special three-line classified ad you are running asks $1,500.

    Anne: I will pay you $1,000.

Hit the rewind button and let's start over again.

Take No. 2

With a lump in your throat and a tear in your eye, you are selling your old oak rolltop desk. The weekend-special three-line classified ad you are running asks $1,500.

    Anne: I love your desk and it is probably worth every penny you are asking. However, I have a decorating budget and I cannot afford to pay more than $1,000.

Let's compare takes.

In Take No. 1, no explanation accompanied Anne's offer. It appeared that the worth of the desk was in dispute. As the seller, your intuitive response would be to decline the offer while extolling the desk's numerous virtues to justify your price.

In Take No. 2, Anne's explanation makes it clear that worth is not an issue. Anne's budget is the barrier. A budget, unlike worth, is so personal that it is beyond rationale dispute.

Soft touching: Anne's real or fictional budget has enabled her to avoid antagonizing you, the seller, with a worth confrontation.

The Missing Man Maneuver

You know the drill. As you walk into the car dealership, Mr. Smooth comes over, shakes hands, and introduces himself—an unctuously overplayed personalization tactic that registers negatively on your *persuade-o-meter.* Your knee-jerk reaction is to tell him your name too.

You find a car that does it all for you. After a half-hour of flipping through esoteric loose-leaf binders and punching an adding machine, Mr. Smooth tells you the deal looks in place. A thousand hallelujahs.

As a formality, Mr. Smooth excuses himself to get management approval. Oh oh. When he returns, he tells you he has bad news. Because a philanthropically low price was quoted for the shiny new car, he must now reluctantly knock $700 off his allowance for your lackluster trade-in. If you prefer, the deluxe wheels can come off the new car—a mind-boggling notion because he got you with those wheels to begin with.

No Holds Bard

You know you will feel better about the whole experience if you can only write a poem about Mr. Smooth. The problem is you can't think of a word that rhymes with "nausea." Mr. Smooth did apologize eloquently without hesitating or groping. The Clarence Darrow of new-car sales. But this is a role he has gotten to play so many times before. The culprit? Higher authority: the *missing man.*

Sometimes the *missing man,* imagined as a cigar-chomping heavy hitter in the back room, is nothing more than an illusion. While you are trying to entertain yourself by looking at third-place golf trophies, Better Business Bureau plaques, and Chamber of Commerce certificates, some of these salespeople who are supposedly seeking approval from "higher authority" are enjoying a cup of coffee in the back room with other salespeople.

Long before Ken Norton became a client of ours, we were retained by the Venezuelan government to negotiate on its behalf the Ken Norton–George Foreman heavyweight boxing match. This first heavyweight prize fight ever held in South America was to be the inaugural event at a lavish new government-owned sports facility in Caracas. The terms and conditions of the fight were approved by one department subject to the approval of another department, which was subject to the approval of still another.

As the deal—which everyone other than the Venezuelan government thought was concluded on at least five separate occasions—moved from bureaucrat to bureaucrat, additional concessions were extracted systematically along the way. The fight agreement was subject to approval by so many officials that is was literally negotiated and renegotiated a piece at a time. The culprit? Escalating higher authority!

Practice tip: Accountability to someone else means being on a short leash. If you call on escalating higher authority, be miserly with your concessions. Granting too many concessions or too large a concession will destroy the tactic's required appearance that you are acting under another person's instructions and have little negotiating latitude.

Defensive tip: Reach an agreement that is subject to approval by someone else's management, partner, spouse, department head, committee, board, or whatever, and you are only negotiating against yourself.

To seal the other person's limited-authority escape hatch shut, ask at the very outset, *Do you have full authority? If not, who does? Do you have authority over price? terms? delivery? style?*

The "William L." Principle

My new client introduced himself as General William L., United States Marine Corps, retired. His fiftyish appearance was central-casting perfect: crew cut, tan, and sternly businesslike.

I am not the only person who held this Marine Corps general in special esteem. The City of Long Beach had offered him two highly prized concessionaire locations on the soon-to-be-opened Queen Mary. A Marina Del Rey yacht company had sold him a luxury thirty-five-footer COD with no money down. Within a month, the boat was fully outfitted to his very exacting specifications.

If you haven't figured it out already, I should tell you that the "general" was a three-star phoney. William L. had been an enlisted Marine once upon a time, but that was about it.

A man wearing a white jacket and stethoscope walks into a hospital room and lethally places a pillow over a patient's head. A man with a toy badge is allowed behind locked doors by a woman he then victimizes.

A Palestinian agent puts on an Israeli uniform to penetrate a command post.

The doctor, cop, foreign agent, and "General" William L. can be successful because they operate under a guise of *legitimacy*.

One savvy group of clients hired me to draft the toughest landlord-oriented lease ever uttered into a dictating machine. My lopsidedly biased effort was then printed as a form. The clients added two words at the top, in large print: STANDARD FORM. Whenever a prospective tenant balks at an onerous lease provision, the response is, *Sorry, but this is our Standard Form.*

How often do people try to negotiate a change to printed bank loan forms, store credit agreements, and similar contractually binding documents? Most folks won't even bother to read something so ordinary as a Standard Form. Those two words, the expense of printing, and the other person's erroneous assumptions give the deal a nonnegotiable sense of legitimacy. People will unhesitatingly accept the written word if the printing is first-class.

Defensive tip: Standard Loan Agreement, Standard Installment Purchase Agreement, Standard Service Agreement, Standard Rental Agreement, Standard Financing Agreement, Standard Construction Agreement, Standard Architectural Agreement—I have never read a contract prepared by a business or trade association that isn't slanted in favor of the folks who paid to have it drafted and printed. The printed word is just as negotiable as the typed or spoken word, and there is nothing sacred about a three-part form.

The luggage store where I bought a briefcase that I later didn't care for refused a cash refund. That was their return *policy*. I could, however, exchange the briefcase for a storeful of other things I didn't care for either.

Policy is a word that creates an aura of legitimacy by implying: *The die is cast and please don't bother me with your requests.*

Defensive tip: When you are on the defensive end of a policy argument, try to show the other person that the policy is not always enforced and is therefore not really a policy at all.

If there is a truly existing policy, then show why it should not be applicable to you:

Customer: I know that you have a no-refund policy, but the salesperson assured my wife that any man would love to get this sweater as a gift. He was wrong. I hate the sweater.

Play the perfection game when you are up against a fixed-price policy. Points are scored by finding as many imperfections as possible—a scratch, a bump, a blemish, a dent, an imperfect match, a minute spot, an unexpected but brief delay in expected delivery.

A top-seeded player will use these imperfections as the persuasive wedge to extract a special concession, discount, or break.

> **Customer:** I know this is a one-price store, but this washer is not in factory-perfect condition. If it were, I wouldn't be asking for a price adjustment. Doesn't your no-discount policy really apply only to mint-perfect merchandise?

Defensive tip: The parts of a house are not going to have the same precision fit as the parts of a fine Swiss watch. Colors can never be matched exactly, and a Chevrolet will not have the same quality of paint job as a Jaguar. But what do you do with the nitpicker who even in bad light can spot angels dancing on the head of a pin?

No one is entitled to more than reasonable perfection. A $100,000 house has one standard and a $1,000,000 house has another. A steak at Denny's is not going to be as good as a steak at the city's finest restaurant, and neither will the service.

If the other person's expectation level is objectively unreasonable, then be calmly firm. You can't allow negotiations to focus on matters so trifling that each side is running for its microscope.

■ ■ ■

The printed equivalent of a verbal policy is a *Procedures Manual*. My neighborhood service station manager brought out his manual to show me why I would get only 20 percent of the amount I paid 10,000 miles ago for a set of tires I was told would last 30,000 miles.

And then there is the *price list*. Quoting your prices verbally invites haggling. Print them as part of a price list and *presto!* They are granted an immunity from any bargaining.

The Gidget Gambit

You have probably heard this one before. Maybe because it's reminiscent of a Gidget movie: boy makes deal, boy loses deal, boy fights to get deal back.

My neighbor's newly pruned trees made my yard suddenly look overgrown and neglected. I felt enough shame that I decided to call the same gardening outfit. A tape machine answered: "International Environmental Corporation, formerly Henry's Tree Service." My reaction was the same as if a limo had pulled up and someone in a polyester double-knit leisure suit had got out. Imagery requires a consistency of style.

John from the pruning service came out the next Saturday. He looked around and quoted a fee of $1,000. As we talked, the price drifted downward to $950 and then $850. My family had already retreated back to the house under the mistaken belief that bargaining is a tell tale sign of a peasant lineage.

Feeling I was on a roll, I pressed on.

John suddenly backtracked: "I don't think I want to do the job for less than $1,000."

"John," I said, "you have a deal at $850. When can you start?"

Rising Sum

Usually, you keep bargaining to get something better than what you already have. John's about-face maneuver was causing the price concessions to disappear altogether. Suddenly starting to breathe thin air, I readily agreed to $850, thanking my lucky stars that John was still willing to do the job for the "old price."

In Istanbul, I was a four-time shopping award "winner." Here's how I did it. By entering a shop anytime before late morning, I was awarded a "first customer of the day" discount. For arriving late in the day, I was awarded the "last customer" discount. And in between, I was awarded "just before lunch" and "just after lunch" customer discounts. It didn't matter whether I was shopping for a silk carpet, a custom-made suede suit for my wife, or a meerschaum pipe. Just about every shopkeeper in the city has mastered this "buy right now to avoid a price increase" *disappearing concession* tactic.

> **Hard-bargain tactics aren't necessarily nice. Soft touch is about using not-necessarily-nice tactics in a very nice way. Technique is about making soft touching and hard bargaining compatible.**
>
> **Your best defense against any hard-bargain tactic is your ability to recognize it. Never assume that the other person has your standards of conduct. They have their own rules. But then they may have none at all.**

20

TIMING, TEMPO, AND TURBOCHARGING
Making Time Your Ally

Negotiating is a process, not an event. The difference between a process and an event is time. Time can be your worst enemy or your best ally.

Timing is not a formula. It's a feeling.

Every situation has a pulse.

A "final offer" at 3:00 P.M. may not have much impact. Make that same offer in a smoke-clogged, trash-filled negotiating room twelve hours and twenty cups of coffee later, at 3:00 A.M., and your persuasiveness quotient is considerably increased.

You don't ask your employer for a raise on the day the firm loses its biggest account.

You don't talk to a customer about extending your contract on a day when you have done nothing right for him.

A top-notch Beverly Hills real estate broker refuses to show homes in the middle of a summer day. She knows that with a bright sun overhead, swimming pools can look more blotchy than inviting.

Generally, Friday afternoons and month ends are stressful. Will this stress mean there will be more resistance to your proposal or less? Does the proper presentation of your proposal require a low-key and relaxed setting?

Automobile sellers, lenders, collection agents, and others who have to prepare month-end reports for higher management may feel a need to get your deal completed *now*.

Timing is about intuition. It is always a judgment call.

Time is a force because circumstances and expectations change with time. If you can't reach an agreement *today*, under *now* circumstances, then try *tomorrow*, under *later* circumstances.

To make time an ally, you must learn the other person's time constraints. There is probably no information easier to obtain. Usually, all it takes is one simply question: "What is your time frame if we are to reach an agreement?"

Practice tip: It makes no sense to divulge *your* deadline unless that revelation will work to your favor. If you are in doubt as to whether to answer, your best response may be, "I am not sure."

Time Vampires

Have you ever noticed how labor disputes are most often resolved minutes before present contracts expire?

Or how things get done more expediently if the seller or buyer or a lawyer on either side is going out of the country on business the next morning?

Or how you raced through negotiations because you had to be somewhere else for an important meeting that you couldn't be late for? How, in your anxiety to "finish up," you made concessions that you would not otherwise have made?

Deadlines are an acceleration device because they create a sense of immediacy. A sense of immediacy creates pressure. Pressure causes action to be taken. And, often, that action will be in the form of concessions given to meet the deadline.

Deadlines can be *personal* or *external*. You use personal deadlines when you tell the other person that your partner, who must also sign the papers, is going into the hospital for surgery tomorrow, or that your wife, whose name is also on the deed, is leaving for Paris on Friday. If you tell the other person the deal must be completed by year-end for tax purposes, you are tying your cutoff date to an external deadline set by the IRS.

The closer and more specific the deadline, the greater the motivation for the other person to take action. *Negotiations must be completed by the 10th or we will have no deal.*

If you are not sure that a fixed time limit will properly serve your purpose, then a flexible deadline may be the order of the day. *Negotiations must be concluded in the near future* (or *soon*, or *shortly*) *or we will have no deal.*

The Out-of-Towner's Deadline Ploy

A classic deadline ploy was sprung on me. I was in Costa Rica negotiating for some American business interests. Their project was the construction of a distillery that would convert cane into alcohol. On the night of my arrival, I was invited to a party at the home of the cane grower with whom I would be negotiating. In seemingly idle conversation, he asked how long I would be in San José, the capital city, and I told him I would be leaving in three days.

It seemed that only I wanted to talk about cane availability, price, and terms. It was thrust and parry. No sooner would I initiate a business conversation than he would change the subject.

After two and one-half sun-drenched days filled with coffee plantations, the Mercado Central, country club lunches, and city tours, he finally initiated the discussions that I had been waiting to pursue. He knew my deadline. I did not know his. He also knew that:

- I had other commitments back in Los Angeles.

- I would feel pressure to make concessions in order to take home a deal.

- Clients don't like flying their lawyer to Costa Rica only to have the lawyer come back empty-handed.

Now, when out-of-towners visit me, I am always self-servingly polite enough to ask when they will be returning home or whether I can assist them by having my secretary confirm their return flight.

The Short-Fuse Deadline Ploy

The person on the other end of the telephone was Joe Howe, a collection agency pro. He was very brief and to the point. Yes, he would settle the claim against my client, a golf pro who had been out of the money too long, provided that I made a satisfactory offer of compromise within the next three minutes. When my time was up, he would hang up—even in midsentence—refuse any future calls, and proceed directly to suit. Tick. Tick. Tick.

Joe's tactic was a short-fused, arbitrary deadline. I wondered how many people would use their precious time with Joe to make their on-bended-knee best possible offers—offers that probably would never have been made if they hadn't been playing "beat the clock." (Knowing that Joe's ego wouldn't allow him to call me back, I told Joe I'd telephone the next day hoping he would be willing to have a less threatening dialogue. The following afternoon, the matter was resolved to my client's delight.)

Practice tip: Demanding immediate action without a stated reason may be an unwarranted use of horsepower. With Joe, I felt more alienated than motivated. Justifying your deadline will help maintain linkage and alignment. *I need to know by 3:00* P.M. *today whether we have a deal because . . . .*

The Evaporating Offer Ploy

Whenever I think about "Linda" and "R&R Records," I can't help but think of those late-night slicer-dicer television commercials. You know the ones: you get steak knives as a free bonus, available for a "limited time only."

Linda, a recording artist, was suing R&R in a down-and-dirty breach-of-contract dispute. The case was far from being a slam dunk for either party. R&R made several settlement offers to Linda who, wanting her day in court, refused to settle.

When Linda rejected an offer of $215,000, R&R decided to try an evaporating opportunity offer: $225,000 if their offer to settle was accepted within five days, $210,000 if their offer was accepted within ten days, $200,000 if their offer was accepted within fifteen days, and $150,000 thereafter.

Time was marching on. Linda was being dragged right along with it. Linda's opportunity to settle for $225,000 was evaporating before her very eyes.

Linda could give R&R's proposal all the thought and consideration she wanted. Her indecisiveness, however, would cost her dearly—R&R had made procrastination unbearably expensive. Linda had to ask herself: *Would more be accomplished by continuing to negotiate than would be lost as the settlement offer started to evaporate?*

■ ■ ■

As a society, we have a cultural bias in favor of fast foods and fast deals.

Stop.

Take a breath.

Analyze your deadline before you race to meet it.

Generally, deadlines are like the seasons. They come and go. Negotiations seldom come to an abrupt halt at the stroke of midnight, and few arbitrary deadlines are ever enforced. If the other person threatens to pull the deal, so be it. For every golden opportunity lost, you will save yourself from a dozen *I never should have* bummers.

There's No Business Like Slow Business

Does the other person have interests that can be crippled by a standstill? If so, don't make any moves. Orchestrate a deadlock. Let the deal collapse.

Put the burden for making a deal entirely on the other person.

If the other person genuinely believes the deal is dying, their negotiating limits may be revealed. Because any deal is better than no deal at all, the other person will, in effect negotiate against themselves.

Is the other person anxious?

Lightly brake, to discover why the other person seems to be in a rush.

Is there a desperate need? A hidden deadline? Another deal pending which is dependant upon an agreement with you being cut first?

Putting the negotiations on the back burner will reveal the relative balance of negotiating power.

Light braking is calculated stalling:

- *Frank, a few questions have been raised by the City. I need additional information from the architect.*

- *Frank, I would like to continue our negotiations but I just won't be available for the next few days.*

By slowing, but not stopping the momentum, Frank's frustrations may well be translated into concessions.

The Great American Breakfast Tactic

Waffle!

Pull out of the diamond lane.

Drag your feet. As discussions get closer to a handshake, play on Frank's eagerness to finish up the negotiations. All of a sudden, the signed agreement that Frank thought was just a breath away is really somewhere up the street.

- *By the way, Frank, I forgot to mention that . . .*

- *Oh, one small thing that needs to be dealt with, Frank . . .*

- *Of course, Frank, I expect that . . .*

Timing tactics are a negotiator's braking and accelerating devices. They govern whether negotiations will be on a fast track, a slow track, or over on the sidelines.

PART IV

THE DEAL-MAKER'S PLAYBOOK
Low-Impact, High-Yield Tips, Tricks, and Tactics

The Deal-Maker's Playbook is a unique action guide of hands-on, real-world *how to* and *what to* instructions. Use these tips and tactics to be a master deal-maker in thirty-six common negotiating situations.

These step-by-step instructions do not need to be followed in their suggested sequence. They have been set out as a by-the-numbers progression so you will be less likely to skip key points and will be more prepared to proceed methodically rather than emotionally.

The Deal-Maker's Playbook cannot and does not:

- Raise every possible deal point or issue.
- Have universal applicability—laws, industries, and community customs vary.
- Replace the need for the services of capable, knowledgeable professionals. The right people will save you money up front and aggravation later on.

Apartment Lease

Negotiating an Apartment Lease

As Miss America, my goal is to bring peace to the entire world and then to get my own apartment.—*Jay Leno* (*parodying the beauty pageant*).

Step 1. Make a Good First Impression

Dress and act like you're being interviewed to win the right to live there! Landlords are more likely to grant concessions to people with whom they feel comfortable.

Look like a slob and you will be perceived as a messy housekeeper.

Be overly critical and you will be thought of as a complainer.

Look down and out and no matter how much your paid for your painstakingly tattered jeans, to the apartment owner or manager you may look as if you are unable to pay your rent.

Step 2. Lower Rent, or Something Else?

Put on your landlord's negotiating hat—you know, the practical one you got on sale. Of the following things a tenant may negotiate, which would you, as the landlord, prefer?

- Lower monthly rent.

- Recarpeting the apartment.

- One month's free rent up front.

Free rent up front is a risk. The tenant may be history by the second month.

Lower monthly rent helps the tenant but does nothing for the landlord. Besides, if existing tenants find out, it will be harder to renegotiate their leases.

The recarpeting is a win–win alternative. The landlord has improved the investment in the premises, and the tenant has gotten something in the bargain.

Maybe you can get all three. They're worth negotiating for. But landlords *need* tenant harmony, and it might be disrupted with super deals for some and not others. Landlords also *need* to improve the image and condition of their units, and to know a tenant will be a good renter before they agree to too many extras.

Step 3. If It's Not Chiseled in Granite, It's Negotiable

Printed lease forms have not been handed down from the Mount and there is no such thing as a "standard" form.

Standard is standard only for that landlord. Standard is standard only for an apartment owners' association whose mission is serving its landlord members, or for a real estate brokerage firm which, with a single form document, struggles unsuccessfully to fully serve the best interests of both its landlord and tenant clients.

Standard is in the eyes of the beholder and is always negotiable.

Step 4. Consider Your Options

Negotiate one or more successive options to renew.

In a tenant's market, when rents are low, a landlord who hopes rents will go up will want the renewal rent to be at rates in effect at the time of renewal.

A tenant, however, will want to use a tenant's market to negotiate and lock-in a fixed, low rent for the renewal term.

But what if the landlord won't lock-in a fixed renewal rate?

Ask for a share of the savings the landlord realizes when you renew. When a tenant renews, the landlord does not have to pay a realtor's commission to find a new tenant (although the original broker may get a commission on the renewal). He or she has no dead time before finding a new tenant, does not have to give "free" or concession rent inducements, and does not have to paint, recarpet, or make tenant improvements to lure a new tenant.

If the landlord insists that the renewal rent must be the rate in effect at the time of renewal, negotiate for a statement that the rate will be *less* commissions saved, *less* the value of rent concessions being given others in the building at that time, and *less* the then-average cost of the landlord's new-tenant restoration and repair improvements.

Step 5. Build in an Escape Hatch

Change is the only constant. People are transferred by their employers, lose their jobs, find the house of their dreams, drop out of school, divorce, become ill, marry and move on, suffer business failure.

Thus, negotiating a right of early termination may make a lot of sense. For example:

- The right to leave after three months if you pay a penalty equal to one month's rent.

- The right to leave if you give six months' advance notice.

- The right to terminate if you lose your job, you become disabled, your business fails, and so on.

Step 6. Negotiate a Right of Change

Negotiate the right to move, during the lease term, to a larger unit in the building—or to a smaller unit; or to a unit with a better view; or to a unit on a higher floor; or to a quieter unit—when it becomes available.

The reason your broker never told you about early termination or apartment change provisions is because brokerage commissions are paid up front and are based on what is locked-in and certain. Rights of termination or change put the scope and duration of your lease in doubt.

Step 7. Managers Are as Good as Their Word—As Long as It's in Writing

Leasing agents and apartment managers change, buildings are sold, memories fade. If you are promised anything—a repainted wall, a new garbage disposal unit, whatever—get that promise in writing.

Appliances

Negotiating Major Purchases:
The TV/Treadmill/Tires/Computer/Refrigerator/Stereo Game

Step 1. Make a Salesperson Invest in You

Get your salesperson to invest time in you, the customer.

How can you cause that investment to be made? Ask questions. Compare the various models available—warranties, colors, finishes, specs, features, sizes, ease of operation, style, price, special incentives—whatever it takes.

What is the worst that can happen? You will know a lot more about what you are doing than when you started.

And the best . . . ? It is a behavioral truth: the more time invested in you by the dealer, the more likely that concessions will be granted to make a deal.

Step 2. Don't Be Swayed by Printed Prices

Tire stores, appliance stores, and computer retailers are just a few merchants that use printed price lists as marketing tools. These lists may show the *manufacturer's suggested retail* or *wholesale* price, or both.

Whenever you are being shown a printed price list, *wholesale* will seldom be the dealer's true cost, and *manufacturer's suggested retail* is a selling aid, not a reflection of worth.

Printed price lists are almost always designed to set arbitrarily high prices so discounts from those prices appear generous. This discourages any bargaining. Instead of being discouraged, counter with Step 3.

Step 3. Ask "What Is Your Best Price?" and Anticipate the Response

The treadmill I was interested in was advertised by a national chain of fitness equipment stores at a weekend special price of $3,395.

The dialogue I had with Tracy was typical:

Bob: Does this store have a competitive price policy?

Tracy: If we didn't, we couldn't stay in business.

150

The stage had been set. It had been acknowledged that the price was not set in stone.

Bob: If at all possible, I prefer not to do comparative shopping. What is your best price?

Tracy: $3,200.

Bob: If $3,200 is your best price, I guess I will have to look around.

Tracy: If you can show me this item advertised for less, we will match the price.

Bob: What is the least amount you or this store has sold this treadmill for?

Tracy: Well. Ugh. Well, to be honest with you, $3,100.

Bob: If I buy this treadmill for $3,100, will you write on the receipt that you haven't sold it for less than $3,100?

Tracy: That's not fair.

Bob: What is the reason it's not fair?

Tracy: OK. I will tell. I sold one for $3,000.

Bob: Did that include free delivery and installation?

Tracy: Yes, but we usually charge extra for that.

Bob: Are you saying you will sell it for $3,000 including delivery and installation?

Tracy: Yes. But that is the best I can do.

Bob: Who in the store is authorized to sell it for less than that?

Tracy: The manager.

The manager has been brought over at my suggestion.

Bob: Hi. Tracy has been very helpful but she says you're the person to talk to. I'm trying to avoid a lot of comparison shopping and would like to do business with your store. But Tracy says only you can authorize a price below $3,000.

Manager: I really can't go below $3,000.

Bob: Tracy said I need a $75 carpet board to go under the treadmill and I know an extended warranty is $100. Can those be included in the price?

Manager: OK, if you buy today.

Step 4. Pave the Way for a Graceful Retreat

Business is not great every day.

A merchant's cash needs are never constant.

Managers in various stores of the same chain are in competition with each other.

Often, a merchant will be willing to sell to you for less but has no room to gracefully retreat from a fixed price policy or from the discount that has already been offered.

Many dealers will sell anything on the showroom floor—yes, even if it has been there all of five minutes—as a "demo." It's a face-saving way of circumventing their own nondiscount policies.

Here are other face-saving deal-clinchers:

I know this is a fixed-price store and you don't discount. However—

—you don't have your normal large selection of colors and models to choose from.

—you are unable to deliver immediately and, because you are back-ordered, you won't be able to deliver for three weeks.

—the merchandise is not in perfect condition [or is shop-worn, or is scratched]. It looks as if it should be priced as a demo.

Step 5. And One for the Road

What is the discount if I pay cash?

Automobile Lease

Driving a Hard Bargain

Sometimes lease can be more. But sometimes you can't win for leasing.

Step 1. To Buy or Not to Buy?

Gone are the days when leasing was an option reserved for doctors, lawyers, and businesspeople who could deduct part of their lease payments as business expenses.

Leasing now makes sense if you want to drive a new car and lack the money for a down payment or costly monthly loan payments.

If you keep a car more than three or four years, drive more than 12,000 to 15,000 miles a year, or are rough on a car, then leasing may not be for you. Remember, no matter how good it sounds, leasing is just a long-term rental, and at the end you own nothing whatsoever.

Step 2. Consider the Leasing Company

Generally, you will do better leasing from a new car dealer than from an independent leasing company. To roll out excess stock on certain models, manufacturers will often give special incentives to their leasing divisions, which in turn offer attractive lease deals to drivers.

Step 3. Understand That Low Payments Are the Bait

Leasing involves four pivotal dynamics:

a. The price (capitalized cost) of the vehicle when the lease commences.

b. The used vehicle (residual) value when the lease ends.

c. The amount of the down payment (*capitalization reduction* payment, or CRP).

d. The term of the lease.

Assume the car you are leasing for 24 months has a price of $25,000. There is a $2,500 CRP. The residual value is $10,000.

153

By leasing, you are depreciating or "using up" $15,000 in value ($25,000 price less $10,000 residual value).

The down payment is part payment for the value you are using. There is still $12,500 of value for which you will have to pay. This $12,500 of value, which you will enjoy along with the leasing company's cost of money, taxes, overhead, and profit divided by 24, will be your monthly lease payment.

Step 4. Negotiate a Selling Price

If you are leasing through a dealership, negotiate the car's price and your trade-in allowance *before* disclosing you are a leasing prospect. If asked whether you are interested in buying or leasing, don't tip your hand. Respond, "I am thinking about buying."

The selling price will almost always be less than the sticker price or manufacturer's suggested retail price (MSRP). (To get a bargain selling price, review the negotiating tips in the next Playbook section, "Automobile—New.")

The lease capitalization cost generally should never be more than 5 percent above the amount for which you could purchase the vehicle.

Step 5. Negotiate the Residual Value

There are two primary types of leases: open-ended and closed-ended.

With an *open-ended lease,* you are speculating on the vehicle's residual value—what it will be worth at the end of the lease term. If this residual value is higher than expected, you will get money back. If it is less than its projected value, you will be stuck paying money to the leasing company.

Chances are you will be negotiating a *closed-ended lease:* both you and the lessor are committed to a fixed sum—the forecasted residual value that you negotiate.

Why negotiate the residual value? Vehicles selling for the same price may have dramatically different residual values. *Think about this:* A car that sells for $28,000 may be cheaper to lease than a car selling for $25,000.

Why? Assume the expensive car has a residual value of $16,000 and the less expensive car has a residual value of $12,000.

Price	$ 28,000	$ 25,000
Residual value	$-16,000	$-12,000
Value used by driver (to be paid to leasing company)	$ 12,000	$ 13,000

Tip: You can determine the residual value yourself by looking at the reference book, *Automotive Lease Guide*.

Step 6. Negotiate the Down Payment (CRP)

It's a lessor's worst nightmare: a low-money down payment followed by the customer's defaulting a few months later. The leasing company is stuck with what is now a used vehicle.

The CRP protects the leasing company by cushioning its loss exposure if the lease is prematurely terminated. The amount of the CRP will, in large part, depend on your creditworthiness.

Leasing companies encourage large CRPs by telling customers, "The larger the CRP, the lower your lease payments." A CRP payment, however, doesn't have the same tax deductibility potential as a monthly lease payment, and business users should consult with a tax professional in regard to the amount of the CRP.

Step 7. Negotiate a Deal That Includes a Low Rate for Additional Miles

A closed-ended residual value is based on the assumption that you will not drive more than a certain number of miles during the lease term—usually, about 12,000 to 15,000 miles per year times the number of years in the lease.

To compensate for the unanticipated wear and tear associated with greater mileage, leases typically provide that mileage in excess of a negotiated number of miles is surcharged by the mile (about 10 to 15 cents per mile). Negotiate more noncompensable miles and a lower per-mile rate for compensable miles.

Step 8. Negotiate Excess Wear Provisions

Somewhere in the contract there will be provisions about your obligation if the car is returned with "abnormal damage" or "excessive wear and tear."

These are hard terms to define. Negotiate lease provisions that are as specific as possible. What exactly will happen if you bring back the car with a ding in the door, a stain on the front seat, or bad brakes?

Step 9. Negotiate a Way Out: Escapes and Transfers

You can't unload a leased vehicle as you would an owned vehicle. Therefore, be sure to negotiate the following in advance:

- The *amount charged* if you terminate the lease at various points in time. On a two-year lease, the cost of returning the car at the end of one year will be different from the cost of returning it at the end of 18 months.

    Leasing companies calculate unearned lease charges in a number of ways (sum-of-the-digits; rule of 78s; net present value; or actuarial method minus any surpluses). In one survey of ten leasing companies, the cost of terminating a four-year lease of a particular model at the end of one year ranged from $10,998 to $2,151. Number crunchers recommend negotiating an "actuarial method minus surplus."

- The *ability to transfer* your lease to someone else. Some leasing companies will not allow a lease assignment or transfer even though you remain responsible in the event your successor fails to make payments.

Step 10. Negotiate a Lease Extension Option

It can happen. You may love that trouble-free, incredibly dependable car and want to extend the lease term. Negotiate lease extension terms prior to the commencement of the original lease.

Step 11. Negotiate a Right of Purchase

At the end of the lease, you may want to buy the vehicle for yourself or a member of your family. It is important to negotiate an option price when you lease, in the event you later decide to purchase the car outright.

The purchase option price should be the *lesser* of the residual value or the "true value" at the end of the term. True value could be Blue Book wholesale. Because residual value is nothing more than a projection, it is possible that Blue Book wholesale will be less than the residual value.

Step 12. Negotiate Gap Insurance

If the vehicle is stolen or if you have an accident early into the lease and the vehicle is totaled, there will most likely be a big difference between what the insurance company will pay and what you have to pay the leasing company. Gap insurance should not be expensive—a couple hundred dollars over the term of the lease—but negotiate to have it included at no charge as a part of the deal.

Step 13. Loaners and Lemons

Be sure that the leasing company will provide you with a loaner if your car spends time in the shop, or will replace it if it turns out to be a lemon.

In many states, leased cars aren't covered by the "lemon laws." In those states, negotiate what constitutes a lemon. For example, if the car is out of service for repairs more than 30 days within the first year or 12,000 miles, it will be deemed a "lemon" and the dealer will have to replace it with a comparable new car for the balance of the lease term.

Step 14. Be on the Alert for End-of-Lease Fees

There is no reason to pay a *disposition fee* or *lease termination fee* if you keep the car the whole term. As often as not, these fees are a marketing gimmick. The leasing company will later agree to "forgive" them if you lease another car or buy the car you have been leasing.

Step 15. Read the Fine Print

The fine print may tell a very different story than the headlines in the ads. Don't be pressured into signing on the spot. Take the contract home and look it over carefully. It will be lengthy and it won't be exciting, but reading the fine print is a must. If the lessor's promise isn't in writing, it isn't worth anything.

Automobile—New

How to Make Your Best New Car Deal Ever

Frankly, I am getting a little weary of making great new-car deals for all of my friends and relatives. So, folks, here they are: my secrets for getting a great deal on your next new car.

Step 1. Know What You Want

Take test drives. Look at the color charts. Learn what is standard in various models, what is offered as a package, and what is optional. Only then decide the exact make, model, equipment, and color you want.

Step 2. Head to the Bookstore

Books listing the dealer's *base* cost (*"invoice"*) for every car as well as the dealer's cost for each piece of optional equipment are readily available in paperback in public libraries and the business section of most bookstores.

Check out the value of your old car if you think you might be trading it in instead of selling it yourself. If your library or bookstore doesn't have that information, look at your banker's used-car valuation bible, *Kelley's Blue Book*.

Step 3. Try to Go Fleet

When you are unequivocally ready to buy, *telephone* a dealer and ask for the *fleet sales department*. Introduce yourself and indicate the model, equipment, and color you are interested in buying.

Why fleet? A fleet sale avoids a showroom salesperson's commission, making it possible to cut a closer deal.

Why would the fleet department sell to you? First, as a separate profit center within the dealership, it must maintain a profitable sales volume. Second, the fleet people like winning sales contest prizes.

Can you ask for a test drive and generally take up the fleet department's time asking zillions of questions? No! That is why you must know in advance what you want. Think of the fleet people as no-frills order takers. Period.

If you are buying fleet, do not visit the fleet salesperson until you have made your telephonic deal and are ready to write a check. A

158

premature visit will take away the essential auction/bid character of your negotiations.

Although you will always do better through the fleet department, some dealerships either will not have a fleet department or will redirect you to retail sales.

If you have been talking with a retail salesperson, the fleet department of that same dealership will probably redirect you back to that salesperson.

In either event, fleet or retail, the steps are the same.

Step 4. Ask About Invoice Cost, Incentives, and Holdbacks

Unless you know what the dealer's *actual cost* for the car you're interested in, you don't know how much room there is for negotiating. The dealer's actual cost is its invoice cost less *factory-to-dealer incentive rebates* and *holdbacks.*

- Ask about the dealer's *invoice cost* of the car. This is not the dealer's *actual cost* but the dealer's base purchase price from the factory.

- Ask about *factory incentives for dealers.* Although the dealer has the option of pocketing these rebates they do lower the dealer's cost below invoice, encouraging and enabling the dealer to sell cars more cheaply. If the salesperson is vague with her or his answer, insist she or he find out and tell you. If an answer is refused tell them you will find a different dealer.

- Ask about *dealer holdback.* Almost all manufacturers give the dealer a further quarterly rebate based on the price of the car. This holdback also reduces the dealer's actual cost. Holdback rebates to dealers generally range from 2 percent of base invoice to 3 percent of the total sticker price.

Tip: Consumer Reports Auto Price Service lists all current invoice costs, holdbacks, cash rebate offers, and factory-to-dealer incentives.

Step 5. Ask the Dealer to Bid the Car

Asking the dealer to *bid* is asking the dealer to propose a selling price. You will want the bid to be *expressed as dollars above or below dealer's invoice* ("We will sell any XL model in inventory, for $200 over invoice"). A pro will negotiate from that figure rather than from the sticker price.

The word *bid* puts the dealer on notice that you will be shopping around. It creates the important psychological aura of a pseudo-auction, thereby prompting a lower price from the dealer.

Remember, incentive rebates and holdbacks may make it possible for a dealer to sell to customers profitably at or even below invoice.

A bid that is dollars above or below dealer's invoice establishes a *negotiating commonality*. The invoice price of similarly equipped cars will be the same at the city's dealerships. Actual cost may vary among dealers because some incentives will be tied to a dealer's sales volume.

Step 6. Clarify the Bid Price

Have the bid exclude add-ons that are not on the factory window sticker. These are strictly for the unwary. By discounting the padding, dealer discounts appear greater than they really are. Some common add-on bargaining traps are:

- "Dealer preparation" charges for waxing, paint sealing, rust proofing, fabric spraying, and undercoating. These are expensive, high mark-up dealer extras.

- ADP (added dealer profit), ADM (added dealer mark-up), and AMV (added market value).

- Conveyance fees charged for paperwork.

If you are negotiating for a *cash-back* car, proceed as if there was no *factory-to-customer* cash rebate. When you have agreed on a price then deduct the cash-back offer.

Ask about *factory incentives for customers.* One manufacturer, for example, offers recent college graduates a $300 incentive discount.

Step 7. Play on the Power of Competition

Now is *not* the time to bargain because you want to play on the power of a pseudo-auction. Tell the dealer you want to make a few calls to other dealers and you will call back.

When you make calls to other dealers, solicit their bids *expressed as dollars above or below the dealer's invoice.*

Once you know the exact model, color, and equipment you want, it may be more convenient to send a fax to the dealers in your area asking them to submit their best deal by return fax.

Call back the dealer who made the best bid, confirm the *exact selling price* of the specific car you want, and ask, "How much flexibility is there if we close our deal today?"

What is a good price? Usually, about $150 to $300 above the dealer's invoice is a reasonable bargaining goal. You will probably pay more if you are eyeing a hot new model and are asked to take a number as you enter the showroom. If your model choice is a slow seller or the factory will soon announce styling changes to that model, then paying invoice or less is a reasonable goal.

Step 8. Negotiate the Other Financial Terms

In all likelihood, before bidding, the dealer will ask you about these other dollar dynamics: financing, extended warranty, and trade-in.

Financing. Are you going to finance? If so, will you finance through the dealer?

Arranging financing through either the dealer's bank or the manufacturer (i.e., GMAC, Ford Motor Credit) is a profitable activity for the dealer, who receives a fee from the financing company.

If you are going to finance, know what your bank or credit union is willing to do for you—before calling the dealer. Your own financing resources may be more attractive than the dealer's.

Extended Warranty. Are you going to buy an extended warranty?

The dealer would prefer to sell you an "insurance company" warranty rather than a manufacturer's warranty. The profit margin is greater. Most insurance company warranties are filled with escape clauses and oppressive conditions regarding when and where routine service is performed.

Your cost for either warranty *is negotiable.* An extended warranty does *not* need to be purchased the day you buy the car *nor* does it need to be purchased from the dealer who sold you the car.

Trade-In. Until the price of the new car is established, don't get into trade-in discussions. This helps keep negotiations simple. Besides, you don't want to lose the benefit of a bargain on the new car by getting a low price for your trade. If asked, say you aren't sure of your plans for the old wheels.

Step 9. Avoid Dealer Game-Playing

Showroom game-playing usually starts with your being asked the sucker-punch question: "What would you be willing to pay for this car?" Ask for the dealer's bid instead.

What if the friendly folks in the showroom aren't friendly enough to bid in terms of cost-above-invoice? You are left with two easy choices.

Choice No. One: Stand firm, letting them know you will do some shopping around. My bet is they will respond with one of the following lines:

- *How much do I have to discount this car to get you to buy right now?* (Respond with a question of your own: *What is the least amount this dealership has sold this car for?*)

- *We will quote a price after you have visited the competition.* (Refuse to shop around. On your return, they will ask about the best deal offered.)

Choice No. Two: Offer "*$150 over actual cost,*" then stand back and watch the salesperson scurry off to a "take-over" manager for further instruction.

Practice tip: After negotiations are concluded, verify the invoice price by asking to see the invoice. If the dealer has been candid, the invoice will be shown to you.

If the dealer refuses to show you the invoice, fall back on the *Pinocchio Test.* Insist that the dealer must write on the final contract: *Dealer represents that the purchase price of this car is $_____ over (or under) dealer's invoice.*

A few years back, I purchased a car and the dealer made this written representation. Months later, I found out I had been misled. When confronted, the dealer promptly wrote a check for the difference.

Practice tip: Yes, what you have always heard is true. You will do better buying a car just before month-end sales reports are due.

Generally, the best time of year to buy is in September and October (at the end of the model year if the dealer has a large inventory and needs to make room for next year's models) and December when dealers want to reduce inventory taxes and give a last minute boost to annual sales.

Negotiating alert: What about "no-haggle" discount dealerships? Professional shoppers report you will do better bargaining with a "traditional" dealership if you know how to play the game.

Automobile—Used

Negotiating the Purchase of a Used Car

When you purchase a car from a dealer, you are dealing with sales pros. Buy a used car from a private party, and you must contend with the seller's emotional and personality makeup.

A new car that you like can be found at dealerships all over the county. Finding just the right used car is a matter of luck. Buying that used car at the right price may mean overcoming the seller's misconception of worth.

Let's start with a scenario illustrating the used-car game.

The ad was in the Saturday classifieds. You follow the directions given to you over the phone. And there it is! The Mustang that you want to buy is parked right before your very eyes.

You play it cool. You're not overly enthusiastic. You never give the car's owner the impression you are a slam-dunk buyer.

Despite all of this, the price is way too high.

You have looked at Mustangs for three weekends and you don't want to lose this opportunity. But then you don't want to play positional *my price vs. your price* hardball with some amateur who may tell you to take a hike.

Wisely, you opt for an oblique run—a nonpositional approach.

You: I feel that the $7,000 you are asking for the car is awfully high.

Seller: I saw some ads in the Sunday classifieds, so I know the going price for this model and year.

You: You used the paper as a guide to determine fair market value?

Seller: Yep.

Your tactics have succeeded: The seller has acknowledged that he is interested in selling his car at its fair market value. The seller's reason for asking $7,000 is his belief that $7,000 is fair. The classified ads were only a guide in making this determination.

You: I have been looking at those ads too, and I saw some where the asking price is a lot less. Do you think we can find some criterion of fair market other than the classifieds?

163

You have suggested to the seller that ads were chosen selectively to support his price position and that there is usually a big difference between newspaper asking prices and selling prices. The seller has agreed to sell the Mustang for its true fair market value but there is a *worth* conflict: What is really the fair market value?

Seller: What do you have in mind?

You: Well, the *Kelley Blue Book* is the used-car pricing bible. I will pay wholesale *Kelley Blue Book*.

Seller: I agree that the *Blue Book* is the bible. But I am a retail seller and I want a retail price.

You and the seller have acknowledged a credible external criterion, *Kelley Blue Book* value. But there is still the issue of whether wholesale or retail book is applicable.

You: Retail *Blue Book* is usually what is charged by a dealer who is willing to guarantee a car's condition and who would assist in arranging financing and transfer of title. What about a price that is halfway between wholesale and retail *Blue Book?*

You are offering the seller a basis of compromise that will be transformed into dollars. Offering money before the basis of compromise is accepted will cause the seller to become more position-oriented.

You offered the seller *an eternal standard* (the *Blue Book*) *and an objective approach* (the 50/50 split). Both contribute to resolving whether wholesale or retail book should apply.

Here are the steps for using this *externalization tactic:*

Step 1. Get the Seller's Reasoning for the Position Taken

The $7,000 asking price was, in the seller's mind, fair market value.

Step 2. Have the Seller Explain Why That Position Is Considered Fair

The classified ads were the seller's benchmark of fairness.

Step 3. **Confirm That the Seller Is Interested in True Fairness**

The seller confirmed an intention to sell the Mustang for its *true* fair market value.

Step 4. **Show Why the Basis for the Position Is Unfair or Biased**

Selected classified ad prices are unreliable determinants of value. Unlike the seller, retailers offer warranties and other benefits to justify a top-dollar price.

Step 5. **Suggest Seeking a Mutually Acceptable Fair Standard**

Kelley Blue Book value is the agreed upon choice.

Step 6. **Convert the Mutually Agreed-On External Criterion to "Price"**

A price halfway between wholesale and retail *Blue Book* should be workable.

■ ■ ■

Practice alert: Beware of a practice known as curbstoning. A person selling a car through the classifieds may be a front for a used-car dealer. Ask: *Who is the title owner? How long have you owned the car?*

In many states, a vehicle's chain of title, showing historical ownership, is available from the Department of Motor Vehicles.

Bargaining and Haggling

The Bazaar/Marketplace/Swap Meet/Street Vendor/Shopping Game

This section is not about chiseling.

It is about being at the top of your bargaining game and is the result of my having interviewed over 200 merchants on six continents, gathering bargaining and haggling tips for shoppers headed for art fairs, flea markets, swap meets, and bazaars around the world.

These are the secrets I have shared in lectures to cruise ship passengers over the years. I have watched those passengers in action, and their results have been incredible.

FROM SI TO SHINING SI

A peasant lineage isn't a prerequisite to becoming a top-seeded shopper. The secrets of success are pretty much the same whether you bargain for brass Buddhas in Bangkok, an amber necklace in Kenya, reindeer gloves in Helsinki's dockside market, or earrings on Berkeley's Telegraph Avenue.

Step 1. Engage in Bargaining Foreplay

Bargaining foreplay is the difference between a great deal and an ordinary one.

Cairo's Khan Al Khalili Bazaar has local color you can cut with a knife. As he watched me scan his wares, a stall owner observed my body signals. When my eyes and hands momentarily came to rest on a mosaic box, he made his move. I should have known better than to show interest in any particular item.

The key to the credibility of a low *I don't care if I buy it or not* offer is appearing not to be too anxious.

Here are a few of the comments I have heard made by shoppers who lost all bargaining credibility by not understanding the importance of bargaining foreplay. Do any of them sound familiar?

- *Wouldn't this look great in the family room?*

- *I saw a necklace just like this at Saks for ten times as much.*

166

- *This is just what Jim and Alice told us to bring them back.*

- *Wouldn't this look great with my turquoise outfit?*

Step 2. Nothing Ventured, Nothing Discounted

Watch other shoppers in action.

Pay particular interest to the spread between initial asking prices and the amounts actually paid. Ask other shoppers what they paid for things that are of interest to you.

Then make an extremely low offer.

A representative from the Indian tourist bureau told fellow cruise passengers sailing to Bombay that "a shrewd shopper's opening offer should be 50 percent of the asking price." The speaker knew that most Americans are too moderate, too "polite" to ever offer less than 50 percent.

But, in Bombay, as in many other places in the world, many of our 80 percent and 90 percent discount offers were accepted.

OK, maybe your extremely low offer won't be accepted. But you have done the groundwork for driving home the best possible bargain because *your low offer has impacted the seller's expectations and price goal.*

Step 3. Build a Budget Ceiling

Your low offer is the seller's cue to extol the virtues of the goods. Once you let *value* or *worth* come into play, you will hear about the untold hours spent weaving, carving, or painting the object you have admired. Instead of questioning worth, I build *a budget ceiling*, knowing that my budget, unlike worth, is a figure so personal it can't rationally be disputed.

A budget ceiling can be your own or someone else's. Bargaining in off-the-beaten-track native markets throughout the world, I will tell a vendor in St. Petersburg, Acapulco, or Rhodes that I am shopping not for myself but for a (fictitious) neighbor back home who asked me to bring back a necklace, serape, or carving but not to spend a ruble, peso, or drachma more than . . . .

The amount specifically "authorized" by the fictional neighbor will, of course, be a fraction of the asking price.

An imaginary neighbor's *budget*, rather than *worth*, becomes my irrefutable fixed ceiling. This tactic, which allows the vendor to save face while retreating from an announced position, works almost everywhere almost every time.

Step 4. Test the Bottom

My bargaining credo is simple: *There is no such things as a final offer, a best price, or an arbitrary purchase deadline.*

- *This special price is available only if you buy now.* Don't be swayed by a disappearing discount. Disappearing discounts *always* miraculously reappear.

- *But I am already offering it to you at my cost.* Once I reach what I think is a rock-bottom price, it is time to test that bottom: *How much of a discount would there be if I bought two? Or three?* Although I may intend to buy only one, the dropping price point gives me a better feel for the seller's flexibility.

The bottom may not be the absolute bottom. Ask:

- *What is the discount offered if I buy with cash instead of a credit card?*

- *What is the discount if I use U.S. currency instead of the local currency?*

Practice tip: The question *What is the discount if . . . ?* presupposes a discount. The question *Is there a discount if . . . ?* makes it all too easy for the seller to say "No."

Step 5. Increase Your Offer

If necessary, quote a higher price. Bargaining is expected. Failing to counter is impolite in some cultures. Keep your increased offer below the anticipated closing price. Remember the secrets in Chapter 17. Posture yourself for a "let's-split-the-difference" offer.

Step 6. Make It Clear That You Are Prepared to Walk

Chances are you won't have to walk very far.

Step 7. Exotic Aisles: Bargaining Traps

- *Please sit and have a little tea.* Store owners in many parts of the world will invite you to sit and have tea with them. An experience to write home about? More likely a *personalization tactic.* Personalizing the negotiating process makes it harder for you to turn down their offer.

- Recall the anecdote about Barbara and the velvet painting, in Chapter 19. Avoid being swept up in the back-and-forth of bargaining. Getting the best possible price isn't great bargaining. Great bargaining is getting *something you want* at the best possible price.

- Remember, somebody is buying what the apprentices are making. Be alert to the possibility that what you see is not necessarily what you get. To avoid switches, never allow your purchase to be out of your watchful sight.

- Except in the very finest stores, don't trust shopkeepers' description of age or quality. Never buy anything important from sidewalk vendors.

- If your tour guide takes you to a store or factory, it's not because the best merchandise is sold there at the fairest prices, it's because the guide is getting a commission. (Those colored stick-on dots tour guides ask you to wear tell the cashiers which guide receives the commission for your purchase.) "Factory" prices are not wholesale prices, and the quality is not always the best.

- Don't assume that store signs proclaiming "Factory Outlet" or "Duty Free" are anything other than come-ons.

- Did you get the right change? Was it in the right country's currency? Was it in the currency in use now? Sleight-of-hand when returning change is not uncommon in Third World countries.

- Street merchants and marketplaces often sell "seconds" and rejects. Examine merchandise (including fabrics and clothing items) from top to bottom, corner to corner.

- *Wanna buy a watch?* Beware of fake designer goods in all but luxury and department stores.

Business—Purchase

Negotiating the "No Surprises Later On" Purchase of a Business

Step 1. Ask Yourself . . .

Before you buy a going business, make sure you understand the prospects of *this* business, at *this* location, in *this* condition.

- Is a national competitor starting to dominate the market? Many independent merchants are being pushed aside by "category killers" such as Staples, Foot Locker, and Home Depot.

- Is new competition around the corner? Stores "on the avenue" are losing customers to malls that offer security and easy parking.

- Is it a trendy business whose time is over? Cookie and yogurt stores were hot for a while, but are now in a fade. Every fad will ultimately suffer the same fate.

- Is it a business impacted by changing health concerns? Red meat, ice cream, fried foods, and tanning salons are falling from favor.

- Is it a business dependent on an anchor or neighboring business to generate traffic? Anchor tenants don't stay forever.

Step 2. Lock in Your Expectations

Ask yourself: *Why am I buying this business? Am I getting what I think I'm getting?*

Warranties are written guarantees that certain representations made by the seller are true.

Common seller's warranties to negotiate are:

- Financial statements are complete, correct, prepared in accordance with generally accepted accounting principles, and fairly represent the financial condition of the business.

- Since the date of the financial statements, there have been no adverse changes, financial or otherwise, in the business's operations, properties, or prospects.

- Accounts receivable are genuine, valid, good, and collectible.

170

- Inventory items are current and salable except for those items specifically scheduled as obsolete or slow moving ("*carve outs*").

- Customer lists are accurate. There are no disputes with any customers nor do any of the customers intend to cease doing business or substantially decrease the volume of business they are doing.

- Fixtures and equipment are in good working condition and repair.

Consider: What representations must you have in order to maximize your comfort level with the deal? *Negotiate* to have all important representations set out in your agreement as warranties.

Step 3. Negotiate the *Scope* of the Seller's Warranties

Warranties can be *absolute*. For example: *All accounts receivable are collectible*.

Warranties can also be *limited* to what the seller knows. For example: *To the seller's knowledge, all accounts receivable are collectible*.

Suppose a large account receivable is uncollectible because a customer has filed bankruptcy. Your seller hadn't received notice of the bankruptcy at the time you bought the business.

If the seller's warranty is *absolute*, the seller would be obligated to indemnify you for what you lost. The warranty is *unequivocal*.

If, however, the warranty is *limited* to the seller's knowledge, you would have no claim because the warranty is *conditional* on the seller's having known about the bankruptcy.

- *Negotiate* absolute warranties rather than being put to the task of proving what the seller may or may not have known.

- *Negotiate* that the warranties will not be affected or limited by any preclosing investigations made by you or someone else on your behalf.

- *Negotiate* that the representations and warranties contained in the agreement *survive the close* of the transaction and the transfer of the business. This will enable you to make future claims subject only to applicable statutes of limitations.

Step 4. Be Ready When the Seller Says . . .

Our business expenses are really a lot less than shown in the books. I run a lot of my personal expenses through the business. Hey, I even vacationed in London last year and charged the whole trip to the business.

Or says . . .

Look, we do a lot of cash business. To be honest with you, we don't report all of our income. Business is really much better than what is shown on the books.

If a seller is lying to the IRS about the business's income and expenses, what makes you think you're getting the straight story?

- *Negotiate* to key a portion of the purchase price to the business's future earnings or profitability. This tactic protects you if the seller's projections or historical earnings representations prove untrue. For example: A part of the price may be based on a percentage of the increase in future earnings over the prior earnings shown on the books.

- *Negotiate* a definition of earnings that excludes extraordinary items such as the sale of noninventory equipment.

Step 5. Can the Seller Become Your Competitor?

Will your business be hurt if the seller suddenly starts competing with you? Don't take that chance.

- *Negotiate* the seller's promise (*covenant*) not to compete by attempting to influence or divert customers from the business.

But what if the seller opens a similar business and doesn't try to divert existing customers, who nevertheless flock to the seller's newly opened door?

- *Negotiate* restrictions as to *when* and *where* the seller may open a similar business. For example: The seller agrees not to engage in the catering business in Los Angeles County for a period of five years.

Negotiating alert: Is it necessary to negotiate with the seller's key employees for a similar covenant not to compete? If so, will the employees' covenant not to compete be enforceable under state law? If necessary, check with your attorney.

Step 6. Keep Trade Secrets Secret

Trade secrets are proprietary information that is vital to the success of a business. Depending on the nature of the business, they may include:

- Customers' names.

- Suppliers' names and prices.

- Unique techniques, methods, or procedures.

- Special formulas or recipes.

- Source codes or computer software.

- Salary and employee information.

Prevent the seller from making trade secrets available to others who could use them to your competitive disadvantage. Negotiate covenants that prohibit the seller from:

- Disclosing to third parties specifically identified lists, data, processes, and so on, that are vital to the effective and successful conduct of the business.

- Removing or duplicating drawings, plans, software, lists, and documents that are specified as trade secrets.

Step 7. Put Teeth in Your Deal

To bite hard, negotiate a broad *indemnification agreement* under which the seller will *hold you harmless* by reimbursing you for any claims, demands, or losses that result from the seller's misrepresentation or breach of warranty.

No matter how artful your indemnification agreement, if the seller is tapped out, you might as well have had no indemnification agreement at all.

To bite harder:

- *If you will be giving the seller your promissory note,* negotiate the right to offset and deduct from future payments the amount of any claim you may have against the seller.

- *If you will be paying all cash,* negotiate a *hold-back*—a portion of the purchase price (the amount negotiated) held by you in a reserve account for an agreed-on period. Your claims against the seller would be reimbursed from the hold-back reserve.

  The seller will want advance notice of your intent to claim a hold-back portion, in order to contest the merits of your claim in accordance with your agreement's dispute resolution procedures.

Reality bite: keep in mind that—

- People are less cavalier in making representations when there is a potential for personal liability.

- The more folks who are on the line, the more likely you will be successful in asserting your claim for money.

To bite the hardest when the seller is a corporation, limited liability company, or partnership, negotiate that each of its officers, shareholders, partners, and principals must join in as co-warrantors and indemnitors.

Step 8. Avoid Asset Purchase Surprises

Here is a sampling of some of the unexpecteds:

- *Surprise:* The seller's license and permits may not be transferable. You may have to make new applications.

- *Surprise:* Motor vehicles, trademarks and trade names, accounts receivable, leases, inventory, fixtures, contracts with third parties, boats and real property are each transferred differently. Determine what is required for the proper and legal transfer of assets.

- *Surprise:* Failure to follow applicable laws may enable the seller's creditors to levy or foreclose on the assets which you paid for and received. Determine what is required under local law to obtain lien-free, clear title to assets. Understand your state's *bulk sales laws* and the required filings at state and county levels.

- *Surprise:* If the purchase price you are paying is not fair and for a "reasonable equivalent value," it has the potential of being overturned by the seller's creditors.

- *Surprise:* Under state law, you may inadvertently assume the seller's liabilities to former employees. Ascertain the law in your state.

- *Surprise:* You may be held accountable for the business's environmental liability and defective product claims, even though the terms of your purchase agreement provide otherwise. Negotiate for the seller to indemnify you from any *successor liability* claims.

- *Surprise:* The accounts receivable being purchased may not be as collectible as represented. Negotiate for a seller's obligation to repurchase from you past-due receivables.

- *Surprise:* Equipment and furnishings that are not inventory are generally subject to a sales tax. Tax obligations most often are the responsibility of the seller. The seller, however, will typically seek reimbursement for the sales tax from the buyer. Generally, absent a contractual obligation by the buyer to reimburse the seller, the buyer is not liable for the sales tax.

  Negotiating tip: Between the parties themselves, determining which party will bear the sales tax burden is negotiable.

- *Surprise:* Key employees often quit after a business changes hands.

  Practice tip: Get assurances from key personnel that they will remain with the business. Clarify whether those employees will be looking to you to honor accrued vacations and other benefits.

Step 9. Talk to a Pro

Maybe you are best off buying the assets that comprise a business: inventory, accounts receivable, equipment, trade name, leases, and so on. As part of the deal, you may agree to assume certain obligations and payables.

Maybe you are best off buying the shares of a corporation(or limited liability company), that owns the assets that comprise the business. Corporations have assets, but they also have obligations, debts, and adverse claims.

Engage the assistance of professionals who can guide you through the maze of tax, legal, and dispute resolution considerations.

Business—Sale

Negotiating the "No Surprises Later On" Sale of a Business

Step 1. Remember the Scotts

The Scotts spent their lives building up a small but profitable and very creditworthy gift boutique. They were justifiably proud of what they had accomplished and looked forward to their pending retirement.

Wolfe offered them a surprisingly large price for their prized business. The purchase would be funded by a small cash down payment plus a very sizable promissory note.

The Scotts had no insight into Wolfe's objective—to loot the Scotts' business.

Wolfe used the boutique's fine credit for the purpose of obtaining loans and buying merchandise for which no payment was ever made. The Scotts never received a penny more than the cash down payment.

People are funny. I know the Scotts; they are like a lot of other good businesspeople. If Wolfe had wanted $1,000 in customer credit, they would have gotten all kind of information about him. But the Scotts were not "programmed" to obtain information about a business buyer.

Step 2. Preparing for the Other Shoe to Drop

Whether you are selling your shares in a corporate-owned business or selling the assets that comprise a business, your buyer will demand from you certain warranties and representations. Examples of common warranties are in the preceding Playbook section, "Business—Purchase."

In agreeing to indemnify the buyer, you are promising to reimburse the buyer for losses that result from the breach of those representations and warranties.

As a seller, you will want to limit the scope and extent of your liability. This can be accomplished if you:

- *Negotiate* an aggregate dollar limitation on the amount your buyer can claim from you for breach of warranty. For example, in no event can the buyer recover more than $25,000 as a result of a breach of warranty claim.

- *Negotiate* that indemnification payments will be limited to amounts remaining to be paid to the buyer from future note

176

installments or from "earn-out" payments if part of the purchase price is keyed to future earnings.

- *Negotiate* that, for indemnification purposes, the buyer's reimbursable losses are calculated on an after-tax basis. The buyer's actual out-of-pocket losses may possibly be reduced by a tax benefit resulting from a tax deduction.

- *Negotiate* a limited time period during which the buyer may bring an action for breach of warranty. For example, no claim for breach of warranty will be valid unless made within six months from the date the business changes hands.

- *Negotiate basket limitations* to avoid arguments over relatively nominal breaches. For example, no claim will be honored until the buyer's aggregate claims exceed $10,000.

- *Negotiate* the *scope* of your warranties by limiting them to what you *actually know*. For example, instead of representing *absolutely* that "the financial statements are complete," your warranty would be one of limitation: "To the Seller's actual knowledge, the financial statements are complete."

- *Negotiate* the apportionment of liability among the sellers if there is more than one. For example, if you own 30 percent of the business being sold, you will not want to have potential responsibility for 100 percent of the buyer's claims.

Limit your liability for faulty or defective goods or equipment to reimbursement of what your buyer *actually paid* for particular items. This will eliminate the buyer's potential claim for lost profits or other losses that are a consequence or result of your breach.

Practice tip: Rather than warranting the condition of equipment being sold, allow the buyer to thoroughly inspect that equipment and sell it in *as is* condition.

Step 3. Getting Off the Hook, Staying Off the Hook

If you are selling assets, chances are you will want to negotiate the buyer's assumption (and payment) of all or some of your business's debt. This is particularly true if you have a postsale obligation to an equipment lessor, landlord, or installment purchase financier.

- *Negotiate* for the buyer *to secure* its promise to you that these assumed obligations will be paid. The buyer's security can be real estate, the equipment being sold, or other good collateral. If the buyer later reneges by not paying the assumed debt, you will be in a position to foreclose on the collateral that secures the buyer's promise of payment.

Is the buyer a corporation or limited liability company?

- *Negotiate* for the buyer's principals to *personally* guaranty that assumed obligations will be *timely* paid. If you are concerned about the financial ability of the guarantors, these personal guaranties can be secured by the personal assets of the guarantors.

Step 4. Protect Yourself from Earn-Out Manipulation

Is a portion of the purchase price based on the buyer's future earnings (*earn-outs*)? Safeguard yourself against earn-out manipulation. Until you are paid:

- *Negotiate* that the business being purchased is to be operated as a distinct entity separate from the buyer's other operations, which could impact earnings.

- *Negotiate* that equipment and fixtures necessary for conducting business can't be disposed of without your consent.

- *Negotiate* that there can be no material changes in the type, scope, or manner of operation of the business.

- *Negotiate* to restrict allocations of expenses for overhead if the business being purchased will be operated as a subsidiary.

- *Negotiate* the right to regularly review the buyer's financial statements and earn-out calculations.

Step 5. Make the Buyer's Promissory Note as Collectible as You Can

- *Reality Bite No. 1: Now-you-see-it, now-you-don't collateral.* You can lose the benefit of having a secured note if the inventory, accounts receivable, and/or equipment serving as collateral can be readily sold or collected with your knowledge or consent.

- *Reality Bite No. 2: You may get your business back.* Having a note secured by the inventory or fixtures of a business means you have to be emotionally and financially prepared to take the business back if you are forced to foreclose on your collateral. (And this assumes the business is still intact.)

- *Biting Back.* Negotiate for the equity in the buyer's home or other real estate to be posted as additional collateral securing payment of the note you are being given.

What if the buyer can't provide satisfactory additional security? Demand that the buyer's note obligation be *guarantied* by others who do have financial substance.

Practice tip: The guaranty should not be for *eventual payment* of the note obligation but a guaranty of *timely payment.*

Consider: Does it make sense to collect receivables yourself rather than sell them? Selling good accounts receivable is like selling cash.

Negotiating alert: If the buyer insists on purchasing your receivables, it may be a sign that the buyer is in shaky financial condition.

Step 6. Talk to a Pro

Selling a business requires the assistance of professionals versed in business and tax.

Cohabitation Agreement

Negotiating an Agreement Between Unmarried Cohabitants

Just when you thought divvying up closet space was the hard part . . .

Step 1. It's Time to Get Real

Now is the time to discuss your expectations and concerns forthright-fully. These discussions can be a rewarding and enriching experience that will lead to a new understanding and appreciation of your relationship. They can also be a revealing and disappointing tug-of-war.

Step 2. Understand What Is and What Isn't

Generally speaking, there is no automatic right to property or support merely because a person was once a nonmarital partner.

In states where any rights of nonmarital partners are recognized, those rights have nothing to do with alimony. They do, however, have everything to do with contract law.

In these so-called "palimony states," the "rights" granted by courts are nothing more than the right every individual has to enforce a lawful contract even though the contract provides for typically "spousal" benefits.

In some of the states where cohabitation agreements are enforceable, the law is further evolving to protect the expectations of cohabitants who do not have a written contract. The courts in those progressive states are willing to examine the conduct of the cohabitants to determine whether an "implied contract" or an "implied partnership" existed. But a nonmarital partner may be unable to establish an implied contract or an implied partnership. A written agreement is therefore imperative.

Step 3. Negotiate the Character of the Relationship

If it appears that your agreement is primarily for sexual services rather than for love, companionship, health care, or sharing of financial resources, a court may deny enforcement of your cohabitation agreement on the grounds that its primary purpose was the procurement of immoral and illicit acts. Negotiate and document with specificity the *purpose and character of the relationship*.

180

Step 4. Negotiate Specific Support Rights and Obligations

A written cohabitation agreement to "support" or "take care of" may be too vague to cause a division of property or a court order of support.

If your agreement is to be upheld, the negotiated respective *rights* and *obligations* of the parties must be clear and specific.

Consider negotiating and including the following in the cohabitation agreement:

- Who will pay all or a greater part of living expenses?

- Will earnings and income be pooled?

- Who will pay taxes, upkeep, and maintenance on property owned by one of the parties?

- Will payments be made to the "pal" periodically—for example, X dollars per year on the anniversary of cohabitation?

Step 5. Negotiate What Happens If There Is a Mutual Breakup

Consider negotiating and including in your cohabitation agreement what will happen if the relationship breaks up:

- Will there be post-cohabitation support? If so, will the support be keyed to how long the partners lived together—for example, one month of support for each month of cohabitation?

- Who will vacate the premises and who will stay?

- Who will keep furniture and other items jointly purchased during the relationship?

Step 6. Negotiate What Happens If a Partner Receiving Financial Benefits Calls It Quits

What happens if the partner seeking to enforce the cohabitation agreement was the one who ended the relationship? A financially benefited partner should negotiate and document what will happen in this eventuality to avoid a defense based on breach of contract.

Step 7. Negotiate Death Benefits

A nonmarital partner's will can be changed at any time without the other partner's knowledge or consent. A cohabitation agreement is a two-party contract that can be changed only by mutual consent.

Consider negotiating and including in your cohabitation agreement:

- Upon a partner's death, the surviving partner will receive a stipulated allowance per month for a specified period of time.

- The partner will own and be the beneficiary of an insurance policy on the life of the other partner.

- Upon a partner's death, the surviving partner will continue to live in the deceased partner's residence for a specified time.

Step 8. Get a Lawyer

Your cohabitation agreement will be better able to withstand a challenge if it has been reviewed by your partner's lawyer. The lawyer should acknowledge in writing that the cohabitation agreement was read, understood, and entered into by your partner free from duress or undue influence.

Collecting Money

Negotiating the Collection of Money Without Sounding Like a Wimp or a Self-Righteous Money Grubber

Nobody likes to collect money. It's the worst job in the office.

Who wants to hear yelling, threats, poor-mouthing, a diatribe of how you could have done something a little better, a little faster, a little differently?

Who wants to be embarrassed and have unjustified feelings of defensiveness when someone asks, "Don't you trust me?"

Everybody knows it's hard enough to get business, much less chance losing it to a competitor because you are being pushy about your bill. Won't people be dissuaded from doing business with you if they see you as relentless and uncaring in your collection policies?

Not necessarily. It's possible to collect what's coming to you while preserving important relationships. Here's how.

Step 1. Have a Creditor's Mindset

Remember that the money is *yours*. You earned it. You are entitled to receive it when promised. You are not looking for a contribution or a handout.

Step 2. He Who Hesitates Loses

The longer you wait to call a potential problem account, the less likely you are to collect. The time to start is within a few days of when the payment has become overdue.

Step 3. Don't Be a Wimp

Let's face it. The following bad-move lines are wimp-outs.

- *Bad Move No. 1: Can you send a partial payment on account?* A partial payment can be $20 on a $1,000 balance, which is hardly what you had in mind.

- *Bad Move No. 2: Look, we have bills to pay, too.* Who cares? And besides, your needs have nothing to do with collecting what is morally and legally yours to collect.

183

- *Bad Move No. 3: How much can you send us?* Discussions should focus on how the bill will get paid, not on what will be sent this week.

- *Bad Move No. 4: If it's not too much trouble, would you send us something today?* The wrong person is on a guilt trip and it shows. Why are you apologizing for asking someone to keep a promise?

- *Bad Move No. 5: I'd like you to pay your bill or at least half.* Name one person who will send 100 percent if there is an invitation to pay 50 percent.

Step 4. Ease Your Tension

If you feel anxiety or discomfort in asking for your due, reestablish *linkage*.

- Start with *chit-chat* if you can make it sound natural and unscripted. Sports and natural disasters are great icebreakers: *Did you see the game Saturday? Did you have wind damage to your house?*

- State why you are uncomfortable: *I hate calling you about your bill and I wish we didn't have to discuss money. If you would rather talk later, tell me when I should call back.*

The offer to defer the discussion shows you really are sensitive to your customers as persons and are not viewing them as collection statistics.

Step 5. Negotiate a Definite Course of Conduct

Being promised "a payment" is not good enough. If you are not getting a full payment, then be *definite* about the *amounts* being sent and the *time frame* for payment in full.

- *I need to know exactly how much you are sending, when it is being sent, and how the balance will be paid off.*

- *How much time do you need to pay off the account?*

- *How short of the full payment are you?*

Without a definitive, specific understanding, you will be pleading for money on a weekly basis.

Step 6. How to Avoid the "P" Word

If you can't say *pay*, then use weasel words: *I need you to clear this account; I need you to bring your account current; I need you to take care of the balance.*

Step 7. Ask About "How"

You have requested the debtor to pay your bill. The next step is a question: *How do you want to clear (take care of, pay) the account balance—by cash, credit card, or check?*

Step 8. Say Nothing

The debtor will respond to your question in Step 7 if you say nothing more.

The response may be a promise of payment (not good enough unless specific) or an excuse for not paying (now is the time to put the excuse on the table for discussion, compromise, or rejection).

If the debtor asks to discuss the situation later, then get a commitment as to when and where: *I understand that this is an inconvenient time. When should I call back?*

Negotiating tip: It is harder to say "no" in person: A face-to-face meeting may be more productive than a phone call. If the amount is significant and it is not physically inconvenient, meet at the debtor's office. Your customer will not have a *Let me reexamine my records at the office* excuse for dodging payment. And even better, that's where the checkbook is!

Step 9. It's Not Over Until It's Over

If you've used the tactics described above and payment still isn't made, consider these money extractors:

- *Joe, our controller pulled your account as one of the ones to be turned over to the lawyers for collection. I retrieved your file and said that I wanted to talk to you myself about your balance.*

- *Joe, our controller pulled your account to go to collection. I understand things are tough and you aren't sure when you can make payments. I can give you some slack if you will sign a promissory note.*

Unlike open account relationships, a note generally will have a definite payment structure, accrue interest, and provide for late payment penalties and the reimbursement of legal expenses. Traditional defenses (late delivery, product defects, and so on) may not be available to the debtor once the obligation is memorialized in a note.

Negotiating tip: Is there a dispute as to the amount owed? Perhaps delivery was late or specifications were not met.

Consider this: Assume a $4,000 claim is reduced to $2,000 and will be paid in monthly installments. To put teeth in the deal, cast the note as a $4,000 note which provides for $2 of credit for each dollar *timely* paid.

If all the payments are timely, only $2,000 would be due. If half the payments are timely, $3,000 would be due. And if none of the payments is timely, $4,000 would be due and you would possess all the rights and abilities of a note holder.

Practice tip: If the business is a corporation or other entity, request the owner's personal guaranty of payment. Talking big numbers? Consider having the note secured by company assets, by the owner's home, or by other good collateral.

Are these requests overreaching? Not when your customer is asking you to forbear from collection action or is seeking more credit.

Contractors, Negotiating with

Negotiating with a Pool/Building/Masonry/Roofing/ Painting/Landscape or Other Type of Contractor

Your preliminary discussions with possible contractors should be treated as job interviews. Ask about qualifications, similar jobs done recently, and references.

For bigger jobs, find out who would generally be supervising your project. Unless you have a comfort level with that person, you will not have peace of mind until the job is over.

Consider tossing out bids which are 10 percent or more below the other bids you receive. Low bids are a sign of an inexperienced or desperate contractor.

Step 1. Negotiating the Quality of Work

Avoidable disappointment: It was an exciting project—paneling your den and installing bookcases and cabinets. But now that it's done, all you can say is that the workmanship and materials are not nearly as good as you expected.

Negotiate that the quality of the completed job will be *first-class, professional,* and *workmanlike.*

Job materials (for example, the type, quality, and size of wood moldings, the brand, model, and finish of door hardware) can be described with *objective* specificity.

Workmanship, however, is *subjective* and not easily defined. Finish carpentry considered first-class in a $300,000 house may be considered third-rate in a $1,500,000 house.

Ask to see the contractor's completed jobs that are similar to your own. If you like what you see, negotiate that those jobs will be your reference point—a visible, tangible, preagreed standard of the workmanship you are buying. For example: *Paneling, bookcases, and cabinets will have the same quality, workmanship, materials, and finish as in the Joneses' remodeled family room.*

Step 2. Negotiate the Use of Specific Subcontractors

Avoidable disappointment: You are landscaping. A friend has a stone walkway that looks just like a meandering stream bed. You decide to install a

187

similar walkway. Somehow your friend's walkway seems special and yours looks very ordinary.

Most general contractors employ their own laborers and carpenters. Everything else is subcontracted. To prepare a bid for your job, subcontractors will be called in by the general contractor to estimate their portions of the job.

If you are using a general contractor and know of subcontractors (cabinetmakers, masons, wallpaper installer, and so on) whose work you admire and want incorporated into your job, then *negotiate* and contract that your general contractor will use those specific subcontractors on your project.

Step 3. Insist on a Detailed Contract

Avoidable disappointment: You signed a contract to have your office's interior walls painted. The day before the painter is to start, he asks when the file cabinets will be moved away from the walls and whether you want to pay extra for removal of brackets and filling in the holes.

Imagine being in a legal dispute with your contractor. Now ask yourself: Is the contract sufficiently detailed to support your position?

Painting a room involves a lot more than putting paint on a wall. How will the wall be prepared? What is the type of paint? Is it a quality brand? How many coats will there be? Will the color be custom? Will electrical outlets be painted the same color as the walls? Will hooks and brackets be removed? Who will move heavy furniture pieces?

Request that your contract contain a room-by-room breakdown that specifies exactly *what* will be done and *how* it will be done.

Your contract should contain *specification sheets*: brands, model numbers, quantities, thickness of wood, sheetrock (dry wall), number of coats of paint, size and type of wood used for moldings and other millwork, and similar details.

Step 4. Negotiate Change Costs and Credits

Avoidable disappointment: The contractor's bid for the room addition was reasonable. During framing, you requested a few changes. The charge for adding another exterior door and expanding the size of two windows was unreasonable.

Some contractors will bid low to get your job. They know that most owners will request changes as the job progresses. Once the initial contract is signed, you are truly a captive customer. High-priced "extras" help offset low bid prices.

- Negotiate change order costs. To avoid being a victim, negotiate up front the *cost* of unforeseen charges by using a formulatic approach. For example, any additions or modifications during the course of the job will be charged at the contractor's actual cost of materials and labor plus 15 percent.

- Negotiate change order credits. You are remodeling a bathroom and decide to install one bathroom sink rather than two. How much will you be credited for the second sink?

  The *credit* you will receive if you decide to delete a contracted item can also be formulatic. For example, if you delete an item, you will receive a credit equal to 85 percent of the cost allocated to the materials and labor associated with the deleted item.

Step 5. Negotiate Time Schedule Penalties

Avoidable disappointment: It is now the end of July and your job, which was to be finished in May, has a way to go.

Find a contractor that offers a *specific completion date* and negotiate a per-day monetary penalty for each day the job goes unfinished after that date. For example, except for delays beyond the contractor's control, the job price will be reduced by $100 for each day the job remains incomplete after June 1st.

Step 6. Negotiate a Way Out

Avoidable disappointment: That amiable contractor who won you over before you signed his contract is now just plain impossible. His work is shoddy and he's behind schedule. Some days, you sit around waiting for him and he doesn't show up at all.

Firing a contractor during the course of a job can be a real problem if a way out is not negotiated and documented up front.

Most contracts provide for "progress payments." For example, if you were doing a room addition, the contractor would receive a percentage of the contract price at signing, an additional percentage when the foundation is installed, an additional percentage when the framing is done, and continuing payments as each stage of the work is completed.

What if you terminate the contractor between progress payments?

What if you terminate the contractor just after a progress payment, but the contractor has now received more money than is represented by the amount of work done so far? (This is the way contractors structure progress payments.)

Negotiate and contract that:

- In the event of a breach, you may terminate the contractor upon X days' written notice, during which time the contractor has an opportunity to remedy the breach.

- If the breach isn't cured, you can have the work completed by another contractor of your choosing.

- Upon final completion of all work by the replacement contractor, the original contractor will be paid the difference between the contract price and what it cost you to complete the job.

Step 7. Negotiate a Progress Payment Schedule That Makes Good Business Sense

Avoidable disappointment: Your roof replacement payment schedule provides for a 75 percent payment when roofing materials are delivered to your home. The tar paper and roof were delivered two weeks ago. You made the 75 percent payment. Now you are learning that the job probably won't be started for another week or two.

You do not need to accept the contractor's job progress payment schedule. Negotiate a schedule in which the size of the payments is representative of the *value* of the work completed as of the date of payment. It's OK for the contractor to always be a little bit ahead.

For example, if you gave the contractor a 10 percent down payment for your room addition, you wouldn't pay 30 percent more when the foundation was set, because the job would not be 40 percent underway.

A common "trick" is to condition some progress payments on delivery of materials alone. This encourages delivery of materials long in advance of when they will be used.

Practice alert: Prior to making each progress payment, have the contractor supply you with a copy of a *lien release* form, which releases your property from any lien arising from the contractor's having furnished labor or materials to your job.

In most states, the release should be signed by each of the contractors, subcontractors, laborers, and materialmen who have filed the appropriate preliminary notices. Determine the law in your state.

Step 8. Make Yourself Surprise-Proof

Avoidable disappointment: You thought your $20,000 swimming pool contract was just that, a $20,000 swimming pool contract. But the contractor says, "Excavation problems have been discovered and $5,000 more is needed to pickax through a layer of rock."

Try to avoid leaving any part of the job "open" until the contractor can better determine what needs to be done when the wall is opened, the ground is broken, and so on. Pros will generally know what needs to be done at the time the contract is prepared. Open-ended contracts are an invitation for trouble.

If the job is different than expected and left partially "open," suggest to the contractor that he shouldn't profit from your misfortune. *Negotiate* that "open work" will be at the contractor's actual cost without profit.

Practice tip: If appropriate, have your contractor acknowledge that it has independently (and not through you) ascertained the geographical conditions of the job property and the general and local conditions pertaining to your job.

Step 9. Negotiate a Completion Bond

Avoidable disappointment: Halfway through a room addition job, your contractor announces he is quitting. The job was underbid and every day of work means he is losing more money.

Completion bonds are issued by bonding companies. They will see to it that your job is finished at the original contract price if your contractor hops into his pickup and is never heard from again. Negotiate to have the completion bond premium borne (at least in part) by the contractor.

Negotiating alert: If the contractor refuses to get a completion bond, check out his reputation. The bonding company may not consider him bondable.

Step 10. Negotiate Warranties

Avoidable disappointment. You just spent $15,000 for a new roof. The first heavy rain brought leaks and water damage to your grandmother's piano.

There will be times when you will negotiate for the inclusion of a warranty in your contract.

For example:

- For six months, newly planted trees and bushes will survive, in healthy condition.

- For five years, your roof won't leak (the warranty could be for leak repair as well as reimbursement for interior water damage caused by the leak).

- For six years, pool plaster won't flake or break.

- For seven years, exterior paint won't peel.

Step 11. Negotiate a Fast, Cheap, and Efficient Dispute Resolution Procedure

Avoidable disappointment: On balance, you like your contractor and don't want to terminate the contract. However, you and the contractor often have heated disagreements. The contractor has told you that you are a perfectionist and, with your zero tolerances, you are asking too much in a kitchen remodel.

Quality is in the eyes of the beholder. You and your contractor may not see things the same way.

To resolve differences through litigation, arbitration, or mediation causes mid-job delays and is costly, time-consuming, and emotionally draining.

Now is the time to agree on a *fast*, *cheap*, and *efficient* dispute resolution procedure. For example, if you have an architect, negotiate that both you and the contractor will accept the architect's decision as final and binding. If there is no architect, consider naming a mutually trusted industry professional who could serve as the arbiter of disputes.

Step 12. More Tips to Consider

As applicable, negotiate for your contract to provide that:

- The contractor, at its own cost, will maintain a policy of *liability insurance*, insuring you against loss or injury connected with the performance of the contract. Ask to see evidence that this insurance is in place before work commences.

- The contractor will *indemnify* and hold you and your property harmless from claims and losses arising from death or injury or damage to another's property.

- The contractor will, upon completion, *remove debris* and surplus materials from your property, leaving your property in *broom-clean* condition.

- The contractor may *not assign* your contract or delegate its duties under the contract to a third party without your written consent.

- *The title to all materials* delivered to your job site will be deemed to have passed to you.

Practice alert: Check with your insurance agent to see if you should have "course of construction" vandalism, malicious mischief, and material theft insurance.

A *final note:* That printed contract you are being asked to sign was prepared by an association whose only function is to protect and serve contractors. Read the small print front and back. Make whatever changes are necessary for you to be properly protected.

Contracts

Contract Negotiating

The macro pivotal points of an agreement have been agreed on. A symbolic handshake has indicated that the parties are in sync. But total consensus is a long way off. The micro terms and conditions are now up for negotiation.

Step 1. Repush Motivator Buttons

Reconfirm your understanding of those deal points that *satisfy* the other person's *needs*. It was the desire to satisfy those needs that led to an agreement in principal.

Step 2. Move from Agreement to Agreement

Discuss other major issues on which you *already agree*. Positive feelings are reinforced and rapport is enhanced as you move from *agreement to agreement*. When issues in conflict are tackled too early, there is a greater chance resistance and hostility will result.

Step 3. Reach Agreement in Principle

If you don't totally agree on a major issue, then try to reach a broader, more general understanding as to that issue. This understanding will become the basis for further discussion.

Step 4. Tackle Nonmonetary Issues First

Once a positive feeling is in place and a collaborative spirit is established, turn to major issues in conflict, beginning with *nonmonetary* issues.

Step 5. Divide and Conquer

Break conflict issues into components that can be dealt with individually. Start with those components on which agreement is more likely.

Step 6. Put Preservatives in Your Deal

If is the magical give-and-get concession word. The easiest *if* to ask for and get may turn out to be your most important—a *compliance concession*.

Compliance concessions that make for a sturdier deal can take many forms:

- *Liquidated damage* provisions stating an agreed-on sum certain to be paid to you in the event of breach. The time and expense of proving the extent to which you were damaged by the breach are eliminated.

- A *high interest* rate on a note, which is *retroactively reduced* if all note payments are timely made.

- A *price increase* for each day that a scheduled sale closing does not take place.

- A *price discount* if the ordered goods are not delivered on time.

- A *late payment fee* for payments not made on time.

- A *revocation of rights* if payments are not made on time, for example, nullification of an option to renew if rent payments are not made in a timely fashion.

- *Enforcement cost recoupment* provisions that discourage breach by making it possible for you to recoup your lawyer fees and related costs in a legal action to enforce the contract.

When you are being assured prompt and faithful payment, completion, or delivery, it is hard to be denied your compliance request. If the other person really means to keep the promises being made, he or she has nothing to lose.

Step 7. Favored Nations Negotiating

Favored nations contract provisions are negotiating devices that can:

- Assure the best possible price. *The seller agrees that he will not, during the next year (quarter, month), sell to another buyer an XYZ unit on more favorable terms or for a lesser price than is provided for in this contract.*

- Test your negotiated bottom. *The seller warrants that he has not sold an XYZ unit during the previous 90 days on more favorable terms or at a lesser price than is provided for in this contract.*

Step 8. Negotiate a "Stock Yard" Clause

One client calls it my all-purpose "stock yard being built down the road" clause. Whatever you call it, it has served me well through the years.

The safety net language to negotiate is to the effect that *the seller (e.g., landlord) has no knowledge or information which if made known to the buyer (e.g., tenant) would discourage or dissuade the buyer from entering into this agreement.*

- For a client negotiating to buy an upscale apartment building, the clause flushed out the rumor that a halfway house would be the new neighbor down the block.

- For a client negotiating to buy acreage in Denver next to a Target store, the clause forced the seller's revelation that water wouldn't be allocated to the site for two years.

- For a tenant negotiating a restaurant lease, the clause compelled the landlord to disclose that the neighborhood had become an evening gang hangout.

Step 9. Negotiating Through Documentation

Deals are cut on *macro* deal points. There are *always* lesser *micro* issues that go undiscussed. If your side drafts the agreement, then your side will be able to deal with all those unattended issues in a manner most favorable to you. The other person may request some changes, but your side's language will in large part go untouched.

But then—there was the exotic animal-breeding deal. There was a deal to bankroll a group searching out Noah's ark. And a U.S. astronaut wanted me to negotiate a deal involving a commercial project in outer space.

I confess: sometimes I find myself on unfamiliar turf. In those instances, after the most basic terms have been agreed on, I have found that it makes good sense for the other side—assuming the principals are more knowledgeable—to prepare the contract. Why? First, I don't want to tip them off as to how little I know about the subject matter. Second, their document will raise points and issues that I may not have considered and can now negotiate.

Step 10. Red Line

Contracts will be reviewed and changed. If your side drafts the contract and changes are requested by the other party and are agreed to by you, then send along an additional copy of the revised contract on which you have red lined (underlined) where the changes have been made.

Red lining *channels* and directs the other party's focus to the underscored changes, obviating any need to reread the entire contract. When the entire contract doesn't need to be reviewed, you have lessened the chance that previously accepted terms will be revisited and renegotiated.

Crisis, Public Relations

Finessing a Public Relations Crisis of Confidence

A death resulting from poor food handling procedures at a restaurant; toxic waste dumping; unsafe products; price gouging at a convenience store . . . acts perceived as threatening safety, public health, or the environment, or as being unfair business practices can throw any business into a crisis mode. Here's how to handle such a crisis.

Step 1. Gather Facts Quickly

You must dispel any impression that you are unconcerned or have lost control. Hard facts will help you avoid the temptation of making a blanket denial that later may be proven inaccurate or untrue. Hard facts will enable you to avoid conflicting explanations that would exacerbate the loss of public confidence.

Step 2. Avoid a "No Comment" Response to the Media

It's the easy and natural thing to say. But when you are confronted by the media, a "no comment" response:

- Gives the impression that something is being hidden.

- Implies that the questions being asked are unworthy of an answer.

- Suggests that the public is not entitled to information.

- Forces the media to look to alternative sources of information— sources that may be less accurate or may have interests adverse to your own.

Calmly explain why you aren't making comment: "We are still investigating." "That's a trade secret. We can't reveal it." Then give out any information you are free to divulge.

Step 3. Designate a Spokesperson

Keeping your own personnel informed builds a sense of organizational unity. However, it's important to control alternative sources of information. Give your staff instructions to refer inquiries to a designated

198

spokesperson. Even if a conversation or interview is "off the record," make it clear to your personnel that they are not to divulge or share information.

Step 4. **Containment Versus Control**

Your lawyers' job is *containing* the crisis. By nature, lawyers are reactive. They think about defending against lawsuits. As spokespersons, they tend to be protective, restrictive, and rigid.

Your *public relations pros'* job is *controlling* the crisis. They are proactive. Public relations pros will set a "forgive and forget" agenda.

Should you move toward *containment* or *control?*

Ask yourself: Will governmental investigations or probing media inquiries make it very unlikely that damaging information can be concealed for any significant time? If the answer is *yes,* then opt for control.

Step 5. **If Your Choice Is Control, Acknowledge There Is a Problem**

Denying that the problem exists will erode credibility. For people to "forgive and forget," they must believe they are dealing with essentially honest people who are genuinely trying to remedy the problem.

Step 6. **Demonstrate Concern**

Losing public credibility may have more damaging long-term impact than is presented by the crisis at hand. Show a dedication to the problem's prompt resolution by promising and demonstrating cooperation with investigative authorities.

Make the public aware of the progress of your investigation into the facts.

Step 7. **Set the "Spin"**

Impressions are made in the media. Negative impressions, once formed, are hard to dispel. When you are proactive, you modulate the agenda, tone, and mood of your story.

Set the "spin" by controlling the public's perception of the situation as well as your response and attitude toward it.

Get your information out frequently and quickly.

Tell your side of the story, discussing the problem in the context of your business record. This can be done through ads, letters to editors, press conferences, and press releases.

Most importantly, apologize if appropriate.

Step 8. The Never Evers

- *NEVER EVER* take a reporter's call unless you know the reporter or know what he or she wants, and why.

- *NEVER EVER* be goaded into a fast-response, reactive comment you will later regret. The more inflammatory the question, the more composed and collected you must be when answering.

- *NEVER EVER* be hostile or condescending. Hostility fosters contempt. Being condescending may come across as apologetic.

- *NEVER EVER* speak to the media without being thoroughly prepared (preferably by a public relations or media pro).

- *NEVER EVER* answer complex or hard questions with long answers. Long answers often have unintended response components which in themselves create new issues.

Here's how you can cool down too-hot-to-handle questions.

- Deflect hard questions with a tough or complex question of your own. (For example, *On what specific facts are you basing your question?*)

- Postpone answering. *There are some things I need to confirm before I can give you an accurate answer.*

- Answer briefly. The longer the question, the shorter your response should be.

Cruises

Negotiating a Super Cruise Fare

Rich or just comfortable. Native or foreign-born. It seems that all passengers on board like to talk about the good deal they got on their cruise fare.

On my first cruise, I discovered this phenomenon the hard way. To my horror, apparently only I and an elderly couple from Montana had actually paid full fare.

Since then, as a shipboard lecturer and frequent cruise passenger, I have finally figured out the secrets of "cruise control."

WHAT'S THE MAIN GAME?

You are about to understand why your travel agent is always so nice in arranging for champagne on ice to be delivered to your cruise ship cabin.

The "base" commission paid to travel agents by the cruise lines is 10 percent. If you and three friends book a $5,000-per-person cruise, we are talking about a $2,000 commission to make a phone call. And the phone call is toll-free!

THE PREFERRED ACCOUNT GAME

Some travel agents have a *preferred account* relationship with various cruise lines. These folks are the bigger cruise brokers who advertise and sell a lot of cruises. The more cruises they sell on a particular line, the more "preferred" they are by that line. In addition to the 10 percent base commission, preferred agents are the first to get up to an *additional* 30 percent or more commission on certain cruises.

What do the agents do with these mega commissions? They have three options:

1. They may try to keep the entire commission as profit.

2. They may act as *wholesalers* or *cruise brokers* to smaller travel agencies, making it possible for these agencies to book fares at a higher commission rate than if they had booked their passengers directly with the cruise line.

3. They may try to sell even more cruises by advertising "special cruise fares." If it's a 20 percent special discount, the agent may make 20 percent, and the passenger saves 20 percent. Don't confuse these specials with the specials offered by the lines themselves.

For which cruises do preferred accounts get the largest commissions?

With new ships being launched every year, there is a competitive scramble to sell cabins, and both cruise line and agent specials are becoming more common. The deeper discounts are usually for:

- Spur-of-the-moment specials when it appears several months in advance of sailing that there will be unsold cabins.

- "Repositioning cruises" (i.e., the segue cruises between seasonal European ports and Caribbean ports). Repositioning cruises cross miles of ocean and hit fewer ports. They are a bargain only if days at sea are more important to you than ports of call.

THE CONSOLIDATOR GAME

Consolidators go after the block bookings business of *affinity groups* like the Masons, Rotarians, or alumni associations. Consolidators generally have the highest profit margins to play with.

To avoid alienating the cruise lines and other travel agents, most consolidators won't negotiate an *affinity group* fare for anyone who is not a member of the group. You can't get an Elks Club fare if you aren't an Elk. But consolidators are too smart not to take advantage of their volume buying power, and so they form their own affinity groups and call them *travel clubs.* "Club members" pay nominal annual dues to get a shot at bargain fares that may not otherwise be available.

EIGHT STEPS TO THE DOCK

Step 1. Decide Where and When You Want to Go

Study the brochures of different cruise lines. You will be surprised at their similarity—photos of sunny beaches, shipboard entertainers in sequins, couples standing on a deck awash in moonlight, and buffets to die for. You will also notice a similarity of itineraries and departure dates in various parts of the world.

Decide your destination and a sailing date range. You are now ready to choose a ship and cruise line.

Step 2. Check Out Cruise Line Promotions and Incentives

Which lines are currently advertising a "sale" on their usual fares?

Those two-for-one advertised cruise line specials are usually not two-for-one for the airfare portion of the cruise. You will find this fact buried in the smallest type at the bottom of the ad.

Call 800 information and get the phone number of the lines whose cruises interest you.

Ask each line about special incentives and programs that are not in their brochure. What are they offering for your time frames and destinations?

Ask each line which agents have blocked bookings for the special-incentive cruises. Some lines will tell you, others will not.

Step 3. Ask Preferred Suppliers About Their Own Promotions and Incentives

For years, you have had an agent who books your trips west to see the kids for the holidays. But shop around. Buying a cruise is becoming more like buying a car or refrigerator.

In addition to the cruise line incentives, preferred suppliers will have their own incentives. Give them your dates and destinations and see what they come up with.

Different agents are willing to offer different concessions, depending on the relationship they enjoy with any given cruise line. Try out-of-state cruise brokers that advertise in the Sunday travel section.

Practice alert: If you buy through an agent you don't know, pay with a credit card just in case the agent heads south.

Step 4. Negotiate a Super Fare

The basic question to ask your agent is: Are you competitive? No agency still in business will answer "no" to this question.

Use the power of competition. Let the agent know you *believe* you can get a better fare elsewhere, although you would prefer to deal with this agency if at all possible. Don't accept superlative service as an alternative to a deep discount. You are buying a ticket—this is not a service-intensive activity. Once your ticket is delivered, the travel agent is pretty much out of the picture.

All travel agents, big and small, who want to be a part of the new, savvy, price-conscious, competitive market will negotiate commissions and price breaks.

Step 5. Negotiate a Cabin Upgrade

Study deck plans and decide which cabin location best suits your needs and budget. Forget about the status aspect. It's not a big thing on cruises.

Upper deck vs. lower deck: Here's the paradox—the smoothest sailing is in the lower decks. The more expensive cabins are on the upper decks.

How is the paradox explained?

Status is being close to upper-deck dining areas and bars. With the exception of very expensive cabins (the ones closest to God and the Captain), most outboard cabins (the ones with a window or porthole) are pretty much the same size.

Interior vs. exterior cabin: If you have an interior cabin, negotiate for an outside cabin at an interior cabin price. Sometimes the views are wonderful, sometimes they aren't. But with a porthole at least you know whether to put on a jacket when you meet the tour bus.

Front, back, or in the middle: The best ride on any given deck is amidship (in the middle). If you must deviate substantially from center in either direction, opt for cabins toward the bow (the pointy end). The stern (the blunt end) cabins have more engine vibration and noise.

In addition to a discounted fare, suggest a free cabin upgrade as part of the deal: *The discount you are offering isn't as much as we had expected. We would consider your proposal if you are able to bump us up into the next cabin category.*

Step 6. Negotiate Prepaid Gratuities

Generous end-of-cruise tips to cabin attendants and dining room servers are a must. The amount is so strongly suggested by the cruise lines that, as a practical matter, it's an obligatory hidden-cost extra.

As a negotiating perk, travel agents will often pay these suggested gratuities for you. You in turn receive a shipboard purser's acknowledgment of the payment to hand these hard-working people.

Step 7. Negotiate Shipboard Allowances

Another perk worth negotiating for with the travel agent is prepaid shipboard spending allowances good for bar tabs, shore excursions, and other shipboard extras.

Why would a travel agent sponsor a cabin upgrade, gratuities, and allowances in addition to a fare discount?

The cruise lines *may* make these perks available to your agent by way of pass-on promotional incentives.

Fare discounts have to be big numbers to make an impact on a potential passenger. Less costly incentives in kind—upgrades, tips, allowances—can be more psychologically enticing. You know the syndrome: It's hard to get excited about winning $50 cash, but winning a dinner for two worth $50 has a special impact all its own.

Step 8. Now Is Not the Time to Buy Shore Excursions

Do not book port-of-call shore excursions in advance.

Is the excursion just a bus trip to a site that doesn't need a historian's long-winded narrative? If so, you will generally save money and time by grabbing a few other passengers and hiring a dockside taxi. You can *always* book the excursion on the ship. To find out if the taxi idea makes the most sense, ask the ship's concierge, not the shore excursion salespeople (usually independent concessionaires).

Why am I mentioning this? Because your travel agent receives a 10 percent commission on any day shore excursions booked *before* you sail.

Debt

Negotiating Your Way Out of Debt

Just about every occupation, profession, and industry imaginable has experienced financial distress in recent years.

I have filed more chapter 7 and chapter 11 cases for clients in crises than I can recall. And I have fought to preserve the rights of creditor clients when others have sought the sanctuary of the bankruptcy courts.

The insights that follow are firsthand, direct from the trenches.

Step 1. Delays Are Costly

Negotiate debt problems *before* they are turned over to a collection agency or lawyer. It is harder to negotiate with a creditor when someone else is getting up to 50 percent of what is collected from you.

Step 2. Swimming Through Mud

Your creditors have heard them all:

- *If I get this new job, I should be able to pay you something in 60 days.*

- *We have cut operating costs and will pay our bills soon.*

- *We have increased our advertising and will pay when the new orders start to come in.*

- *I am trying to find a financial partner.*

Reality check: Most people in financial crisis are not able to turn things around without having their *debt reduced.* Debtor tactics to delay creditors are just that—a delay of the inevitable.

Want to make your pennies-on-the-dollar debt reduction offer attractive? Let your creditors know in an *unthreatening* way that *unless something can be worked out you have no apparent alternative to bankruptcy.* That reality and that alone is the greatest single source of your negotiating leverage.

It works.

206

Every day, banks take major hits in loan settlements. American Express, Visa, and Master Card debts can be settled for a fraction of what is owed if you are *credible, are prepared to prove* you are *tapped out,* and have *no clear prospective* ability to pay.

- *The "credibility" factor:* Made-up excuses for nonpayment ("defective goods" or "late delivery") sound just that way—made up. They bring emotions into play and make principled creditors less inclined to settle. Cry poverty later on and your veracity will be suspect.

- *The "prepared to prove" factor:* Your offer to supply financial information without being asked will shore up credibility lost through unkept promises of payment.

- *The "tapped out" factor:* "Tapped out" doesn't mean living-in-the-park destitute. It suggests that if you were forced to file bankruptcy, that creditor who is hounding you would receive little if anything.

- *The "no clear prospective" factor:* It is not enough to be tapped out if you are starting a big bucks job next month. Your settlement leverage is highest when your future prospects are lowest.

Step 3. It Ain't Fudging

You may call it "fudging." The courts call it fraud.

Desperate people do stupid things. Loans induced through false financial documents may not be excused in bankruptcy. Super negotiating power flows from the *possibility* of bankruptcy and the discharge of your indebtedness. This possibility is lost when false financial documents are part of the scenario.

So what's left if you need money?

Step 4. Don't Be Quick to Borrow from Friends and Relatives

You can unemotionally negotiate a debt reduction settlement with a stranger. You will feel emotionally obligated to repay friends and relatives in full, no matter what.

People in crisis borrow to keep a dying business alive a little longer. Throwing good money after bad is the alternative to admitting failure to themselves and to others.

If you do borrow from family and friends, collateralize those loans by giving them security: a lien on a house, car, or other lienable property in which you have equity (a residual value after deducting other liens against that same property).

Liens will enhance a favored lender's chances of repayment.

Practice alert: Liens that are not filed or recorded at the time the loan is funded are in jeopardy of being stripped away in a bankruptcy proceeding.

Step 5. Spend Wisely

Use available funds to pay obligations that can't be legally excused in a bankruptcy or readily discounted through negotiation. These include retail sales taxes, employee withholding taxes, and income taxes due on returns filed less than three years before the bankruptcy.

Step 6. Bad Idea

Giving your creditor a postdated check is generally a bad idea. It's a no-win situation.

- If there are insufficient funds to cover the check on the day it is dated, you will be facing criminal prosecution. Your negotiating leverage will never be lower.

- If you stop payment on the check to prevent it from being "NSF," you will have angered the creditor, making it harder to negotiate.

Step 7. Guarantied Trouble

Is there insistence that a family member or friend guaranty your obligation? You may not want to agree to this suggestion. Guaranties are designed to strip away negotiating power. Any settlement leverage created by your personal inability to pay and possible bankruptcy will be lost because of the guarantor's commitment and ability to pay your debt.

Step 8. A Note of Caution

Creditors to whom you owe money on open account may ask that you sign a promissory note. It will be harder for you to negotiate a settlement once your debt has been memorialized in a note because:

- A note will preclude you from future nonpayment defenses based on defective goods, late delivery, or misrepresentation.

- A note, unlike open account debt, will provide for the reimbursement of creditors' legal fees if suit is brought and they win.

- A note enables a creditor to receive interest—or more interest than would otherwise accrue on an open account.

Step 9. Untapped Negotiating Power

An unsecured lender or trade creditor who is paid on a previously existing debt must disgorge the funds received within 90 days of a bankruptcy filing. In some cases, that 90 days is extended to a year if the creditor is a close friend, relative, or "insider."

If you have made partial payments to a creditor within the past 90 days, you have the negotiating power to settle the balance of your debt.

Why? Because if you were to file bankruptcy, that creditor could be forced to disgorge the money previously paid. Call it *settle-now-on-the-balance-or-be-forced-to-give-back-what-you-have-already-gotten* power.

Step 10. The Preference Trap

There will be a temptation to pay some creditors but not others. Every industry is a small industry, and the word will get out. When others find that squeaky wheels are being paid, they too will squeak.

Creditors who feel they are being given short shrift while other creditors are being paid may be motivated to drag you by the ankles into an involuntary bankruptcy. Why? Because *only* in a bankruptcy context can a preferentially paid creditor be ordered to turn over what has been already paid.

Step 11. Preserve Your Future Credit

If a debt is settled, negotiate with the creditor as to how the creditor will report the debt to credit reporting services such as TRW and Dun & Bradstreet. If the debt was paid for pennies on the dollar, request that it be reported only as "paid," with no additional detail.

Step 12. How to Get Faster Delivery Than the Customers with Good Credit

If you are forced to pay COD for goods to stay in business, it is best to buy from suppliers to whom you already owe money.

Few things irritate a supplier more than watching someone who owes them a bundle giving cash business to a competitor.

Consider this: Offer that creditor 105 percent of the COD purchase price for new goods, with the extra 5 percent being applied to the old debt. Your supplier will be encouraged to keep you in business, and, if it comes down to a choice, who do you think will get merchandise first: the customer paying 105 percent cash or the customer paying 100 percent on terms? Case closed.

Divorce

Negotiating a Divorce

The trend of divorce courts is to encourage or *require* that battling spouses try to resolve issues through mediated negotiation before going to the economic and psychological expense of a protracted trial. Most states have now mandated that the parties try to reach a mediated outcome in child custody disputes.

This trend toward mediated negotiation presents a unique opportunity. Through negotiation, you can shape the outcome you want rather than having that outcome determined unilaterally by a judge.

Step 1. Consider the Tactical Advantages of Mediated Negotiation

Mediators are not decision-makers.

They are nonadjudicative problem solvers. Unlike judges, they are presenters and testers of alternative creative solutions. They are facilitators who help the parties *negotiate* their own joint face-saving decisions.

Controlling the divorce process is different from trying to control your spouse and kids.

If mediated negotiation will best advance your goal, encourage its use. Here's the pitch that will make it enticing:

- In a trial, one of the spouses is bound to be disappointed. An outsider, rather than the negotiating parties, decides the outcome of a disagreement.

- Trauma, anxiety, and uncertainty are associated with a trial. They can be avoided in mediated negotiations.

- A joint decision of the spouses can, with the consent of the parties, become as binding as a court determination.

- Decisions made by the parties themselves, in mediated negotiations, are emotionally easier to live with. These decisions are less likely to evoke retaliation or avoidance maneuvering than are decisions forced on them by an outsider.

- Mediation prevents intimate marital details from being discussed in a public courtroom.

Assume that your spouse agrees that mediated negotiations make sense.

211

Step 2. What Type of Mediator Will Best Serve Your Needs?

Determine the major areas of contention.

Mediators can be independent lawyers, therapists, family counselors, or businesspeople. Decide the principal issues to be dealt with, and then encourage using a trained mediator who can best understand and serve *your* needs.

If the issue is child custody, then a therapist or psychologist makes more sense than a businessperson. If the issues involve determining the value and goodwill of family businesses, then an accountant, banker, or businessperson may be most effective.

Step 3. What Mediation Personality Will Best Serve Your Needs?

Mediators are people. How you influence them will in turn influence the result they are trying to "objectively" achieve.

- *Is your spouse easily intimidated or influenced by signs of authority?* Consider a mediator with an aggressive personality who will ramrod home the negotiating result you want.

- *Is your spouse more likely to be influenced by reason?* Consider a mediator with a more low-key personality who will be better able to guide and direct negotiations toward your settlement goal.

- *Is your spouse more likely to capitulate if the mediator is empathetic?* A mediator, unlike a judge, can be sympathetic and allow a free expression of feelings. Often, this pressure release can lessen festering animosity and enhance the possibility of your negotiating an accord.

Negotiating alert: Mediators, though neutral and unbiased, are businesspeople who may subconsciously favor the side that suggested hiring them.

Step 4. Do You Want Lawyers Present at the Mediated Negotiations?

The answer is *yes* if:

- Your spouse's lawyer is more objective and reasonable than your spouse.

- Your spouse's lawyer is able to control your spouse's exhibitions of aggression, hostility, or anger.

- The issues are so complex that a lawyer will be necessary.

- Your spouse's lawyer has a reputation for cooperation.

The answer is *no* if:

- Your spouse's lawyer has a reputation for aggressiveness and belligerence, or has a win–lose persona.

Step 5. Do Not Appear Too Accommodating, in an Effort to Placate the Mediator

Mediators are more likely to seek negotiating concessions from the more malleable party.

Step 6. Preserve an Aura of Mutuality

Try to match your spouse's significant concessions by what appear to be your *seemingly reciprocal* concessions.

Step 7. Justify Your Proposals

Whenever possible, supply the mediator with a rationale that can be used to convince your spouse of the reasonableness of your proposal.

Step 8. Consider the Benefit of Procrastination

Lengthy mediation sessions may break down a recalcitrant spouse. The fatigue factor frequently causes people to become more yielding.

■ ■ ■

Negotiating tips:

- Support and alimony are generally based on present income. If you are going to file for a divorce, do it when things are about as bad as they will get.

- Want a bitter spouse intent on revenge? Then clean out checking and savings accounts and cancel all credit cards.

    Consider leaving your spouse with half the cards but removing your name as a responsible party. As for that bank account, leaving a reasonable amount of money in the account for your spouse will pay off in later negotiations.

- *Tax, legal,* and *bankruptcy* considerations are associated with the characterization (spousal support/alimony, child support, property settlement) of payments made by one spouse to another. Seek professional advice in negotiating the characterization of monetary obligations.

Employees, Negotiating with

Negotiating Tips for Employers

I like hard work. Especially when I'm paying for it.

■ ■ ■

Here's a lab experiment every employer should try.

Required: Two young children and a handful of nickels.

Part One: Offer one of the children the choice between taking a stack of three nickels or a stack of five nickels. Any child, in a heartbeat, will surely choose the stack of five.

Part Two: Offer a stack of three nickels or a stack of five nickels to the same child. Tell the child that if he chooses the stack of three, the second child in the experiment will also get three nickels, but if he chooses the stack of five, the second child will receive ten nickels.

Analysis: What would the result be at your house? Would your child define winning as absolute or relative gain?

One of our law firm's senior staffers was thrilled about her annual raise all morning and depressed about it all afternoon. During lunch, she discovered that another very valuable but newer employee had also been rewarded with a sizable, although smaller, salary increase. The fact that there was still a big salary gap between the two wasn't as important as the closeness in the raise differential.

Most of us are secretly envious—or perhaps resentful—of a coworker who experiences unusual financial good fortune. And why not? *People gauge their own success by comparisons. How we are doing is not always an absolute but is often relative to the success of our peers and fellow employees.*

Consider this: Mega-raises for your company's superstars become ascertainable goals for your other employees to shoot for.

Step 1. Negotiate Terms of Separation

When Ed resigned from his position, he gave himself one heck of a good-bye gift: the company's plans and processes; supplier and pricing information; present and prospective customer lists—a goodly part of the company's ongoing value and the result of his employer's 20-odd years of sweat, sacrifice, and risk taking.

People are funny. Employees who wouldn't be trusted to repay a $5,000 loan are handed the keys to "the vault." They are given ready

215

access to the proprietary and confidential information that sets a company apart from the rest.

Employers often focus their negotiations on what the employee will get: vacations, perks, insurance, or whatever. They should be negotiating what they will get from the employee. This is especially true when trade secrets are at risk.

It is NEVER TOO LATE to negotiate—as part of, or independently of, an employment agreement—what a "trusted employee" can no longer do when that employee is fired or walks.

- *Negotiate* that company trade secrets cannot be given to others or used by the employee during or after job termination.

- *Negotiate* that the company's customers' names, processes, plans, prices, lists, formulas, methods, suppliers, and information about other employees are all trade secrets. Unless trade secrets are defined between the parties, there is a possibility that a court will not construe them as such after termination.

- *Negotiate* how and in what ways a former employee can compete. Define "competition" and negotiate what would not be permissible in terms of *conduct* (can't sell wholesale medical equipment), *specific geographic area* (in the state of Nevada), and *time frame* (for two years from the date of termination).

Practice tips:

- *"Anywhere, anytime, anyway"* restrictions are so broad that they may be deemed by a court as unconscionable or overreaching and therefore not enforceable. Tell a software engineer that, for two years following her termination, she can't get near a computer, and you are prohibiting her from making a living in the only profession she knows.

  The broader the exclusions, the more likely the employee will not abide by them and the more likely a court will not enforce them.

- *Check the baggage:* Find out what restrictions from a former job the employee-applicant with whom you are negotiating is bringing to your company. That knowledgeable, well-connected salesperson may be useless to you unless you are planning on opening Iceland as a new market.

Step 2. Consider Whether to Negotiate an Employment Contract

Are your company's best interests served by not having an employment contract?

Here are some thoughts pro and con:

Pro: Employees who are secure in their jobs perform best and have a greater sense of commitment to their employer.

Con: The company is obligated to a salary commitment even though the employee is no longer needed OR is not performing as well as expected OR the company can no longer afford the employee.

The employee can walk at any time. A contract can physically tether the employee to the job, but an employee who doesn't want to be there will always be a liability.

Step 3. Beware of the Sayonara Syndrome

It has happened to every employer: a valued employee announces a departure for another job and a lot more money.

Here is what not to do: Match the other company's offer. In so doing, you create a pseudo-auction negotiating environment. Other employees will bring in offers, hoping those too will be matched or bettered.

Here is what to do: Ask about the departing employee's long-term career plans. Although he or she may get more money elsewhere next year, or maybe the year after, explain the long-run advantages of the career-building opportunities you have to offer.

Point out that "hire-away" big bucks salaries don't always increase as hoped. Ask:

- *Have you considered the chances that the new employer may not be around in a few years?*

- *Is the "hire-away" salary the price being paid for competitive information which, once divulged, will lessen your value?*

Family and Friends, Negotiating with

Tips for Negotiating with Family, Friends, and Partners

Preserving special relationships can be more important than driving home a hard bargain. The key is in being an "I win–you win" negotiator without being a wimp.

■ ■ ■

Betty wants to spend her vacation in Hawaii.

She has been looking forward to spending endless hours on a beach. She can't wait to indulge herself with good food, a high-rise luxury hotel, entertainment, and dancing. Betty has no intention of packing and unpacking every day of her vacation. When she isn't shopping or carpooling, Betty's job keeps her on the road. Staying put for a while sounds wonderful.

Her husband, Bill, has had too many business lunches and dinners, and gourmet dining isn't that important to him. Sunshine is great, but Bill's dermatologist has told him to limit his hours under the rays. Big luxury hotels are too reminiscent of the building housing his offices. He already spends too much time waiting for elevators. Hula dancers and swaying palms have their place, but he would like his vacation to be an educational and cultural experience. Besides, Bill has been tethered to his desk. Stretching out sounds pretty good. Driving through Italy would be Bill's ideal vacation.

The arguments between Bill and Betty have become more heated as summer approaches.

Betty says that she would consider Italy if Bill's mother does not move in with them for three weeks in December.

Bill would consider Hawaii if the sewing room was converted to an office when they redecorate the house.

Betty and Bill have become literalists.

Each is taking the other's requirements at face value, making demands, counterdemands, and conditional concessions. Literal demands, not true interests or needs, have become the focal point of their attention and energies. Betty and Bill are engaged in a one-dimensional tug-of-war. The winner of their contest of wills will be the spouse who pulls the hardest.

218

It is a behavioral truth that people become committed to their stated positions, their announced points of honor. Egos and personalities are wrongfully summoned into play when defending those positions becomes a matter of personal pride and self-esteem.

Could either Betty or Bill be a winner by forcing one position down the other person's throat?

If Betty were miserable in Italy, would Bill really enjoy his well-earned vacation?

Betty and Bill fought over their stated positions. Tunnel vision prevented them from identifying or reconciling their compatible needs or interests.

Instead, Betty and Bill can use their energy to create ways to collectively gain rather than to defend and assert a demand or a position. This is the *art of optimization*.

Step 1. Ascertain the Other Person's Interests and Needs

The other person has underlying needs, desires, and concerns of varying degrees. Some of these needs will be apparent and some will be hidden.

Your continuing inquiry will be welcome. How can there be antagonism toward you when you are trying to understand the other person's needs?

Step 2. Communicate Your Concerns, Fears, Needs, and Wants

Letting the other person know where you are coming from lessens the chance that you will be misread. This doesn't mean telling all. It means giving the other person important information if an *optimizing solution* is to be reached.

Step 3. Focus on Interests That Are Compatible

Betty and Bill are confronted with a very basic choice: to emphasize their areas of conflict or to emphasize their compatible interests.

Betty and Bill's stated positions are geographically a world apart—Hawaii versus Italy. They have individual interests to support their respective vacation positions. But just because Betty and Bill's positions are dramatically opposed does not mean that all their needs and interests are opposed.

Betty and Bill's compatible interests are:

- Going on vacation and getting away.

- Sharing a vacation they can enjoy together.

- Going a long way geographically from home.

- Being gone about two weeks.

- Having a vacation that would be relaxing and would revitalize their spirits.

- Not doing anything that would harm their relationship.

Step 4. Turn to Interests and Needs That Are in Conflict

Deal with conflicting interests in piecemeal form, a bit at a time.

Break big problems into component problems that can be reckoned with individually.

Separate monetary and nonmonetary segments and discuss nonmonetary issues first.

Betty and Bill's conflicting interests are:

- Endless hours on the beach versus sightseeing.

- A big luxury hotel versus no high-rise building.

- Entertainment, dancing, and fine food versus a cultural experience.

- Staying in one place versus being on the go.

Step 5. Balance Conflicting Interests and Needs

Separate vacations together?

Betty and Bill's conflicting interests could be balanced with a Mediterranean cruise. Betty would have the luxury and amenities offered by a hotel; Bill would not be reminded of the twenty-six-story building housing his office. Fine food and dancing are available on the ship. Betty could sun while Bill toured classical ruins on the Greek Isles. Betty would not be put to the task of frequent packing and unpacking.

Perhaps the Mediterranean cruise would have been neither Bill's nor Betty's first choice. Other balanced alternatives could be explored, such as staying at a small hotel on Italy's cost, where they could spend part of the time on the beach and part of the time touring.

■ ■ ■

When my seminar students are first presented with Betty and Bill's dilemma, over 90 percent of the proposed solutions suggest separate vacations, a week in Italy and a week in Hawaii, or a biennial choice by each spouse.

Long term or short . . . business or family . . . whenever any relationship is at risk, consider optimizing possibilities. That consideration, that thought, that flexibility of determination is the essence of the art of optimization.

Franchisors, Negotiating with

Tips on Negotiating with Franchisors

One out of every twelve business establishments is a franchise. A new franchise opens every eight minutes of each business day.

Here is what you need to know and what you need to do, if you are considering joining this trend.

Step 1. Evaluate the Three C's

Ever hear of Victoria's Bakery . . . Sun Studio . . . Your Attic . . . Playful Parenting . . . or Send a Cookie International? They are a few of the franchises that didn't make it.

In 1983, there were 138 companies that began selling franchises. In 1993, all but 34 of those companies were defunct. Today, the market is more saturated, making the risk of failure even greater.

Where do you begin when there are thousands of franchised businesses spanning 65 different industries? Begin with the three C's: the Company, the Customer, and the Competition.

The Company

- What are the company's objectives, vision, and values?

- Does the company have the talent, capital, and facilities to develop?

- What are the company's strengths and shortcomings?

- Is growth needed for the company to fund national advertising, develop new products, or retain key executives?

- Does the company have growth strategies other than franchising, such as sales in supermarkets, company-owned stores, mail order?

The Customer

- What is the market for the company's products and services now and tomorrow?

- Is the customer base definable by gender? Ethnicity? Age? Geography? Education?

222

- How will you approach the market? If it is a service business, can you "sell" both yourself and your service to others?

The Competition

- Is the company's major competitor gaining or losing market share?

- What are the competition's strengths and shortcomings?

- In what ways do competitors' products and services differ?

- How will the company be able to maintain or increase its market share?

Step 2. Disclosure Document Alert

Federal law mandates that, as a potential franchise purchaser, you must be provided with a *disclosure document* presented in a Uniform Franchise Offering Circular (UFOC) or Federal Trade Commission (FTC) format.

A disclosure document describes the company, its franchisees, working capital requirements, pending litigation, and franchise obligations such as equipment, signage, leases, insurance, preopening purchases, site selection, and advertising.

The disclosure document is only a place to start. A company's use of an approved disclosure document does not signify that any state or federal authority *approves* or *recommends* the franchise investment.

The franchise business could be selling sand in the desert, but if the required information is in the disclosure document, the franchise offering would be in compliance with federal law. The information presented in the disclosure document is *not* verified by any governmental authority. Franchisee suits alleging that disclosure documents presented false or misleading information are not uncommon.

Most state laws and the FTC rules are *disclosure*-oriented. As such, they are solely designed to ensure that prospective franchisees have the data needed to make informed decisions about franchise opportunities. Often, there is little, if any, *regulation* of the ongoing franchisor–franchisee relationship.

A successful prototype doesn't guarantee a successful franchising system. The skills needed to operate a franchising system are very different from the skills needed to operate a single store or restaurant.

If you are looking at the earnings claims of prototypes (one or two company-owned stores), then consider:

- How do the locations of those stores differ from your prospective unit in geography, climate, and demographics?

- Did it take years to build the company store's customer base to its present size?

- Is much of the company store's success attributable to the personality or special ability of its operators?

Step 3. Talk to Former Franchisees

Disclosure documents will list people in your state who have voluntarily or involuntarily terminated their franchise. Don't accept the franchisor's explanation, "They could have succeeded if they had tried harder."

Locate these former franchisees. Listen to what they have to say about their negotiating experiences and negotiating successes with the franchisor.

- Did the franchisor modify the standard agreement?

- Did they lose money when they sold their business?

- How were they dealt with, both before and after entering into the franchise agreement?

- What did they like and dislike about the operation?

Step 4. Talk to Present Franchisees

Ask about their negotiations with the franchisors, their frustrations, their concern for the future. Would they still have invested in the franchise if they knew then what they know now?

Work at a franchise store for a few weeks, even if it means being an unpaid volunteer.

Step 5. Negotiate the Franchise Agreement

Franchisors don't *sell* franchises. Franchisors *grant licenses* allowing others to use their well-known name, operating system, and support system for a *defined period* of time. The controlling and operative document is the *franchise agreement.*

Franchisors will tell you that, to preserve continuity, franchise agreements will usually be identical for *identical groups* of franchise during any given time frame. Most franchisors will, however, deviate to some degree from their standard agreement despite the fact that their disclosure statements project an image of strict uniformity.

Negotiating tips:

- Franchisors in a start-up time frame will almost always be more flexible in negotiations than a well-established operation.

- Explore with the franchisor the ways in which your franchise would not be *identical* to its other franchise units. For example:

  a. Will your unit be located in a ski area, where you can conduct business profitably only during the snow season?

  b. Will your unit be in a complex that is open only on certain days or has restricted hours of operation?

  c. Will your unit be smaller than that of the company's other franchisees?

- Show that changes to the standard agreement were made for present or former franchisees.

To preserve the quality and consistency of its products and services, a franchisor tilts franchise agreements in favor of itself. Be alert to agreements that are so slanted that you can later be unfairly treated.

Following are some of the issues you must consider—and, if possible, negotiate.

Territory

- Are the territorial boundary lines clear? Can the franchisor open a company-owned store in "your" territory? Or place another franchise unit so close to you that it will impact profits?

- Can the franchisor sell its products in "your" territory through nonfranchise outlets? (For example, is the company's ice cream being sold in supermarkets?)

- "Exclusive" territories are not truly exclusive. Antitrust laws permit franchisees outside your boundaries to sell to customers within your boundaries.

- If the exclusivity of the franchise territory is expressed in miles (for example: *No other competing unit will be installed within three miles*), does that mean as the crow flies (preferable) or road-distance miles?

Financing Assistance

- Who is providing financing? A franchisor's promise to "assist" in obtaining financing may mean nothing more than help in completing loan applications.

- If the franchisor is providing the financing, what will be the terms? What collateral and/or guaranties will be required?

Site Selection

- Can you turn down a prospective site selected by the franchisor? Will the franchisor assist in site selection? Or will the franchisor just approve or disapprove your selections?

- Does the franchisor have its own site selection staff or does it employ local brokers? Local brokers may be familiar with the real estate market, but may not have the "feel" needed to select a site that will make your unit a success.

- Will the franchisor guaranty your lease in order to assist you in negotiating the best possible lease terms?

Site Development

- Who will build out your location?

- Will the franchisor's plans be generally accepted by your local building department?

- Are there local building ordinances or other prohibitions that impact architectural style? Signage? Build-out elements essential to the franchise's image and ready customer identification?

Royalty Fees

- Can royalty payments be raised later? If so, how and when?

Training

- Visit the franchisor's training facilities. Are they what you expected? How comprehensive is the training program? What are the qualifications of the people conducting the program?

- Who bears the expense of travel and lodging during training? Can additional people from your franchise unit attend training? At what cost?

- Is there a requirement for periodic retraining? If so, at whose expense?

Standards of Conduct

Operating standards are often expressed in vague terms: "Courtesy," "Cleanliness," "Adequately Staffed." Be aware that a requirement for "refurbishing" (at your expense) can mean changing roof colors or picking up the tab for installing a new look mandated by the franchisor.

Operating manuals are often no more specific. The results can be a difference in expectations and franchisor complaints that you, the franchisee, are not in compliance.

Advertising

Advertising is an area where franchisees are often unfairly treated. Each of the following questions should be considered critical:

- Can advertising obligations be changed by the franchisor from time to time?

- How much must you spend on local advertising? What type of advertising? How frequently?

- How much must you contribute to the national advertising campaign?

- Will the franchisor spend all of the money that franchisees contribute within the year it is collected? Will excess funds be refunded or spent the following year?

- Is there a franchisor advertising fund administration charge? Will the franchisor supply an advertising fund accounting to the franchisees?

- Will the company-owned stores contribute on the same basis as franchisee-owned stores?

Purchase of Products

Franchisors provide product specifications and the names of vendors whose products meet those specifications. Be aware that the franchisor's specifications may be so restrictive that no products other than the franchisor's own or those of a favored vendor will be acceptable. In that situation, franchisees can be charged unfairly.

Audits

Find out how often franchisees are audited by the franchisor and who pays the auditors.

Managerial Assistance

- If you need help, will the franchisor provide assistance? At what charge?

- Who will bear the expense of travel or lodging for out-of-town help?

Assignments and Right of First Refusal

If you sell your franchise, your successor will in all likelihood have to be approved by the franchisor. Ask about clear criteria for the approval of your successor or whether rejection can be arbitrary.

Renewal

Franchise agreements typically have terms of ten to twenty years. They are often nonrenewable or are renewable at much higher royalty rates.

- Do you have the absolute right to renew? On the same terms and conditions as before?

- If renewal is not allowed, what will you be paid when the franchisor takes over your business?

If the price to be paid is the *book value* of your business, there is a good chance you will be shortchanged. Most successful businesses are worth much more than their book value.

Right of Relocation

- If your site or territory isn't as successful as you expected, can you "move" your franchise to another site within the territory or to another territory?

- Will there be a relocation fee?

Death or Disability

- Does the franchisor have the ability to acquire your business in the event you die or become disabled? If so, at what price? (Remember, book value is seldom reflective of true worth.)

- If the franchise can be passed on to a family member upon the death of the franchisee, is that family member obligated to sell within a specified time period?

Termination

- Under what circumstances can the franchise be terminated?

- Are elected franchisees part of a panel that will determine whether termination is justified, or will the decision be left to the franchisor alone?

- What rights do you have to appeal or contest termination? To whom is that appeal made?

Covenant Not to Compete

- What restrictions are applicable to your future once you are no longer a franchisee?
  Will you be prohibited from operating another restaurant some day, even though your whole life may have been spent in the restaurant business?

Dispute Resolution

- How are disputes to be resolved? Will other franchisees be sitting as part of a grievance panel? Is the dispute resolution mechanism costly or complex?

- Will you be forced to travel out-of-state to the franchisor's home base to arbitrate, litigate, or mediate?

House—Purchase

Negotiating the Purchase of a House or Condo

It's a perfect little three-bedroom overlooking mammoth payments.

Step 1. Prequalify for a Loan

Even though you haven't found the house of your dreams, now is the time to talk to your bankers. Tell them the price range of houses you will be considering and ask how much you can expect to borrow.

Why jump the gun? Because more deals are aborted over the buyer's inability to get financing than any other factor.

With the financing hurdle and uncertainty largely out of the way, a seller will be more apt to grant concessions to a "prequalified buyer."

Step 2. Decide Whether You Want a Broker to Call Your Own

There are two situations when you may encounter the seller's broker without having a broker of your own: at a seller's open house and at a visit to a new home model.

Those friendly, informative brokers are *not* your brokers. They are *not* your friends. They are *not* your advisers. They have *no* duty or allegiance to you.

They represent only the seller, and it is their job to extract as much money from you as is humanly possible. There are no confidences: whatever you tell the seller's broker about your income, budget, contemplated opening offer, or contemplated ceiling must be dutifully reported to the seller.

At this juncture you have two choices:

a. You can hire a broker to negotiate for you—free. How's that? Sellers pay all brokerage commissions. If there is only a selling broker, the commission all goes to that one broker. If you also have a broker, the commission is split between the two.

b. You can tell the seller's broker that you plan to get your own broker *but* if the purchase price is reduced by the amount your broker would earn, you will go it alone.

230

Why would the selling broker do this? The additional discount enhances the chances of a deal being made.

But what if you need help? You can hire a broker, or retain a lawyer out of your own pocket on an hourly basis, and probably get a more effective result in the bargain.

Step 3. Don't Tip Your Hand

On their second visit to the Michaels' home, Mrs. Black, a lovely lady, in kindness and sincerity said, "Mrs. Michaels, you have such a beautiful home. We have looked at houses all week and haven't seen one we liked nearly as much."

Guess who had the upper hand in the ensuing negotiations between the Michaels and Blacks?

Step 4. Ascertain Why the Seller Is Selling

- Has a job been lost? Is a company transfer imminent?

- Has another home been purchased? Is the seller anxious to move before the start of another school year?

- Is the seller racing to beat a foreclosure auction?

The deal you negotiate will be a function of the seller's *needs* and the situation's *immediacy*.

Power negotiating information is readily available from your broker, from credit reporting agencies, and from public records. (Unpaid property taxes, lender default notices, lawsuits, or court divorce files may have orders regarding the disposition of the house you want to buy.)

Step 5. Ascertain the Seller's Needs

A meeting with the seller may give you a better opportunity to read the seller's needs and assess their immediacy. When you know what they are, look for creative ways to satisfy them. Here are some examples.

- *Psychological Need*

  We put so much work into the house, I still feel I'm underselling it. Offer a higher selling price but a lower interest rate on the note you are giving to the seller.

- *Emotional Need*

  Whenever I think about this house, I'm going to remember that chandelier (or favorite item). Offer the seller the right to remove and take a special chandelier or artistic leaded-glass window.

- *Convenience-Oriented Need*

  Even though the house is on the market we would prefer to sell after the school year ends. Offer a closing date that coincides with the seller's finding and buying another house, finishing a semester, selling a business, and so on.

Step 6. Determine Your Primary Objective

Step back. Take a deep breath.

Before making an offer, ask yourself a critical question: *Is my primary objective to get the best possible* **price?** *Or the best possible* **commitment?**

It was my very first home purchase. Even though the asking price was about the same as the asking price of today's luxury cars, it was a lot of money for a house at the time.

My offer was a low 65 percent of the asking price. For fear of being "embarrassed," the broker holding the open house refused to submit my offer to the seller. After I threatened to deliver the offer myself, he reluctantly agreed to submit it. Much to everyone's disbelief, including mine, the offer was accepted.

Yes, I made an extreme offer. Yes, I got an incredible deal. And yes, I took the chance of losing the house to someone who may have offered even a hundred dollars more. But there was no scarcity of houses on the market, and my sole objective was getting the best possible *price.*

Had the house been one of a kind or had houses been hard to come by, I may have offered more. To do so would have meant that my objective was not nailing down the best possible price but hammering a *commitment* from the seller. The extra money paid would have been my "insurance" premium for lessening the chance of losing out.

Step 7. Ask the Broker for "Comps"

A seller's initial asking price is the seller's dream price. An asking price may be so far over market that, even when discounted, you would be overpaying.

So what if the guest bathroom has great wallpaper or the kitchen has a built-in microwave? You can't effectively negotiate without knowing the true market value of the house you are considering.

Ask the seller's broker (or your own broker) for "comps"—an analysis showing the recent sale prices of comparable houses nearby, as well as the asking prices of comparable houses presently listed for sale. By adding or subtracting the dollar value of the positive and negative features of the house you are considering, you will get a good idea of its true market value.

Step 8. Go Ahead, Change the Printed Form

Brokers have a disincentive to:

- Get you the best possible price: the more you pay, the more they are paid by the seller.

- Make waves that may kill the deal: they get paid only if the deal closes.

- Have you pick the escrow, title company, inspection service, or mortgage broker: these indispensable folks frequently give kickbacks and gifts to referring brokers. Who pays for these kickbacks and gifts? You do, through higher prices and rates.

  That printed form your broker is using, the Purchase and Sale Agreement, is a "one size fits all" document for use by both buyers and sellers. A universal agreement, by definition, can't fully serve the best needs of everyone or anyone. Negotiate changes to the printed form so it protects and serves you.

Step 9. Determine Your "Would Likes"

Light fixtures, antenna, draperies, and other items *attached* to walls, floor, or ceiling may or may not be considered a part of the physical house.

What you see is not always what you get. An unattached, free-standing room divider or free-standing book shelf, a large hanging hall mirror, a potted tree in the patio, or a custom-made furniture unit built to fit in a room wall-to-wall, floor-to-ceiling—all may be whisked away by the Bekins folks.

Determine which unattached items—those that aren't physically a part of the house—you would like to own.

Negotiating alert: Do *not* include *would like* items in your initial offer. Sellers *always* counter. When you counter to the counter, increase your offer *if* those *would like* items are part of the deal.

Step 10. Think of a House as a Machine You Live In

What you don't see is sometimes what you do get—problems. House systems (mechanical, electrical, plumbing, heating/ventilation/air conditioning) and the structural elements of the house, including walls and foundation, should be delivered in good condition and repair when the title passes.

Cars come with a warranty. Refrigerators, stereos, and computers do, too. So, why not a house? There is no reason to buy a house "as is" without warranties unless it is a tear-down or a true fixer-upper and your expectation is that nothing will work and the place could momentarily fall in a heap around your ankles.

Negotiate a *seller's warranty* that each system and all structural elements of the house are in good condition and repair and that they comply to all applicable building codes and safety ordinances.

Practice alert: Review the contract to be sure that the *warranty survives* and *continues* beyond the transfer of title to you.

Negotiating tip: Negotiate for the seller's warranty to be *absolute* (i.e., "The roof is in good repair and leak-free.") Most seller's warranties are not absolute but are made only "to the best of seller's knowledge" (i.e., "To the best of seller's knowledge, the roof is in good repair and leak-free").

Step 11. Negotiate a Right of Offset

Is the seller taking back a promissory note from you as part of the purchase price? A *right of offset* is your right to hold back note payments while negotiating with seller over who will bear the responsibility for undetected postclosing problems. Be sure that your promise to pay does *not* sap your negotiating leverage. Do not state, "I promise to pay without right of offset."

Step 12. Make a Limited Time Offer

"Offering shopping" occurs when the seller's broker uses your offer to coax another prospective buyer to make an offer or to better an earlier offer. In effect, the broker is creating an auction environment.

The best way to prevent offering shopping is to make your offer valid for a very limited time. I've prepared offers that were open for as little as a few hours, when I knew the competition for the house would be intense. Longer time frames, twenty-four or forty-eight hours, may be reasonable under less competitive circumstances. Any longer period may be to your negotiating disadvantage.

Step 13. Negotiate the Terms of Notes and Mortgages

Promissory note and mortgage document forms are provided by title companies or brokerage associations. Like the Purchase and Sale Agreement, the terms and conditions of these printed forms are not immune from your negotiated changes.

Consider these changes if the seller is taking back a note from you:

- Longer notice-of-default and opportunity-to-cure periods.

- Elimination of stepped-up default interest rates.

- More lenient penalties.

- Softer forfeiture provisions.

SPECIAL TIPS IF YOU ARE PURCHASING A NEWLY BUILT HOUSE

Subdivision developers like to keep prices high. Buyers don't want to move into a subdivision only to find their neighbor paid $5,000 less for a similar model the month before. Higher prices today ensure higher subdivision appraisals in the future.

If the builder is resistant to negotiating price, it may be easier to negotiate upgrade concessions such as tile or hardwood flooring instead of carpeting, air conditioning, tile counter tops and showers, landscaping, and all those other wonderful "designer options" you saw in the model houses.

The builder may be a publicly owned, stock exchange-listed company. If so, it will want to present Wall Street with the very best sales figures possible.

Publicly traded home builders are more likely to wheel and deal as it gets closer to the end of their fiscal year. To determine the builder's fiscal year, either ask the builder or a stockbroker, or check your local library.

The important thing is that your closing (when you take delivery of title) must be before the end of the builder's year.

Builders who offer *designer packages* for window coverings, plush carpeting, and the like often charge more than a local merchant would charge for the same items. If you can beat the builder's price, negotiate a credit from the builder for the standard carpeting, appliances, or whatever the builder won't be installing, and have someone else provide and install the upgraded items.

Look for a builder with *standing inventory*—homes built in excess of what the market will absorb. Standing inventory is expensive for builders to hold unsold. As loan interest, insurance, security, and other expenses accrue, builders become more flexible deal-makers.

House—Sale

Negotiating the Sale of Your House

Step 1. No Contract Is Standard

Read and *negotiate* the fine print when presented with a printed form called a Purchase and Sale Contract. (These contracts are called Deposit Receipts in many states. People read contracts, but who reads a receipt?)

Purchase and Sale Contract forms are designed for use by *both* buyers and sellers. By definition, they can't fully serve the best interests of either. Never feel locked in by the printed word. Negotiate what is best for you.

Step 2. Consider at What Point You Want to Be Under Contract

The *wiggle room* in a Purchase and Sale Contract is always with the buyer.

A Purchase and Sale Contract provides that the seller *must* sell if the buyer *decides* to buy after reviewing title, inspecting the house, shopping for financing, and so on.

In a strong seller's market, consider keeping pressure on a buyer by not taking your property off the market or committing yourself to a sale until the buyer has a real commitment to the deal.

Real commitment comes when the buyer (a) makes a sizable deposit and (b) satisfies or waives some of the conditions (*contingencies*) over which the buyer has a measure of discretionary control. For example, tell the buyer you will not sign an agreement to sell until the buyer has first inspected and approved the physical condition of the house.

Or consider, entering into a contract which, for the most part, has very short contingency periods. For example, the buyer has five working days to inspect and approve the physical condition of the house.

Step 3. Read the Buyer's Needs

It may be worthwhile to have a meeting at which the buyer, seller, and broker are present. By being able to *read* the buyer's needs, motivations, and time constraints, you will be better able to determine the relative balance of negotiating power.

237

Sometimes the buyer's need for *mastery over the negotiating process* is more important than the actual *dollars* involved.

If the buyer is firmly insistent about a further price reduction, consider giving in to the reduction demand IF (tax implications aside) there is a dollar-recouping interest rate hike on the mortgage note you will be taking back, or IF the buyer will accept the property "as is," or IF the buyer agrees to an early closing but will allow you to live in the house rent-free for 60 days until your new place is ready.

Step 4. Change Quarterbacks?

Brokers have a need to be in control and to feel instrumental in making the deal. Your broker may be caring, charming, and energetic. Your broker may also be the world's worst negotiator. Strategize how you can work as a team. It's your deal, and it may make sense for you to call the plays personally.

Step 5. Insulate Yourself from the Scottsdale Squeeze Play

The buyers were my clients, and I was embarrassed.

But then they were from another part of the world and their way was, well, their way.

The deal I negotiated was for the purchase of a palatial home outside of Scottsdale. The contract called for a $10,000 cash deposit. There was a standard *liquidated damages provision* allowing the seller to keep the deposit in lieu of a suit, in the event my clients breached their "commitment to buy." Title was to transfer in four months. To me, it was a done deal.

My clients stood on the sidelines as the seller bought a ranch in Montana, made arrangements to move his mother to a convalescent facility in Montana, enrolled his kids in a Montana school for the fall semester, forwarded medical records, and generally got ready for an anxiously awaited move north.

Then the bomb dropped.

My clients decided that the house was too expensive. They weren't going to close. The buyers were prepared to say good-bye to their $10,000 deposit.

As predicted by my clients long before, the panicked seller whose life had been rearranged had no practical choice other than to once again discount his selling price for a timely close.

Here is what I learned later. The buyers were not risking their deposit. Had the seller said "no" to their demand for a further concession, the buyers would have proceeded to close anyway.

Insulate yourself from the Scottsdale squeeze play. Negotiate an escalating deposit—lower at first, if necessary to encourage the buyer to sign the sale agreement, but quickly increasing as inspections are made and title reports are reviewed.

Make sure the increased deposit is large enough so that you, the seller, are reasonably protected and the buyer feels very committed to your deal.

Keep contingency periods for inspections, studies, approvals, or financing as short as possible.

Step 6. Inventory Your Negotiating Chips

Furniture, area rugs, outdoor planters, a large hanging mirror are more than things that "make the house." They are *negotiating chips* in ensuing buy–sell negotiations. Rather than lowering the price, consider "throwing in" furniture and decorative items, or anything that would cost a buyer money.

Step 7. Discourage Delays

Real estate deals seldom close on time. Discourage delays by negotiating a price increase in the event of a delayed closing.

For example: *The sales price shall increase by the equivalent of 10 percent simple annual interest from the date of scheduled closing to the date of actual closing. Tax prorations shall be as of the scheduled closing date rather than the date of actual closing.*

Step 8. Prevent Note Offsets

Taking back your buyer's note as part of the purchase price? *Negotiate* that the note states the buyer's promise to pay you is *without right of offset.* An offset right is the right to withhold or reduce note payments. A buyer *with* a right of offset can withhold note payments long after closing, while squabbling over who is responsible for replacing a leaky roof.

Step 9. Don't Wait for the Postclosing Shoe to Drop

Negotiate that seller's warranties, if any, terminate when title to the house is passed to your buyer.

Step 10. Avoid Your Lender's Prepayment Penalties

The bad news: If your existing loan is from a financial institution, there is a good chance there will be a prepayment penalty if your loan is paid off at the time of sale. The norm for early payment is a penalty equal to six months' interest.

The good news: Most lenders waive the prepayment penalty if your buyer will finance their purchase from your lender. If this is your lender's policy, negotiate to have the buyer finance the purchase through your lender.

Alert: If, by way of formal agreement with your lender, the buyer *assumes* your existing loan, make sure the lender unconditionally releases you from any further loan liability.

A buyer who makes payments on your loan as if the loan originated with him or her is buying *subject to* your loan. You are then *not* being released from the debt and you *will be* held accountable if the buyer fails to make payments.

Insurance Claims, Auto

Negotiating Automobile Insurance Claims

Step 1. Negotiate Which Shop Will Do the Work

Chances are your policy does not require you to:

- Obtain two or three estimates.
- Drive the car into a drive-in claims service.
- Use a body shop chosen by the insurance company.

If you are requested to do any of these things, insist that you be shown where in your policy it is required.

The contract to have repair work done is between you and the shop. The insurance company will not guarantee the shop's work. If things aren't right, you will be dealing with the shop, not the insurance company. It makes sense to go to a shop where you will get a minimum of aggravation and the best possible job.

Shops recommended by an insurance company are the ones that give the insurance company a discount in exchange for a high volume of repairs. They aren't necessarily the shops that will do the best job.

Start off at a drive-in claims office, and the adjuster will encourage the use of an insurance company's "captive" shop.

The best way to *negotiate* having the shop of your choice do the work is to start off by driving or having your car towed to that shop and leaving it there. Call your insurance company and tell them to inspect the car at your chosen shop and to make a repair deal with that shop.

What happens if the repair estimate of your chosen shop is much more costly than the adjuster's assessment of the damage? Compare specific differences in the two estimates. Does one have parts being repaired rather than replaced? Remember, your car must be restored to its predamage condition. *Negotiate* and justify your shop's more costly effort.

If the insurance company is dragging its feet, submit a *Proof of Loss* statement, which is your demand for payment, accompanied by documentation supporting the amount of your loss.

A Proof of Loss form can be obtained from the adjuster or your insurance company.

Step 2. Don't Be Intimidated

If I were you, I would accept my offer now. If my supervisor has to review your claim, she won't be as liberal as I am.

To save money on adjustment and claim costs, some adjusters will try to *cash-out* your claim quickly by assessing the damage based on prices supplied by the insurance company. These cash-out prices are usually lower than the prices you will have to pay to have your car repaired at a first-class body shop.

If the body shop fails to meet your reasonable expectations or if it is discovered that additional work needs to be done, it is up to the insurance company to make things right. If, however, you cash out, the insurance company has no further obligation to you.

Step 3. Negotiate Betterment and Depreciation

Because of a sandstorm, your four-year-old car needs to be totally repainted.

Your insurance company's obligation is to put your car back to where it was just before the damage occurred. With a whole new paint job, your car is in better shape than it was just before the damage. Your *betterment* is in getting back the four years of paint life that had already been used (depreciated) on the day of the sandstorm.

Assume that an *average* car's paint job lasts ten years. Because your car is four years old, the insurance company will offer to settle for 60 percent of the cost of a new paint job. This represents the remaining six years of paint life you lost.

In this example, *negotiate* that your car was garaged, regularly waxed, and so well maintained that the paint had a reasonable life of sixteen years rather than ten. The four years of paint life you used and got back was only 4/16ths or 25 percent of a sixteen-year anticipated life. Accordingly, the insurance company should pay for 75 percent of the paint job.

Step 4. Negotiate Value Diminution

How much *value* has your car lost as a result of being damaged?

Would you buy a car knowing it had been badly damaged and repaired? Even though fully repaired, the value of a car that was in an accident will always be less than the value of an identical car that wasn't in an accident. This increment of decrease in worth is *value diminution.*

How do you measure diminution of value? Ask used car dealers, "What could you have sold my car for, had it not been wrecked and repaired? What could you have sold it for, had it never been wrecked at all?"

Negotiate diminution reimbursement. These negotiations are most successful when dealing with the other person's insurance company. The diminution argument works best with expensive cars, whose owners are usually concerned with their cars being in perfect condition. Owners of less expensive, older cars may only be concerned with the car's drive-back-and-forth transportation value.

Step 5. Negotiate Total Loss Value

Is your car totaled? The *Kelley Blue Book* and other value guides are for cars that were maintained in "average" condition.

There is a big difference between a low-mileage, pampered car and one that sits outside all year, is never waxed, and is not regularly serviced.

To receive the most for your car, *negotiate* that it was in far better shape than the average car of that make and model, and therefore you shouldn't be bound to the insurance adjuster's computerized schedule of depreciated "actual cash value."

Also *negotiate* to be reimbursed for:

- License fees.
- Sales, gas guzzler, and other taxes.
- Extended warranty premiums you paid on the totaled car.

The amount of your license fee and tax reimbursement will be based on what you would have to shell out to purchase a used car similar to the one that was totaled. *Negotiate* your entitlement to this reimbursement, even though you plan to use the settlement money to buy a newer car or go on a Panama Canal cruise this winter.

Step 6. Negotiate Car Rental

You can get car rental reimbursement from your own insurance company only if you have paid a separate premium for it. But if you are dealing with the other driver's insurance company, then in most states you can negotiate to be reimbursed for rental while your car is being repaired.

Negotiate what is a reasonable amount of *time* to have a rental car and the *type* of rental car.

If you are driving a Cadillac or Lincoln, you are arguably entitled to rent a comparable luxury car. You will get a lot of resistance insisting on a luxury car, but you may very well prevail if you push hard enough.

Step 7. Negotiate Liability

If you are stopped at a red light and someone rear-ends you, chances are you were blameless.

But what if you stopped suddenly before you were hit? You may be partially to blame, depending on why you stopped. Did you slam on your brakes because you weren't attentive to traffic? Or to avoid a child darting into the street?

If you are deemed partially negligent and to some degree responsible, the insurance company can fault you with a "chargeable accident," which can result in increased premiums. *Negotiate* with the company as to whether you should be considered at fault and whether the accident will cause your premiums to increase.

Step 8. Negotiate Collision Versus Comprehensive

Collision: the damage done to your car when another car hits you or you hit another car or an inanimate object.

Comprehensive: just about any other calamity that befalls your car—a windstorm, fire, vandalism.

Your car is damaged by a rock on a mountain road.

Did the rock roll down the hill and hit your car? If so, it's *comprehensive* loss.

Did the rock roll down the hill and stop, and then you hit the rock? If so, it's a *collision* loss.

If there is a question as to how your car was damaged, *negotiate* the character of the loss. With a comprehensive loss, there will be either no deductible or a very small deductible. The meeting of car and rock will not go against your driving record, and your premium will probably not increase.

Step 9. Keep the Pressure On

Once a Proof of Loss is filed, the insurance company will have a limited amount of time to accept or reject your demand. Any rejection must be accompanied by the reasons for rejection.

If you are not satisfied with the reasons given, ask to speak to a claims supervisor or the president of the company, write to the State Insurance Commissioner or Department of Insurance requesting arbitration, or do whatever needs to be done to keep settlement pressure maximized.

Step 10. Do Not Sign a Release If You Were Injured

Were you injured? Don't tell the other driver's insurance company of your injury until they have agreed to pay for the repairs to your car in a shop of your choice and have provided you with a rental car. Once the insurance company knows you will be making an injury claim, they will want to settle both the property and injury claim simultaneously, which will slow down the repair of your car.

Do not sign a release of your personal injury claim until you receive adequate payment for that injury claim.

Practice alert: Determine your state's applicable statute of limitations bar date for filing claims as well as your state's Department of Motor Vehicles reporting requirements.

Step 11. The Money Can Go Two Ways

You and your insurance company have agreed on *what* needs to be done, *where* the body work is to be done, and *how much* is to be paid.

Some insurance companies will contract with and pay the body shop. Others will want to cash out—give you the money and have you contract with the body shop.

If you cash out, you are on your own. But if the insurance company contracts with the body shop and the job isn't to your liking, you can look to the insurance company. *Negotiate* to choose the body shop and to have the insurance company contract with and pay the body shop directly.

Insurance Claims, Homeowner

Negotiating Homeowner Insurance Claims

Here's the latest from Los Angeles:

Question: What do riots, fires, mudslides, earthquakes, and ex-wives have in common?

Answer: Eventually one of them will get your house.

The good news is that four of the above can be covered by insurance.

Step 1. Don't Jump the Gun

- Notify your insurance company of your loss.

- Read the *insured's duties* section of your policy.

- Don't have anyone start working immediately "to minimize loss."

- Have an emergency professional board up the house, or move your contents to storage if immediate protection is necessary.

- Save everything. Do not discard anything.

Tip: If you do any emergency work or cleanup yourself, the insurance company will not reimburse you because you did not incur any expense.

Tip: Don't be hesitant to ask for an advance payment. You are entitled to an advance for certain services, supplies, and living expenses.

Step 2. Somewhere Out There Is an Expert for You

You can't negotiate with your insurance company until you know *what* needs to be done and *whom* you want to do it.

The best remodeling contractor is not necessarily the best homebuilder. And neither the remodeler nor the homebuilder is necessarily the best contractor to do specialized water, earthquake, or fire damage repair.

Casualty damage restoration experts come from two distinct industries:

246

a. *Building/remodeling:* structural repair, painting.

b. *Interior restorers and cleaners:* upholstery, contents, carpets, cleaning, furniture.

The two industries meet at your interior walls. There, the applicable expertise will depend on whether those walls are being cleaned or painted.

Determine the appropriate subject matter experts. Talk to various licensed, bonded, and established companies to get a feeling for which ones will best serve your needs.

Ask restoration contractors:

- Can you see their restoration facilities?

- Do they use specialized equipment (smoke deodorizers; probes and meters to locate hidden water damage; dehumidifiers and dryers; sewage decontamination and disposal equipment, and so on)?

- Will they guarantee their work, and for how long?

Ask all contractors:

- Can they produce references from insurance companies, independent adjusters, and other insureds with similar losses?

- Have there been any lawsuits by unhappy customers?

Step 3. Get Bids, Not Estimates

After you have decided which firms best suit your needs, solicit bids from the companies that are prepared to do the work *immediately*.

Request that these bids be specific and detailed. At a minimum, bids should break down the cost of various types of repairs—painting, cabinetry, electrical, and so on. If possible, break those costs down on a room-by-room basis.

Compare bids to determine why they differ. Are the differences reflective of quality? (For example, will heavily smoked or charred wood be scraped or sealed rather than replaced?) Or do they mean that the bidding contractors viewed the job differently?

Why a *bid* rather than an *estimate?* An *estimate* is nothing more than a guess, and there is no such thing as a precise guess. On the other hand, most *bid* forms are binding and enforceable agreements once they are accepted by you.

Step 4. Prepare a Proof of Loss Claim

A Proof of Loss statement, when delivered to your insurance company, serves as your *offer* to settle as well as your *demand* and your *justification* for payment.

A Proof of Loss statement sets forth the issues and items that need to be addressed to resolve your claim: additional living expenses, debris removal, content losses, contractor bids, and so on.

Blank Proof of Loss forms are available from your insurance company.

A Proof of Loss statement should be as detailed as possible. Show that you expect to be compensated accordingly by setting forth exact amounts right down to the pennies. The more detailed your claim, the more money you will be paid. Document your loss with photos and/or video.

A Proof of Loss statement enhances your negotiating power in two ways:

a. The insurance company is obligated to respond to your request within a narrow and specific time frame.

b. You can demand specific reasons if your claim is rejected.

How not to play the claim game: Agree with the insurance company as to the amount of your loss *first,* and then sign a Proof of Loss statement prepared by the insurance company.

How to play the claim game: File a Proof of Loss statement first and negotiate later.

If the damage is substantial, consider hiring a *public adjuster* to assist in preparing a Proof of Loss statement. Public adjusters are pros who specialize in different types of insurance losses and represent victims only.

Alert: Avoid any public adjuster who miraculously shows up on your doorstep, or franchise public adjusters with crash-course training.

Step 5. Negotiate Repair and Restoration

Based on photos, documentation, and your Proof of Loss statement, try to reach an agreement with your insurance company as to the extent of repair.

Step 6. Negotiate Content Losses

A *content* is any personal item in your house that is not nailed down or made a part of the house.

List lost contents item by item (suit by suit, chair by chair). It will take time to compile the list and document replacement costs, but it will almost always be worth your effort.

Negotiate the Price of Content Items

Unless you have *replacement cost coverage,* content losses are paid on an *actual cash value* basis. This means the insurance company has to put you back where you were before the loss.

Insurance companies have computer-generated lists showing the cost of various household items. These lists are sold to insurance companies both as a guide and as a printed reference to get you to settle faster. It shouldn't surprise you that the prices on these lists are low. A *replacement price schedule* is *not* a nonnegotiable authority.

Negotiate the Life of Cost Content Items

If you have a two-year-old Mitsubishi television that was burned, what are you entitled to from your insurer?

If the insurance company's depreciation schedule says your television set had a six-year life, then the fire deprived you of four more years of television viewing. You would be reimbursed two-thirds of the replacement cost because you lost two-thirds (four years out of six) of viewing pleasure.

But what if that set was in your guest bedroom and was seldom turned on? A six-year life expectancy would be too short for a set used so infrequently.

A *depreciation schedule* is *not* a nonnegotiable authority. Negotiate that your television set had a life of twelve years, not six years, and that your two years of use (depreciation) was not a third but only a sixth of the set's life. If a replacement television costs $1,000, the difference is whether the insurance company will pay you $833 or $666.

Step 7. Don't Be Timid or Intimidated

Appearing timid will make you easily compromised by an adjuster whose job is to close files.

Take your time. Don't be pressured into accepting an adjuster's quickie deal. Once released, the insurance company is out of the picture even though things don't turn out as you expected.

Step 8. Don't Allow Adjuster Delays

Many adjusters are freelancers who work for different insurance companies. Their compensation is based on the amount of time they work on your claim. Delays are to their advantage. Beware of delay tactics such as continual requests for documentation and information that you have already supplied.

Step 9. Be Aware of Quickie "Cash Out" Offers

To save money on adjustment and claim costs, some adjusters will try to settle your claim quickly. Watch for these two common negotiating tricks:

- Assessing the damage based on cash-out prices, which will be lower than the prices you will have to pay to restore or replace damaged items. What the insurance company saves, you lose.

- Using former contractors to provide *estimates.* These contractors will never do the work. Their purpose is to provide the insurance company with third-party credibility. Your negotiations should be based on written *bids* from *first-class* contractors who will do the work *immediately.*

Cash-out offers often presuppose that an item will be restored rather than replaced. If the restoration fails to meet your reasonable expectations, you can refuse to accept the work and ask that the item be replaced—UNLESS you cash out. With a cash-out, the insurance company has no further obligation to you.

Step 10. Negotiate Betterment Issues

Assume that your home's interior paint job has an expected (depreciable) life of five years.

At the end of two years, there is a fire in your living room. The insurance company has agreed to repaint two smoke-damaged walls. The cost to paint the two walls is $400.

Should the insurance company pay only 3/5ths of $400 because with a new paint job you are getting back the two years of paint life you enjoyed before the fire?

No.

You weren't *bettered* by getting back the two years of paint life you already used: in three years, you will paint all four walls anyway.

If all four walls were fire-damaged and repainted, you were *bettered.* It would then be reasonable for the insurance company to deduct the depreciation (two years of paint life you enjoyed before the fire).

Step 11. Don't Accept the Insurance Company's Contractor

Builders, contractors, and restorers solicit insurance company work by quoting low prices. To save money, insurance companies will hire these people. But these folks are often younger and less experienced than seasoned, high-quality contractors. This difference is reflected in their prices.

"Our insurance company only has one outfit that we work with." Must you use the insurance company's contractor if the bid is lower for the same work? The insurance company may make you pay the difference.

Remember, *the insurance company's obligation is to put you back where you were before the damage.* Perhaps this can be done less expensively with the company's own contractors, but you aren't obligated to accept work quality or materials that are not as good as what you lost.

Tip: Have your choice of contractor review the insurance company contractor's bid to make sure it specifies the same scope of work and the same kind and quality of materials.

If you disagree and are unwilling to pay the difference between the two bids, then contact your adjuster's supervisors and threaten to initiate arbitration or litigation, or contact your State Insurance Commissioner or State Department of Insurance.

Step 12. The Money Can Go Two Ways

You and your insurance company have agreed on *what* needs to be done, the *contractor* to be hired, and *how much* is to be paid.

Some insurance companies will hire and pay the contractor. Others will want to give you the money and have you hire the contractor.

If you cash out, you are on your own. The insurance company is out of the picture no matter how the job turns out. But if the insurance company hires the contractor and the job isn't to your liking, you can look to the insurance company for redress.

Negotiate to choose the contractor and to have the insurance company hire and pay the contractor directly. Do not accept the job or release the insurance company until everything is at least as good as it was before the damage.

Step 13. Negotiate Extras and Remodeling

You may want to take advantage of the fact that your home is being repaired to do some nonrestorative remodeling.

If you are going to remodel as well as restore, the best way to negotiate with your insurance company is to have each contractor give you two separate bids: one bid for the insurance-related work, the other bid only for additional work needed to remodel your home while the insurance repairs are being made.

IRS

Negotiating with the IRS

The Internal Revenue Code is 1,378 pages long. The Federal Tax Regulations ramble on for 6,439 pages. There are 280 IRS forms. Even the IRS finds the tax laws almost incomprehensible.

As a test, tax pros hired by *USA Today* telephoned the IRS with prepared questions. The IRS's answers were wrong 40 percent of the time.

AUDIT NEGOTIATING TIPS

How They Will Be

Eventually, you will get "the letter"—the IRS is requesting an "interview" for the purpose of verifying the accuracy of your tax return.

Nonbusiness and small business audits are conducted at the IRS offices (*office audits*) by *tax auditors*. Tax auditors generally have no background in law or accounting. They are IRS-trained to examine specific audit items, largely through the use of "Pro-Forma Audit Kits." The kits deal with tax return line items such as casualty losses, rental income and expenses, and contributions. The routine and repetitive nature of their work makes them very proficient.

Revenue agents conduct the more complex *field audits* (on-site examinations). Partnership and corporate returns are almost always audited on-site at the taxpayer's business. Revenue agents are better trained and more experienced than tax auditors. Many have college accounting credits. Unlike tax auditors, their line of inquiry is neither channeled nor item-specific. Any income or expense item is fair game for examination.

How You Must Be

- Never allow any audit meeting to take place unless you are advised in writing of the purpose of the audit.

- If your meeting will be anything other than routine, the IRS must first inform you of that fact.

- If a *special agent* is present at your meeting, stop dead in your tracks. Don't say another word. Special agents are part of the

253

IRS's Criminal Investigation Division (CID). Now is the time to hire a professional.

- You need not personally attend an audit meeting. Your professional representative may appear on your behalf. *Consider:* Should you go to it alone?

    Because taxpayers are more prone to misstatements than their representatives, some agents encourage taxpayers to attend audit meetings even if they have a professional representative in tow.

    If you are easily flustered or are worried you'll say the wrong things, send a professional in your place.

- You can terminate an audit meeting by stating that it appears nothing is being accomplished and you have no desire to continue. Your file will be marked *"Unagreed"* and, if you request, it will then be turned over to a *group manager*, who will try to resolve the areas of disagreement.

Adopt a tax negotiator's persona:

- Be prompt.

- Be seemingly cooperative. Have neat, accurate, and complete records.

- Be cordial, not rude. Be polite, not friendly. Being threatening or antagonistic will only make matters worse.

- Act as if you are in control.

- Set out your position clearly and strongly. Be affirmative. The line between tax avoidance (which is legal) and tax evasion (fraud) is both thin and wavy. The pros themselves are often stymied in determining the boundaries. Claiming an "aggressive" deduction is not fraud. Fraud *is not* making an error or forgetting some item of income. Fraud is knowing what's right but doing what's wrong. It is intentional underpayment.

- Only answer the questions asked, but think about your answer before responding. Don't get rattled.

- Unless you are answering a question, don't speak. Don't volunteer information or documents. Give only information specifically requested. Talk too much and you may raise tax liability issues that hadn't been previously raised or contemplated.

- Leave your attitude at home. Keep politics to yourself. This is not the time to share your views about how the tax system is inequitable and oppressive.

- Auditors are trained to notice body language. Try to look relaxed. If you become concerned with how the meeting is progressing, you may call it to a halt at any time for the purpose of retaining a professional to represent you.

If you don't reach an agreement, you will receive a *Preliminary Notice* giving you 30 days to file with the *Appeals Office*. If you do not appeal, you will receive a *Notice of Deficiency* and you will then have 90 days either to petition the *Tax Court* or to stop interest from accruing by paying the tax and claiming a refund. If you do neither, the tax will be assessed.

The means by which you will initiate an appeal will depend on the amount of your tax deficiency. The IRS will provide you with printed information as to how you must proceed.

APPEALS OFFICE NEGOTIATING TIPS

Appeals officers are an elite group. They are mostly better educated, better trained, more experienced, and more secure in their jobs than office and field auditors.

Appeals conferences are informal meetings. You may represent yourself at an appeals conference or you may be represented by a professional.

Theoretically, the appeals officer, although an IRS employee, represents neither the IRS nor the taxpayer and adopts an objective, neutral approach as to what is reasonable under the circumstances.

What doesn't the IRS want you to know: If you request, the IRS must now disclose relevant portions of your case file. Information you are entitled to see includes the IRS's position relative to disputed items and any audit findings.

The Appeals Office's willingness to settle conflicts largely depends on how it perceives the IRS's chances of prevailing in the Tax Court. The IRS shies away from litigation if it appears the odds are not in its favor. Even with slam-dunk cases, an appeals officer may offer small concessions to save the IRS the time and expenses associated with litigation.

If you lose your appeal, you will receive a *Notice of Deficiency* and will then have 90 days either to petition the Tax Court or to pay the tax and claim a refund.

"IN COLLECTION" NEGOTIATING TIPS

Collection officers are determined, intractable, and unemotional. They are called into play when tax is owed but not paid, or when no return is filed. Given their mindset that they are duty-bound to collect every cent owed, they can be unrelenting.

Certificates and promotions are awarded to top producers. So intense is the pressure to produce that collection officers are hair-trigger-quick to lien, levy, confiscate, or seize property. They can be capricious. They can be arbitrary. They are not above bluffing or harassing. Some collection officers are not above lying.

Here's what you need to know to protect yourself:

- If a collection officer comes to your door unannounced, you do not need to invite him or her in. By law, the officer must be invited.

- Before there can be a valid lien or levy, the IRS must explain the collection process, including how to appeal.

If you take no action, the IRS may file a notice of a federal tax *lien*. A lien attaches to and encumbers your property, making your property the security for the payment of the tax debt. A lien is not the taking of property but it is public notice that the IRS has a claim against you.

After 30 days' notice, the IRS may serve a notice of *levy*. By levying, the IRS can actually take wages owed to you, bank accounts, a boat, car, or other property.

Certain things, however, cannot be levied by the IRS. Included in this exempt category are public assistance payments, a limited amount of furniture, personal effects, tools of the trade, and a formula-determined portion of your wages.

If you are unable to effectively negotiate a settlement with a collection officer, you can *change negotiating levels* by:

- Requesting a meeting with the collection officer's group manager or requesting the manager's name and how to contact him or her.

- Filing an appeal. An appeal officer will then consider the reasonableness of your *previous* compromise proposal. Unless the

IRS has a reason to believe your assets will be dissipated in the interim, it will not levy pending the appeal hearing.

If the IRS's collection action would result in a "significant hardship" (i.e., shutting down your place of business, or denying you the ability to purchase necessities such as food, shelter, transportation, or medical treatment), you may get relief from the *Office of the Ombudsman,* which can quickly issue a binding Taxpayer Assistance Order. The IRS application to file is, appropriately, Form 911 (or telephone 1-800-829-1040).

CRIMINAL INVESTIGATION ALERT

Special criminal investigation agents do not have the power to determine tax liability. Their calling is to search out hidden assets and unreported income sources. In reality, they are federal police officers, even though they may come across as having a laid-back *You can talk to me/trust me* persona. Don't consider second-guessing CID officers, and never underestimate their ability. When contacted by the CID, consult a tax lawyer.

HOW TO NEGOTIATE WITH THE IRS

Step 1. Make Time Your Ally

IRS employees, like everyone else, have deadlines. Postponing a meeting may put pressure on them to finish. The price for finishing timely may be IRS concessions.

Practice tip: A last-minute postponement will only antagonize the person with whom you are meeting.

Scheduling your meeting at the end of the month is best. If the person charged with your file has too many unclosed cases, he or she may be inclined to settle more quickly in order to close your file.

Schedule your meeting just before a long weekend. The chances are pretty good that the person handling your file will show less interest in the audit than in the upcoming holiday.

Schedule the meeting at 10:00 A.M. When it's finally time to talk about adjustments, it will be near the noon lunch break. IRS personnel have been known to make concessions to keep a meeting from interfering with their lunch hour.

Step 2. Keep Your Eye on the Big Picture

An auditor's goal is to collect additional taxes, close your case, and move on. Compromise on some smaller items. Trade allowances and disallowances. Be emotionally prepared to pony up some additional taxes. Don't lose sight of the big picture—it's the more important items that count in the end.

Step 3. Negotiate the Cancellation of Penalties

Negotiate the cancellation of penalties (not interest) by showing that sufficient cause exists for the failure that led to the penalty.

The IRS has historically found that sufficient cause for penalty cancellation exists when: the taxpayer has been ill (alcoholism, now considered an illness, can be grounds for setting aside a penalty); there is grave illness in the taxpayer's immediate family; necessary documents were destroyed or not available; returns were sent to the wrong IRS address or sent with insufficient postage; there was reliance on bad professional advice; the taxpayer did not receive forms requested from the IRS.

Step 4. Negotiate Payment Arrangements

If you acknowledge owing the tax but don't have the money to pay, the IRS will negotiate a payment program.

Step 5. Negotiate a Partial Amnesty

Negotiate to reduce the amount of the tax owed. This is done by demonstrating doubt as to your *liability* for the amount owed or doubt as to your *ability* to fully pay the amount owed.

Be prepared to describe in detail why the IRS cannot collect more than you are offering. Your assets and present and future income will be considered in evaluating your offer. This settlement offer of partial payment and/or a percentage of future earnings in exchange for a release of all taxes, including interest and penalties, is called an *Offer-in-Compromise.*

The Silver Bullet

Show your tax debt is excusable in bankruptcy. Do you have an *income tax* debt for a *tax year* that was more than three years ago? Count from when your tax return for that year *could* have been (not actually was) filed.

For example, if the tax year was 1992, the last date you *could* have filed a return (without an extension) was April 15, 1993. You would count the years from April 15, 1993 (even if you actually filed April 1, 1993), to the present.

If you filed for an extension for your 1992 return, count back to the last extended date your return *could* have been (not actually was) filed.

If the result of your count is more than three years *and* if you *actually* filed your return more than two years ago, then your tax debt and interest on that debt may, subject to other criteria, be discharged (excused) in bankruptcy. Special rules apply to the dischargeability of penalties.

Tax *liens* encumbering real or personal property survive bankruptcy even though the tax *debt* is discharged. In this situation, the IRS can do nothing more than foreclose on its prebankruptcy lien.

For example: The IRS has a $60,000 tax lien encumbering your cabin. You file bankruptcy. The *lien* is not affected by your bankruptcy. The IRS, exercising its lien rights, forecloses and receives $50,000. The IRS cannot collect the $10,000 ($60,000 minus $50,000) balance.

If you have more to gain than to lose in bankruptcy proceedings, the ability to discharge your tax liability may give you significant negotiating power in settling with the IRS.

Bankruptcy and tax rules are complex. Consult with a professional adviser.

FREE FOR ALL

To receive these free IRS publications, call (toll-free) (800) TAX-FORM:

Publication 1, "Your Rights as a Taxpayer"

Publication 5, "Appeal Rights and Preparation of Protests for Unagreed Cases"

Publication 594, "Understanding the Collection Process"

Publication 910, "Guide to Free Tax Services"

Jewelry, Buying

Negotiating Major Purchases: The Fine Jewelry and Watch Game

Whoever said money doesn't buy happiness just didn't know where to shop.

A gold Rolex Oyster Perpetual is a gold Rolex Oyster Perpetual at every Rolex dealership.

Gemstone jewelry, however, is different. The materials used (stones and precious metals) can be compared and valued. But design and labor are *blind item* price dynamics that can't be readily quantified.

Jewelry profit margins ranging from 100 percent to 400 percent and up are not unusual. That incredibly liberal credit you see offered is possible because the down payment can cover the cost of goods *and* throw off some profit. Anything collected beyond the down payment is pure gravy.

Zales will. So will Tiffany. All jewelry stores—the world's great names, national chain jewelry stores, the small shop around the corner—will *gladly* negotiate when you know how.

Step 1. Learn What You Are Doing

If you can't distinguish an emerald from a garnet, a ruby from a red spinel, or 10-karat gold from 18-karat gold, then take the time to learn what you are doing. Then learn even more.

Gold and silver prices are based on their purity: 10-karat gold (41 percent pure) is less valuable than 14-karat gold (58 percent pure), which is less valuable than 18-karat gold (75 percent pure). There is a difference when a label says gold plate, gold filled, or solid gold.

Tiny Baubles

Gemstones come in different grades and qualities. If you believe that the diamonds, sapphires, rubies, and emeralds being hawked on the television shopping networks are anywhere near top quality, you are already in trouble.

For every color you like, there are probably five or six gemstones in that color. With gemstones, it's color that counts. A green chrome tourmaline may look a lot like a green zircon but because of availability may be worth twice as much. Flaws in colored stones will not impact their value as much as flaws will impact the value of diamonds. Gemstones are

260

often treated with oils and heat, to enhance their color. Appropriate inquiry should be made before purchasing.

Diamonds are universally graded by color, carat weight, clarity, and cut. A colorless, flawless stone is the most valuable. Fancy shapes sell for 5 percent to 10 percent less. Size is not the most important factor in diamonds. A half-carat, round-cut flawless stone with excellent color can cost twice as much as a three-carat diamond with poor color and noticeable imperfections.

Negotiating alert:

- The American Gemological Institute's universal grading system denotes *color* in letters (near colorless D ranging downward to a faint yellow K). Clarity grades generally range from VVS_1 (flawless) downward as VVS_2, VS_1, VS_2, SI_1, and SI_2. Many jewelers sidestep the universal diamond grading system by conjuring up their own self-serving grades, such as "deluxe quality" or "heirloom quality." These fictional ratings may in actuality hover close to the bottom of the true universal grading scale.

- Beware of the A-word: "approximately." A merchant's appraisal can be meaningless because diamonds are sometimes misleadingly bumped into a higher grade under the guise of having color and clarity that are "approximately graded _____."

Merchants' appraisals are *always* at *their* retail (why would they give you an appraisal for less?). This is *never* indicative of worth. If you believe otherwise, then ask a reputable jeweler what the piece's resale value would be if you have to or want to sell soon. *Medical alert:* Be sitting down when you get the answer.

If you think of jewelry as an investment, you shouldn't be buying jewelry.

Step 2. Try Not to Swoon

Oh, I just have to own this!

Jewelry is an emotional purchase. It is even more emotional if you are shopping for an engagement ring, Valentine's Day gift, or special birthday or anniversary present. Advertising doesn't tell us that diamonds are a great hedge against inflation (they would be lying). It tells us diamonds are the gift of eternal love.

Let your enthusiasm show and you lessen your negotiating leverage. This is particularly true for unique pieces that can't be purchased readily elsewhere.

Step 3. Link

Merchants like to do more for people they like. A friendly, appreciative attitude gores a long way.

Step 4. Make the Jeweler Invest in You

If you just stick your head in the door, set off the customer entering chime, and ask about discounts, the answer will be, "We are a fixed-price store." (If it was a "discount" shop, there would be a sign in the window.)

Get the jeweler to invest time in you. The more time spent comparing design, quality, and size variations, the more knowledgeable you will be. The more time the merchant spends with you, the greater the propensity to make a deal. Remember: A jeweler's investments, whether in inventory or time, are supposed to pay off.

Step 5. It May Make Sense to Shop Around

If the piece you are considering is a budget buster, ask about the weight of the precious metal (expressed in grams or penny weights) and the size and grade of the gemstones.

Shop around. Stones and precious metal are commodities that have readily ascertainable retail and wholesale prices. Everything else is design and labor. The value is in the eye of the beholder.

Step 6. Go for the Gold

With rapport established and time invested, try these price breakers:

- My *friend bought emerald earrings here a few months ago and received a discount. How much are these earrings discounted?*

  Possible response: *What is the name of your friend?*

  Your reply: *Give the name of your uncle in Des Moines. It's all an accepted part of the face-saving, image-preserving negotiation process.*

- *If I buy the more expensive of these two rings, how much of a discount is available?*

- *This is a beautiful tennis bracelet. Its price is more than I budgeted. May I leave my name and phone number and if it goes on sale, please call.* (It may well go on sale before you hit the front door.)

  Anticipated response: *Open an account with us and we will finance the balance.*

  Your reply: *I prefer not to be in debt by spending more than I have budgeted.*

  Next anticipated response: *Well, instead of the four-carat bracelet, what about the three-carat one—it's beautiful on your wrist.*

  Your reply: *No, I am only interested in the four-carat bracelet.*

- *I will buy these diamond earrings if, in addition to the discount you offered, you will throw in that silver bangle bracelet for my daughter.*

How much of a discount can you expect? It will depend on the merchant's cash needs, profit markup, inventory levels, and desire to make the sale.

PURCHASING A FINE WATCH

Omega, Rolex, Cartier, Baume and Mercier—the list goes on. Their high manufacturer's suggested retail price is designed to add to the prestige of a watch that keeps time with pretty much the same precision as a Timex. But then if you wanted a cheap watch you wouldn't be at a nice jewelry store, you would be at Kmart.

Watch manufacturers sell more than timepieces—they sell strap-on self-esteem and identification. There is no goal attainment, self-satisfaction, or status associated with a cheap watch—even an accurate, cheap Japanese watch that looks like the expensive Swiss real thing.

As with all jewelry, watches are readily discounted if you follow the rules.

Because they are not produced in limited editions, that watch you have been admiring can be readily purchased elsewhere. Your negotiating power flows from the dynamics of competition:

- *You have been very helpful. I would like to buy this Omega from you, but I know that substantial discounts are available elsewhere. How much can you help me with the price?*

- *I would like to buy this watch from you, but I have a friend who is going to St. Thomas (or Hong Kong, or some duty-free port) where the same watch is much less. I know it's hard to be competitive with out-of-the-country prices, but if you can make it more afford-able for me I would like to buy it from you.*

Job Interviews

Finessing the Job Interview

A great resume only gets you in the door. Now you have to ace the interview.

Step 1. Power Generators

If at all possible, free yourself from the pressure and anxiety of a "do or die" interview by having fall-back options in the form of other job offers or opportunities.

The greater the number and the more realistic your options, the more self-confident you will be. Self-confidence is a big part of what the interviewer is buying.

Step 2. Loop In

Open the interview dialogue with chit-chat about the traffic, the weather, the city team moving into the final round of the play-offs, or whatever. Chit-chat will give you a few minutes to be in control. By not feeling immediately put on the spot, you have the time to loop into a relaxed interview stride. Chit-chat doesn't mean being chatty. Keep your comments brief. Let the interviewer run with the conversational ball you have put into play.

Step 3. Don't Drown in the Blur Pool

Look around the interviewer's office. Is there a golf trophy, a Masonic plaque, pictures of kids who are about the ages of your own, travel photos of places you have visited, a diploma from your alma mater?

If you too are a golfer, parent, teacher, or alumnus of the same school, then these objects are tools that make it possible for you to *personalize* the interview by creating, but not belaboring, a *commonality of interest.* Applicants who have linked personally with the interviewer are remembered long after the others have become part of the applicant blur pool.

Step 4. Go for the Fit

So what if it's a drop-dead great-looking sweater in a style you have been hoping to find? If it doesn't fit, you aren't buying.

265

You may have the educational and experiential background being sought, but if you're not an all-around fit, you won't get the nod. An all-around fit includes fitting in with the company culture.

Practice tip: Before the interview, scope out the company's culture. By asking others who are familiar with the inner company, you will be better able to act and dress in a way to make the fit happen.

Step 5. The Unasked Mega Questions

The interviewer probably won't ask them. Nonetheless, the questions that need to be expressly or impliedly answered by you are: *What can you do for the bottom line? Can you get the company back its money plus some? How did you do it for your previous employer and how can you do it for us? (Will it be by bringing in new business? Implementing new cost-saving measures? Introducing fresh insights and innovative ideas?).*

Step 6. Do the "Brieflys"

Briefly demonstrate:

- An understanding of the industry—personal contacts (there is a critical difference between being connected and being a name dropper), technical lingo, the market, industry practices, changing demands, new pressures, and emerging competition.

- A knowledge of the company's business—where it has been, where it is headed, who is its management, what are its plans and goals.

Step 7. Be a One-Minute Hero

Interviewers care more about what you can get done than how hard you work. Offer specific instances of what you have accomplished in a similar position, stressing *results* rather than *activity*. Limit these snapshots to no more than a minute each.

Step 8. Build Bridges of Opportunity

Ask questions about the open position's responsibilities. Use the interviewer's answers as *bridges of opportunity* to show how your skills and abilities can meet those responsibilities.

What kind of things did you do on the last job? View this frequently asked question as an opportunity to shape an answer that shows you have both the experience and the know-how to satisfy the position's demands.

Practice tip: The interviewer doesn't care about your life story, so leave out any information that doesn't clearly and directly show you are the person the company is seeking.

Step 9. The Great "I" Pit

If you are like most interviewees, your inclination will be to focus on what you want (*I am looking for a position with real growth opportunity; I am interested in a position that will challenge me*).

So what? Interviewers are being paid to fill their company's needs, not yours. If you want the job, focus on what the company wants and how you can satisfy those wants.

Practice tip: Until you are offered the position, don't ask "I" questions—vacation and sick day benefits, expected hours, and perks.

Step 10. Making the Cut List

You will have a better chance of making the cut list if you:

- *NEVER EVER* sell yourself as a bargain. Who wants to hire someone who has a "turned down all over town" sense of self?

- *NEVER EVER* say you're sorry about your shortcomings. No one is perfect, so no one need apologize.

Is there something in your history that could crimp your chances? If in all likelihood that "something" will come up in the interview, then you should be the one to raise it—not by way of apology but by way of explaining why it shouldn't be a factor for concern. There is no need to otherwise volunteer information that is best kept to yourself.

If asked *What are your weaknesses?* don't parade the horribles. Instead, finesse the question by answering in the broadest possible terms: *Sometimes I am too focused,* or *There are times when I am overly competitive.*

- *NEVER EVER* memorize the answers to anticipated questions. Scripted answers come across as either wooden and rehearsed or slick and rehearsed.

Practice tip: Have friends or family toss you likely questions in a mock interview.

- *NEVER EVER* talk about your problems. As interested as the interviewer may appear, an interview is definitely not the place to unload.

- *NEVER EVER* be overly flattering or overly complimentary of the company or the interviewer. Your efforts will be transparent, and phoniness is a turn-off.

- *NEVER EVER* come across as having an *Everyone wants to hire me* attitude. You may be good, but you're not so good that you can afford to be arrogant.

- *NEVER EVER* act anything other than your age. Even though you feel a younger person has a better shot at the job, acting and dressing twenty years younger than you are will look foolish.

- *NEVER EVER* be critical of the employers or supervisors where you are now working or where you have worked in the past. Sour-grape comments alert the interviewer that she or he may be the next person to be bad-mouthed by you.

Step 11. Tips à la Carte

- Schedule yourself as the last interview rather than the first interview of the day. You will be better remembered than similarly qualified applicants who, by the end of the interviewer's day, will be part of the blur pool.

- If told you will be called after the other applicants have been interviewed, position yourself to be a caller rather than a callee. *I will be in and out for the next few days. May I call you back later in the day or in the morning?* By being the caller, you have a second-shot opportunity to stimulate interest in your candidacy.

- Spend a few extra bucks on your clothes. Ninety percent of what an interviewer sees is on your back. Making a fashion statement may be inconsistent with the company's culture, but clean, pressed, properly fitted clothing is a very big part of your first-impression footprint. More important, you will feel better and more confident about yourself.

- Watch your body signals. You do not want to subconsciously appear desperate, discouraged, or defensive.

Step 12. With an Offer in Hand, You Are Now Ready to Talk Salary

Don't accept the job offer until all of the components of the salary and benefit package are discussed. See "Salary, Beginning," later in the Playbook.

Lawyer, Hiring a

Hiring a Hired Gun

Lawyers bring objectivity to the table, raise unconsidered issues, contemplate unforeseen problems, and test rationally what was decided emotionally.

Unless the task is small, negotiating a written retainer agreement that spells out the terms of the attorney–client hiring is a must.

We lawyers like to think we are all things to all people.

But the charming senior partner you initially met may be a mediocre lawyer but a great "rainmaker"—the firm's one-person sales force.

Consider whether you need a lawyer to lead the way or to take your direction.

Some lawyers will be compatible with your personality. Others will not.

The unrelenting steel-fisted lawyer you needed to hammer out an insurance settlement last year may not have the soft touch to negotiate the sale of your business.

A creative lawyer with honed people skills may be better able to defuse, finesse, and coax to get the results you want.

Has the deal been verbally cast? Perhaps you need a technocrat who is a skilled and thorough draftsperson.

Step 1. Seek Quality Legal Advice

Don't hire the lawyer whom you met at the last Elks Club meeting, because he seems "pretty good."

Bar Association referrals and "Lawyer Directory" services are of questionable help. No matter what their ads say, there is little or no substantive independent checking.

For more reliable recommendations, ask friends who had *similar cases.*

Every major public library has *Martindale-Hubbell*, the recognized lawyer rating directory. Educational backgrounds and letter-grade rates are all there for the viewing.

270

Step 2. Interview Several Lawyers

Most lawyers will initially meet on a "courtesy, nonchargeable" basis to determine whether there is mutual interest in having the lawyer handle the case.

If your matter is complex, interview several law firms. Ask them about their approach to your case. Wanting to sell themselves, lawyers are quick to map out a strategy. You may be presented with new insights and previously unconsidered novel approaches.

Interview the people who would actually be doing your work. Ask about the number and recency of matters they handled that were similar to yours. Ask about the outcomes of those matters and their clients' costs for obtaining those outcomes.

Step 3. Negotiate a Fair Fee Structure

The most expensive lawyer in town may be the cheapest. One insightful and creative lawyer's hour is another lawyer's entire week.

When can you get the very best lawyer for the same price as an average lawyer?

The answer: In traditional percentage-fee matters—personal injury cases, insurance bad-faith cases, and so on. In those situations, all lawyers pretty much charge the same *percentage* of your gross recovery. The best are the best because they have the reputation and skill to obtain bigger settlements and awards for their clients.

One phone call. That is all it took for a lawyer acquaintance to settle his client's personal injury claim with an insurance company whose insured readily admitted liability. My acquaintance's percentage fee was $440,000!

You guessed wrong: the lucky lawyer is not a high-profile practitioner. He isn't even a personal injury specialist. He is a criminal lawyer with offices in a tacky part of town.

In collection and personal injury claim matters where neither liability nor collectibility is in real doubt, negotiate hiring your lawyer on an hourly fee basis rather than a percentage (contingent) fee basis.

■ ■ ■

Forget how good it feels to be told by a judge that you are right. Judgments are not always collectible. Even if you win, you could lose.

Small suits have many of the same expenses as big suits: a lawyer's time is by the hour; deposition reporters, processing services, filing fees, and other costs are not predicated on how much you are seeking.

If collectibility is in doubt, or the cost of litigation is subject to wide variables beyond your control, consider negotiating (a) a percentage fee, or (b) a low hourly fee with a bonus on collection, or (c) a combination of a low hourly fee and a lower percentage fee.

Bonus benefit: Your proposal to pay something other than a full hourly fee will test the lawyer's expectations of the outcome of your case.

If someone is trying to collect money from you, consider a *reverse contingency fee,* negotiating to pay your lawyer a *percentage* of the money the lawyer saves you.

Negotiate *value-oriented* hourly fees keyed to the relative difficulty or importance of the case components. For example, in litigation try to set a rate of $125 an hour for drafting pleadings, $150 an hour for the lawyer's attendance at depositions, and $325 an hour for the time the lawyer spends in trial. (Note: hourly fees vary dramatically from city to city.)

Retainer Agreements

Retainer agreements provide for a "retainer fee" or initial payment.

- *Negotiate* that the initial retainer payment is not a minimum fee but a deposit for services to be rendered. By doing this you will receive a partial refund if the actual fees turn out to be less than the retainer deposit.

- *Negotiate* which part of the retainer payment will be applicable to fees and which part to costs (filing fees, personal service fees, deposition reporters, and so on).

- *Negotiate* for the retainer to be applied as a credit against the first payment due the lawyer, rather than allowing the retainer to be held as a "security for future payment deposit."

- *Negotiate* and include in the retainer for contingency cases an agreement as to who will front the money required to advance the case.

- *Negotiate* whether certain costs (for example, expert witnesses' fees, deposition reporters, trial costs, and so on) will *not* come out of your percentage share of the recovery but will be paid off-the-top, before any percentage allocation. This negotiation will depend on the nature of your case, the amount of anticipated costs, and the projected award.

- *Negotiate* and include in the retainer agreement when the percentage earned by the lawyer will change: When a lawsuit is filed? When trial preparation is commenced? When trial commences?

  A sliding percentage arrangement with a number of incremental percentage bumps may serve you better than the traditional two-tiered agreement with bumps at the commencement of the suit and again when the trial begins. *Negotiate* what constitutes "the beginning of a trial."

- *Negotiate* and include in the retainer agreement whether the lawyer earning a contingency fee has an obligation to appeal if you lose the case.

Step 4. Avoid Overlawyering

Overlawyering comes in different shapes and sizes.

You don't need a $300-an-hour senior partner to do what a second-year associate lawyer could do just as well for one-third as much.

Large law firms are notorious for "double teaming"—sending two lawyers on a task that can easily be performed by one.

- *Negotiate* and include in the retainer agreement who will be doing your work. Make sure skill and experience levels match your actual needs. You don't need a Perry Mason to try a case against a former tenant who did $3,000 of damage to your beach house.

Step 5. Keep Costs Under Control

When HK, a client, asked me to go to Chicago in April, he made arrangements for a first-class flight and a limousine to pick me up at the airport and whisk me off to a suite at the Four Seasons.

When a corporate client sent me off to Chicago in May, the client's expectations and budgeting were for economy seating and a taxi ride to a simple room at the Holiday Inn.

- *Negotiate* and include in the retainer agreement traditionally unnegotiated *cost* items: per-diem allowances, transportation expectations, and lodging expectations. Make sure you won't be billed separately for secretarial word processing time. Agree on fax and photocopying charges.

- *Negotiate* and include in the retainer agreement traditionally un-negotiated *time* items: How will travel time be billed? Will you be charged for time spent in the air or driving to a meeting across town? This time is often billed at 50 percent or less of the regular hourly charge. Time spent preparing memos to your client file is often not charged. Discuss discounting unproductive time spent waiting in courtroom corridors.

Bonus benefit: Discussing money concerns will sensitize the lawyer to the fact that you will not tolerate cavalier spending or a meter that is always running.

Step 6. Insist on Clear, Frequent Billing

- *Negotiate* to have each activity billed as a separate line item on the billing statement.

  Not acceptable: *"Conference with Smith, telephone call with Jones: 25 minutes."*

  Acceptable: *"Conference with Jones re refinancing: 15 minutes; Telephone call with Smith re construction problems: 10 minutes."*

- *Negotiate* and include in the retainer agreement the frequency of your billing. The more frequent the billing, the better you will be able to monitor what the case is costing, what is being done to advance your case, and who in the law firm is doing the work. In no event should you be billed less often than once a month.

- *Negotiate* tenth-of-an-hour minimum fee increments and a billing format that is very specific and descriptive. Specific and frequent billing will keep you alert to overlawyering.

Don't accept a billing item that refers to some mental activity such as the nondescript, but not uncommon, billing entry: "Attention to file."

Step 7. Make Sure Your Lawyer Keeps in Touch

Do you have an immediate need or a situation that will require a great deal of lawyer interfacing? A lawyer who will be out of town or engaged in a lengthy trial won't be able to deliver the service and attention you expect or require.

Negotiate an understanding as to time frames and accessibility. Will the lawyer be available to meet with you on weekends? On days when he or she can't see you at the office, will you be able to speak to the lawyer by telephone in the evenings?

Instruct your lawyer to send you copies of all correspondence and pleadings. Informed clients are better clients for themselves and their lawyer. A backlogged lawyer will be more inclined to move your work to the top of the stack if he or she knows you are monitoring the effort.

Negotiating tip: Some clients wisely use their lawyers to squelch a deal that the client wants killed. The lawyer is hired to strictly follow the client's script and say "no." By laying the blame on the lawyer, the client is able to preserve important relationships. After all, it's the lawyer who squelched the deal.

Practice alert: In some states, the retainer agreement must indicate whether the lawyer has malpractice insurance. It's a good idea. The day you discover that your lawyer doesn't have insurance is the day to say goodbye.

Litigation, Settling

Negotiating with a Litigation Opponent

Question: How many lawyer jokes are there?

Answer: Only two. The rest are true stories.

Step 1. Decide: Expediency or Valor?

In litigation, winners never win enough. Losers always lose too much.

Litigation is emotionally and physically consuming, brings out the worst in everyone, eats up more time than you ever imagined, is costlier than you ever dreamed, and can easily become the focal point of your being, robbing you of other thoughts, opportunities, and a good night's sleep.

And to make matters worse, it's not enough to be right. Every day, lawyers, great and ordinary, win cases that were "absolute losers" and lose cases that were "dead-bang winners."

Is it time to settle?

It may put you ahead of the game.

Ask yourself: What dynamics are there other than winning? Are relationships at stake? Are prospects for future business being lost? Will your company develop a litigious reputation?

Step 2. Forget Early, Best-Shot Settlement Offers

Personal interests of attorneys vary. Lawyers being paid on an *hourly basis* often try to crank out more work on larger cases. If you voice a *Let's give it our best shot* early-on settlement offer, you help the lawyer on the other side justify the expenditure of additional billable hours and discourages settlement discussions.

Best-shot high offers fuel the other person's recovery expectation and reaffirm his or her feelings of invulnerability and self-righteousness.

Step 3. Come Out Swinging

It's human nature. Lawyers being paid on a percentage or *contingency basis* like to do as little work as is reasonably possible. A strong showing

276

early on, which creates a load of work for your litigation adversary, encourages the contingent fee lawyer to settle sooner.

To the litigation adversary who is paying by the hour, it shows that you mean business and that the prosecution of the case will be long and costly. Your early settlement proposals will appear more attractive when compared to the expense associated with long-term litigation.

Step 4. Keep Your Lawyer on a Short Leash

It may make sense to give your lawyer limited negotiating authority. Weak positions that are inflexible become strengthened.

Step 5. Meet in Person

To defuse the hostility associated with litigation, arrange a personal meeting instead of a phone call. People investing the time and effort to attend a meeting are less likely to quickly say "no" and more likely to consider creative problem-solving approaches.

Step 6. Take Another Look—This Time at Your Lawyer

This is what your lawyer won't tell you.

The fact that your case isn't being settled may be the result of your lawyer's personal style. Your best negotiating play may be to change lawyers.

Style problems are people problems. Most litigation lawyers have competitive personalities. Competitive lawyers tend to negotiate competitively with both their competitive and cooperative counterparts. The most effective negotiators are masters of soft-touch/hard-bargain negotiating: competitive problem solvers who seek competitive results in a cooperative manner.

Step 7. The "Lloyd's of London" Tactic

What amount does your litigation adversary *reasonably* believe would be awarded by a court? What does the other side *reasonably* believe are the chances of winning? Multiply the answers by each other ($100,000 probable award times a 60 percent chance of winning = $60,000). *If* the resulting number is to your liking, explain how it was derived and use it as a *justified* basis for settlement negotiations.

Step 8. Get an Expert of Your Own

Don't argue with your litigation adversary's expert appraisers, geologists, inspectors, physicians, psychologists, or whatever. It seldom works, so why alienate everybody? Instead, get an expert of your own.

Step 9. Change Games

Consider resolving disputed issues in mediation. If the litigation case has progressed far enough for each side to accurately assess the facts, the law, and the risks, the timing may be ideal to consider mediation. Wait too long and both sides will have spent so much time and effort preparing for trial that further preparation will be unnecessary and the prospect of substantial legal fees being incurred will no longer be a threat or incentive to settle.

High–Low Mediation

Set aside all the agreed-on issues. If the remaining issues are financial issues, agree on a ceiling number (what the plaintiff would accept in settlement) and a floor number (what the defendant would pay in settlement).

Mediate the remaining financial issues with this understanding: the mediator can make a binding award that can be neither higher than the ceiling nor lower than the floor.

Last-Chance Mediation

A neutral party acting as an arbitrator gathers facts, hears arguments, and then prepares a written award, which he or she places in a sealed envelope. The neutral party then, acting as a mediator, encourages a negotiated settlement. If a settlement is reached, it is conclusive. If no settlement is reached, the award in the envelope is determinative.

The parties, knowing an award has been rendered, although not disclosed, are motivated to negotiate their own settlement.

Step 10. Look for Trade-Offs

After a preliminary settlement has been negotiated, but before it is reduced to writing, explore tax and other trade-offs that may be to the benefit of both parties.

Loan, Negotiating a

Negotiating a Borrowing Transaction

There are 250 varieties of shark, not counting loan and pool.

Step 1. Put on Your Borrower's Face

No one will lend you money just because you need it. Tales of desperation and bad luck aren't what it's all about. Lenders are businesspeople who make business decisions. Philanthropy is not part of their decision-making process.

Be positive about what the future will hold. Lenders like to think they have a good shot at being repaid.

Look and act the part of a worthy borrower. Dress to reveal a responsible and capable you.

Be well organized. Lenders need to know you have a grasp of your own finances—earnings, assets, and so on. Organized people are more likely to make timely payments.

When you want a loan, have a reason that will make you an even stronger and more able borrowing candidate. Needing the money to go to Maui is a nice idea but not as compelling as fixing up a house, which enhances the value of an asset, or starting a business, or acquiring new skills that increase your earnings potential.

Step 2. Line of Credit or Lump-Sum Loan?

Are you borrowing money and using the equity in your home as collateral? Distinguish between a home equity loan and a home equity line of credit, and then negotiate the type of loan that best satisfies your needs.

A *home equity loan* is a lump-sum loan usually made at a fixed rate of interest. The loan is repaid in equal installments (amortized) over a number of years—usually fifteen or more. If interest rates are low and you need the money for a *one-time transaction* such as remodeling the kitchen, this may be the type of loan to negotiate.

A *home equity line of credit* is a variable interest rate loan. The lender agrees to lend you up to a certain amount of money. You borrow from time to time as needed, repay as you are able, and pay interest only on the amount actually borrowed. If your needs are *ongoing*, such as periodic college tuition, this type of loan may be the one to negotiate.

279

Step 3. Know Where to Go Loan Shopping

Compare *all* terms offered by a number of lenders, not just those with the biggest ads.

You will always be better off starting your loan shopping at a major bank, major savings and loan, or other large lender. The cost of obtaining your loan will be less, and the borrowing terms will be more favorable than with other lenders. Referred to as *credit lenders,* their *primary* lending criterion will be your credit—the ability to repay.

The second most desirable lenders are smaller institutional lenders who are generally willing to make riskier loans. Referred to as *asset-based lenders,* their *primary* lending criterion will be whether you can secure the loan with collateral that can generate the cash needed to repay the loan (accounts receivable, inventory, and so on).

As a last choice, there are direct lenders—noninstitutional companies or individuals who make loans. Referred to as *equity lenders,* they are less concerned about your creditworthiness than they are about real estate equity collateral. Some of these lenders may actually hope you will default, enabling them to foreclose on your home. The most costly loans in terms of both interest rates and loan fees are those made by this third tier of lenders.

Loan Shopping Tips and Traps

- Don't pay any money in advance for a loan except for the cost of a credit report.

- Don't pay for an appraisal until you have a loan commitment predicated on the value of the property to be appraised.

- Be on the alert for hidden loan costs. Ask about all of the lender's loan transaction fees and charges.

- Make sure your financial statement is complete and accurate. If you are forced to file bankruptcy and the financial statement you supplied a lender is materially false, there is a good possibility you will not be able to discharge or excuse your loan indebtedness.

The Lone Arranger

Consider hiring a loan broker who, for a fee, will assist in matching you up with the right lender.

Step 4. Negotiate Interest Rates

Fixed Rate Loans

Are interest rates presently low?

If so, you will want to lock in those rates by negotiating a fixed rate of interest (the rate won't vary during the term of your loan).

Negotiate an interest rate that is *simple* rather than *compounded*. Compounded interest will always cost you more because the lender is accruing interest on interest already earned.

Variable Rate Loans

Are interest rates presently high?

If you don't expect rates to go higher and stay higher, consider a variable rate loan, which fluctuates as interest rates themselves fluctuate.

- Get the details on "special" introductory teaser interest rates. Those attractive rates you see advertised often change dramatically after the first few months of a long-term loan. Look at the variable interest rates with a long-term perspective. *Ask:* When, how, and to what degree can the teaser rate change?

- *Negotiate* an interest rate *adjustment period* that is as infrequent as possible (semiannual or annual rather than quarterly), if it appears that interest rates will go up over the longer term.

- *Negotiate* a *cap* limiting how much the interest rate can be increased in any *one* adjustment period (i.e., a quarterly maximum hike of ¼ percent rather than ½ percent).

- *Negotiate* a *ceiling* limiting how high the interest rate can go during the term of the loan.

When and how much your loan will fluctuate will depend on *external determinants* such as the Federal Reserve discount rate or the prime rate. Compare by asking lenders about the volatility of their variable determinants.

Practice alert: Do not accept a provision whereby you are borrowing both principal and interest but receiving only the principal.

For example, assume a 12 percent interest $100,000 loan. The first year's interest would be $12,000. Some lenders require that you borrow and pay interest on $112,000. The lender would, however, only hand you $100,000. The unfunded $12,000 is deemed the first year's interest prepaid.

Step 5. Negotiate How Your Loan Will Be Collateralized

- *Negotiate* the required *amount* and *type* of collateral, but post no more collateral than is reasonably needed to secure the loan. Don't be intimidated by the standard lender response: *If you are going to pay on time, what difference does it make?* No one knows what the future holds, and you may need unencumbered assets later.

- *Negotiate* the ability to *substitute* the collateral with other collateral of like or greater value. For example, if your loan collateral is General Motors stock, you want the future ability to give your lender substitute collateral so you can sell the GM stock without paying off the loan.

- *Negotiate* that your collateral is *incrementally returned* to you as your loan is repaid. For example, if stock is the collateral, negotiate to have $750 of your stock returned to you for each $1,000 of loan repayment. In real estate collateralized loans, acreage release clauses are not uncommon.

Collateral practice alert: Be on the lookout for these common lender provisions:

- A requirement that you replace or replenish collateral if there is a diminution or lessening of its value.

- A prohibition against removing the collateral from where you will be housing, using, or storing it.

- A prohibition of further borrowing against the same collateral. (Lenders believe that if borrowers have no or little equity in the collateral, they will be less likely to be concerned about its dissipation or condition.)

Step 6. Negotiate Loan Fees

The *fee* you will pay for your loan is commonly expressed in *points*.

A point is 1 percent of the principal amount borrowed. If a $10,000 loan costs 10 points, then your cost for the privilege of borrowing is

$1,000. If it is a one-year, 10 percent loan, the loan is, in effect, costing you 20 percent the first year.

Points are negotiable. The less risky the loan, the fewer the points you will have to pay to acquire the loan.

Step 7. Negotiate Penalties and Defaults

Be on the lookout for and negotiate these common lender penalty and default provisions:

- The length of grace periods. Do installment payments have to be received by the lender right on the dot, or is there some leeway for postal or other unavoidable delays?

- The amount of late payment fees. Late payments are penalized by imposition of an extraordinary fee or surcharge. Negotiate the amount of late fees and when they will be charged.

- The default interest rate. Negotiate whether an interest rate increase will apply to the entire loan balance for the period that loan arrearages are not paid.

- Negotiate under what default conditions the note balance can be accelerated and become suddenly all due and payable.

  Practice alert: Defaults are not always monetary. For example, failure to provide required periodic financial statements or proof of insurance renewal on loan collateral may be an event of default.

- Negotiate whether interest arrearages will themselves bear interest and, if so, at what rate.

Step 8. Negotiate the Loan's Renewal Criteria

Negotiate under what circumstances the loan maturity can be extended. Circumstances may include timely payment, partial principal reduction, an extension fee, or a reappraisal of collateral.

Step 9. Negotiate Away Early Payment Penalties

Early payment penalties are designed to discourage early loan repayment. Lenders who lend money when interest rates are high will want to receive interest from you for as long as possible. Negotiate that the loan can be paid off at any time without a prepayment penalty.

Step 10. Negotiate the Loan's Assumability

Is the loan to be secured by real estate or other property you may sell in the future? If so, negotiate that the loan can be assumed by your buyer without the payment of an expensive loan fee. This locked-in ability of a buyer to take over your existing financing will make it easier for you to sell your house later.

Step 11. Negotiate Guaranty Obligations

Negotiate that there will be no guaranties. Guarantors are usually family or friends—the last people on earth you want stuck with your debt.

But if a guaranty is a must:

- *Negotiate* a limit on the amount guarantied. For example, if the loan is $100,000, negotiate that the guaranty is only for $50,000 of the loan amount.

- *Negotiate* that the guaranty is limited to repayment of first rather than last moneys.

In the above example, negotiate that only the *first* $50,000 of loan repayment is guarantied. If you have paid $40,000 of the loan, your guarantor's liability would be limited to $10,000 because the guaranty is that your lender will receive a minimum of $50,000 in loan repayment.

Practice alert: Distinguish a guaranty for *timely payment* from a guaranty of eventual *collection* (a guaranty that is invoked only when all other avenues and sources of repayment have been exhausted).

Step 12. Negotiate the Length of Your Lock-In

A *lock-in* is a lender's binding commitment that you will be lent money on specified terms: points, interest rate, repayment. Lock-in commitments most often are in letter form. You pay for the privilege of having the interest rate locked-in. How much of a fee you will pay for the "lock" will vary with the amount and type of loan and the length of the lock.

Generally, lock-ins are for fifteen to sixty days. What if a home purchase loan is locked in, but now the closing date to buy the house is unavoidably extended? If interest rates jump, the lender will probably not extend its commitment to loan at the old (lower) lock-in rate. Never knowing when interest rates will increase, it makes sense to negotiate as long a lock as possible.

Office Lease

Negotiating Your Office Lease

The print is small. The sentences go on forever and some paragraphs fill an entire page. Reading them is an exercise in patience. Understanding them can be difficult.

So why go to all the effort? After all, the broker and landlord have already said it's all "very standard."

No wonder small businesses get into so much trouble with their office lease.

MONETARY ISSUES

Step 1. Negotiate Base Rent

Base rent is a function of how many square feet of space you are leasing and how much you will pay per square foot.

To compare per-foot asking rates, understand how the landlord calculates the number of feet being leased.

There are two common ways for landlords to determine square footage:

- Usable footage: You pay only for the number of feet within your office.

- Rentable footage: You pay for the number of feet within your office plus a portion of the common-areas space (halls, corridors, elevator lobbies, restrooms, and so on) on your floor. If your office occupies 10 percent of a floor's usable footage, you would also pay rent on 10 percent of the floor's common areas.

   Before negotiating the per-square-foot rate, negotiate what will be excluded from the footage calculation. For example, in some real estate markets, you can exclude your office's exterior balconies, terraces, and support columns.

Step 2. Negotiate Rent Concessions

Landlords are often willing to grant concessions by arranging for free rent. For example, the first month of each year of the lease term is rent-free. By giving free rent rather than lowering the square footage rate, landlords are able to maintain an *actual rental rate* continuity among tenants.

By averaging concession rent ("free rent") with your actual rental rate, you arrive at a blended lease rate, which is referred to as the *effective rental rate*. For example, if you have a 36-month lease with an actual rental rate of $1,000 per month and you get two months free, your effective monthly rent would be $34,000 divided by 36 or $944.44 per month.

When comparing competitive leasing opportunities, *effective* rental rates rather than *actual* rental rates are the comparison factor.

Negotiate concession rent by convincing the landlord:

- You are considering other buildings.

- You will be a stable, creditworthy tenant.

- You will be improving the leased space at your expense.

- Your business is of a type that would attract other tenants or enhance the building's image.

Step 3. Negotiate When and How Rent Is Increased

Will your lease be longer than a few years? If so, the landlord will want the ability to raise your rent during your lease term.

- *Negotiate* when, if ever, the rent increase would start (for example, the increase would start in the third year of the lease).

- *Negotiate* whether the increase will be a fixed amount ("bumps") or will be tied to an inflationary index (usually the Consumer Price Index).

- *Negotiate* a cap or ceiling on the size of the percentage of increase, if an inflationary index will be determinative. For example: *The increase shall be no more than 5 percent in any one year.*

Step 4. Negotiate Pass-Through Exclusions

Most office leases will obligate you to reimburse the landlord for your proportionate part of the landlord's building costs and expenses ("passthroughs"), such as insurance, management, personnel, repairs, and property taxes.

Negotiate pass-through exclusions. You should NOT have to pay pass-through building costs associated with:

- Retail or garage operations in the building.

- Upgrading the building to comply with handicap, fire, or safety codes that were in effect prior to the date of the lease.

- Real property tax penalties incurred because of the landlord's late payment.

- Increases in real property taxes resulting from a change in ownership of the building.

- Leasing commissions.

- Costs incurred in disputes with tenants.

- Costs for capital improvements or replacements, unless they will reduce building operating costs so there will be a net savings to tenants.

- Landlord's general overhead and administrative expenses.

- Compensation paid to parking attendants or clerks in commercial operations.

- Advertising and promotional expenditures.

- Costs arising from the presence of hazardous materials.

- Repair of latent defects in the building core or shell, or landlord-installed improvements.

- Landlord's own management fees in excess of 3 to 5 percent of the gross rental revenues.

Negotiate a ceiling or maximum ("cap") on the annual amount that can be passed through to you as an added cost. For example: *Pass-through costs cannot be increased more than 5 percent per year.*

Negotiate the right to audit the landlord's records relating to pass-through items.

Step 5. Negotiate Away Charges for Extras

Are building services such as after-hours or holiday air conditioning, heat, and elevators provided only on an "extra charge" basis? If so, negotiate:

- How many free "extra charge hours" you will be allowed each month.

- The price of extra charge hours (e.g., landlord's actual cost plus 10 percent).

Step 6. Negotiate Deposit Issues

What kind of deposit is being requested? A deposit for *rent?* A deposit for *security* that the premises will be returned in good condition?

- *Negotiate* that you are creditworthy enough that no deposit is even necessary, or suggest that a letter of credit can be used in lieu of a cash deposit. With a bank letter of credit, the landlord is protected and your cash will not be tied up. (Note: Brokers discourage letters of credit; their commissions are often paid from the deposit.)

- *Negotiate* whether your cash deposit will bear interest.

- *Negotiate* that your rent deposit can, in whole or part, be applied to rent as you prove yourself creditworthy during the term of the lease. For example, 20 percent of the deposit will be applied to rent in each of the last four years of a five-year lease.

TIME ISSUES

Step 1. Negotiate Renewal Options

Moving into a new office is not only a pain, it's expensive. Now is the time to negotiate an option to renew your lease.

The key issue is the rent for the renewal term. Renewal-term rent can be stated either (a) as a fixed dollar amount or (b) at the downstream market rate in effect when your option is exercised.

If you foresee a strong downstream leasing market with rising rents, you will want to negotiate a low fixed dollar rate now.

If, however, you think the leasing market will soften with decreasing rents, you will want to negotiate a downstream rate based on the market rate at the time of renewal. In that case, NOW is the time to:

- *Negotiate* how the downstream market rate will be determined. Will it be based on the rents then in effect in your building, or in similar buildings in your geographic area?

- *Negotiate* a discount from the downstream market rate. This discount should take into account:
  a. Free or concession rent *then* being given by the landlord to new tenants.
  b. The landlord's savings by not having to pay a broker's commission.
  c. The cost of tenant improvements or improvement allowances being given by the landlord to new tenants at the time of renewal.

Step 2. Negotiate a Right of Early Termination

New businesses often don't always work out as well as hoped.

Ask for the right to terminate the lease early without liability by giving advance notice (*six months' advance notice*) or paying a penalty (*a sum equal to two months' rent*).

If the landlord won't negotiate a right of early termination, negotiate a shorter lease with successive short option periods (instead of a five-year lease, a one-year lease with four one-year option periods).

EXPANSION / CONTRACTION ISSUES

Step 1. Negotiate Expansion Space

If you are confident that your business will expand in the foreseeable future, negotiate the right to acquire adjoining space.

There are three ways this acquisition can be negotiated:

a. A *right of first refusal.* The landlord must offer you adjoining space on the same terms as a prospective tenant has offered to pay.

b. A *right of first negotiation.* The landlord must negotiate with you in good faith before putting the adjoining leasing space on the market. A right of first negotiation, however, does not ensure that a deal will be made.

c. An *option.* The landlord must make adjoining space available to you when the space becomes vacated. The option rental rates issues are the same as in Step 1 of Time Issues, discussed earlier in this section.

If the landlord is willing to grant you any of the three rights listed above, then now is the time to:

- *Negotiate* that the adjoining space lease will expire concurrently with your original lease.

- *Negotiate* that the cost of breaking through walls to the adjoining space will be at the landlord's expense.

- *Negotiate* an allowance to modify or refurbish the adjoining space.

Step 2. Negotiate the Right to Change Offices

Do you have your eye on space presently occupied by another tenant in the building? *Negotiate* the right to move into those offices when they become available.

TENANT IMPROVEMENTS

Negotiate office enhancements: new carpeting, painting, wallpaper, cabinets, a sink, more interior walls, and so on, or a cash allowance to make enhancements of your own.

PARKING ISSUES

Negotiate:

- The number, location, and cost of spaces.

- The landlord's right to raise parking prices.

- Options to increase and to reduce the number of spaces.

- The right to move to other spaces as they become available.

- The cost of client/customer parking (discounted validations, free validation stickers).

SUBLEASE ISSUES

Negotiate the right to sublease or assign your lease and to be released from your obligation to the landlord if the new tenant is financially worthy.

If the printed lease provides otherwise, negotiate the right to keep for yourself any sublease or assignment profits.

The lease, when delivered, will in all likelihood be a form. It may be the landlord's own "standard form" or that of an association. There is nothing sacred about a form. The lease was chosen by the landlord because it protects landlords. Read and understand each and every provision. Make sure that the lease serves and protects you.

Prenuptial Agreement

Negotiating a Prenuptial Agreement

Marriages are made in heaven. But then so are thunder and lightning.

Step 1. Be Prepared for an Emotional Response

"You said the only important thing is that we're together."

Brace yourself. This may be your toughest negotiation ever. It's not the terms and conditions you will be sweating. It's your intended's reaction when you pop the other question, *"Will you sign a prenuptial agreement?"*

Call it what you want. A prenuptial agreement is a *marriage contract*.

Negotiating a prenuptial agreement can be an enriching experience that enhances a couple's knowledge and appreciation of each other's desires, fears, and expectations. Hidden agendas are brought to light. Before they say *I do*, couples are forced to discuss how money will be handled during the marriage.

Prenuptial agreements can also be the stage for a frustrating and perhaps disappointing struggle for domination, power, and control.

Considering the high rate of divorce, prenuptial agreements make sense because they:

- Stipulate what is community or marital property and what is separate.

- Define the estate's rights at the time of death.

- Provide for agreed-on (rather than judicially determined) spousal support or alimony in the event of divorce.

- Help prevent business ownership disputes, which can be disruptive to a business.

- Deal with financial ties and obligations to the spouses' respective families.

Step 2. Don't Negotiate the Agreement as Guests Are Arriving

"Honey, please sign here . . . ."

293

Prenuptial agreements are not a guarantee against a knock-down, drag-out divorce. Like any contract, they are often contested. Even Donald Trump had to go through a prolonged and costly divorce because his wife, Ivana, unsuccessfully challenged their prenuptial agreement.

Prenuptial agreements negotiated and signed under pressure have a greater possibility of being declared null and void. Agreements signed shortly before the wedding are arguably signed under pressure: the only choices are to suffer the humiliation of breaking off the engagement or to accept an unsatisfactory agreement.

Step 3. Negotiate a Fair and Reasonable Agreement

"Don't you trust me? I wouldn't do anything to hurt you, or anything that is unfair."

The enforceability of an agreement with onerous terms that leave a spouse sadly undersupported may be contested as being neither realistic nor fair.

Step 4. Maker Sure Each Spouse Has His or Her Own Lawyer

"Don't worry about having your lawyer look this over. Everything will be redone and taken care of later in a will."

A will is a unilateral document that can be secretly changed at any time by its maker acting alone. A prenuptial agreement is a bilateral document and can be modified only by mutual consent.

The prenuptial agreement you are negotiating will best survive challenge if each intended spouse has a separately retained lawyer review the agreement. Each lawyer should acknowledge in writing that the fiance-client thoroughly read and understood the agreement and that its terms and conditions were agreed to free of duress or pressure.

Step 5. Negotiate with Candor

"So what if I didn't tell you everything? I thought you loved me—not my bank account."

Holding something back? Another basis for contesting a prenuptial agreement is that assets were not fully disclosed and that the agreement would never have been signed had all the facts been revealed up front.

Step 6. Negotiate What Will Happen During Marriage and in the Event of Divorce

"In my mind I believed that . . . ."

Prenuptial agreements are particularly important in second marriages where the new spouses come to the marriage with children, accumulated assets, and a disparity in respective net worth.

Matrimonial laws vary from state to state. Some states recognize community property; others embrace a concept of "equitable distribution" upon divorce. This step and step 7 are designed to serve only as *examples* of negotiating possibilities. It is imperative that the actual prenuptial agreement be prepared by a legal professional who is familiar with applicable state law.

- In the event of divorce, the nonaffluent spouse will receive in lieu of alimony a settlement of X dollars for each month of marriage.

- During marriage, the affluent spouse shall pay all or a greater part of living expenses.

- During marriage, payments will be made by the affluent spouse to the nonaffluent spouse. (This possibility is useful if the nonaffluent spouse is assuming a caretaker role.)

- Assume a spouse has property with a value of X dollars at the time of marriage. At the time of divorce, it has a value of $X + Y$. The spouse who owns that property would, in a divorce proceeding, receive credit for X, and Y would be divided equally or in some agreed proportion, depending on the length of the marriage.

- During marriage, a spouse owning separate property will pay taxes, upkeep, and maintenance on that separate property.

- During marriage, the affluent spouse's income is separate, but a negotiated percentage of that income over a certain base level (i.e., the income during the year prior to marriage) will be gifted to the nonaffluent spouse.

- Professional practice and business are separate, but the earnings during marriage will be deemed community.

- Earnings, rents, profits, and income of separate property shall themselves be deemed separate property.

- During marriage, all debts other than for living expenses shall be the separate obligation of the spouse incurring the debt.

- At the time of marriage, the nonaffluent spouse shall release all rights acquired through a cohabitation relationship with this partner prior to marriage.

Step 7. Negotiate What Will Happen in the Event of Death

"I understand 'til death do us part . . . but then what?"

Examples of negotiating possibilites include the following:

- Upon death, the nonaffluent spouse will receive a stipulated amount per month for the remainder of his or her life.

- Upon death, the nonaffluent spouse will continue to live in the affluent spouse's furnished house for the remainder of his or her life (or until remarriage, or for six months for each year of marriage).

- The nonaffluent spouse would be both the owner and beneficiary of a life insurance policy on the life of the affluent spouse. Premiums would be paid by the affluent spouse. Each year of marriage, the amount of the policy would increase to an agreed maximum.

- The affluent spouse will provide for "allowance" payments to be made to the survivor spouse upon death. The amount and duration of those payments will be keyed to the length of the marriage.

- If the affluent spouse dies first, designated assets received by the surviving spouse will, upon his or her death, revert back to the family of the affluent spouse (for example, family heirlooms, furniture, art, china).

Real Estate—Listing Broker

Negotiating a Broker Listing Agreement

"Your house is wonderful. It is certainly salable for close to the price you have in mind."—Broker soliciting a listing.

"Your house needs a lot of work. The kitchen is twenty years behind the times. Your price expectations just aren't realistic."—Broker now encouraging the acceptance of a low offer.

Step 1. Motivate the Broker

They need cash, or there is a job waiting in another town, or whatever. Sellers confide in their brokers, disclosing why they need to sell.

"Highly motivated" is how brokers describe their desperate sellers in ads or by word-of-mouth. In effect, the brokers are announcing to the world that the sellers are running low on negotiating power.

Turn things around. Motivate your broker.

- *Negotiate* a shorter listing (i.e., ninety days instead of six months). Let the broker know that if *you feel* that the broker is doing a good job, you will extend the listing.

- *Negotiate* for the broker to supply you with a monthly list of prospects who were shown the house by *your broker,* and an update as to whether any of those prospects are presently interested.

- *Negotiate* what the broker will do *at the broker's expense* to get your house sold. Ads? (How often? How big? Where?) Flyers or brochures? Open houses? (When?)

Step 2. Keep the Pressure On

How do you avoid having the broker sandbag you with unqualified buyers?

The chance that your broker will screen potential buyers and will bring qualified, able buyers to your premises is enhanced if you *negotiate* to eliminate from the brokerage listing agreement any provision that:

297

- Allows the broker to share in the buyer's forfeited deposit (the usual forfeiture clause calls for a 50/50 split).

- Extends the listing period by the amount of time your house was off the market in contemplation of a sale that was aborted.

Step 3. Avoid the Commission Paradox

Brokerage commissions are negotiable.

But whatever the agreed-on percentage commission, why pay a commission on the part of the purchase price that the broker receives?

The paradox: If the sale price is $200,000 and the commission is 5 percent, why pay commission on the $10,000 that goes to the broker? You would then be paying a commission on a commission.

Avoid the paradox! Negotiate a commission based on the gross sales price ($200,000) divided by 1.05 percent (in a 6 percent deal, divide by 1.06 percent, and so on). The resulting figure ($190,476) would then be multiplied by the commission rate (5 percent). In this example, the commission would be $9,524 rather than $10,000.

Step 4. Go Multiple

Negotiate that your broker will place the property with a multiple listing service *immediately.* Brokers sometimes will keep your listing a secret— what the industry refers to as a "pocket listing." The secret is to your detriment because you are denied maximum exposure to the market. The secret is to the broker's benefit because a broker who is able to sell a house solo avoids the obligation to share the commission with another brokerage firm or another salesperson in the broker's own office.

Reservations and Tickets

Negotiating Tickets, Reservations, and What Can't Be Gotten

The plans for my parents' July golden anniversary celebration were finally settled. Reservations would be made for five rooms at the Ritz Carlton in Laguna Niguel and for ten seats at the Laguna Pageant of the Masters. It was early April and the celebration was not until the end of July, so naturally I had a real sense of organizational pride for having whipped the plans into shape so early.

Half an hour later, my secretary reported the bad news: Both the hotel and the festival were "sold out."

In my heart, I knew there had to be unsold tickets and rooms. After all, what would happen if the President and First Lady suddenly hit town?

Panicking, I picked up the phone and detailed my fiftieth anniversary plight to Ellen and Loretta, the two ladies who had firmly—but categorically—rejected my secretary's request. Explaining how my folks had spent months considering the very best and most meaningful way to celebrate this special event, I asked each lady for her *help*.

Abracadabra is a magic word. *Please* is not. *Please* is a polite word. Like a breast-pocket handkerchief, *please* has no real purpose other than gentrification. *Help* on the other hand, is a magic word. Remember how you felt the last time you gave elaborate directions or tips to a stranger? People just love to be asked for help. *Help* is the word that gets the results because it is an involvement word.

Did I give Ellen and Loretta too much detail, considering they weren't related by blood or marriage? Yes. And it was all on purpose. I wanted their involvement. I wanted to talk to a person, not a cordial functionary.

Loretta (at the Masters pageant) somehow found ten incredible house seats. Within a half hour, Ellen (from the Ritz Carlton) called back: all five rooms were reserved.

Why were Ellen and Loretta so willing to help a stranger on the telephone when so many before me had fallen and failed?

Because I was a little less of a stranger than all of the others, including those who had gone to the box office in person.

And because of the equally simple reality that *persuasion is more a function of involvement than it is a function of cajoling, hands-and-knees pleading, or saying "please."*

299

Then there were those difficult men and their flying machines . . . .

My usual fantasy that a computer miracle would have me heading into the wild blue yonder seated next to Cher or Streisand had already been abandoned. For this flight, I would have been thrilled to be sitting next to a chatty spinster with chronic sniffles.

You see, when I reached my departure gate, I was informed that my Phoenix-to-LA flight had been overbooked. I was one of seven instructed to wait while the plane was checked for any possible unoccupied seats.

The results were in.

Lo and behold. There was one seat left.

Who amongst our number would be the blessed one?

One of our anxious group must have been an engineer or systems analyst. He had an argument that was based on deliberated logic: His reservation was reconfirmed only yesterday. The gate manager had her own logic: "A reservation is not a seat."

The other five were heavy-handed: argumentative, abusive, threatening. Theirs was the "logic" of the screeching wheel.

My move was neither logical nor boisterous. I knew that I needed the involvement of the gate manager if I was to reach Los Angeles on time.

To personalize, involve, and set the proper climate and mood, I sympathized with her dilemma, for which she was very appreciative. Explaining that I had an important meeting back at my office in just a few hours, I asked for her *help*. A few very sketchy details were supplied so she in turn would somehow feel real involvement with my dilemma.

When the others weren't looking, I was whisked to the waiting plane and a simple reality was again proven to be true: *Persuasiveness is more a function of involvement than it is logic or abuse.*

Salary, Beginning

After a Job Offer: Negotiating Your Starting Compensation

The human race is faced with a cruel choice: work or daytime television.

Step 1. Get a Grip on Reality

The salary you *need* or *want* isn't important. What is important is what the employer perceives as reasonable. Sourcing information is readily available from former and present employees, headhunters, and people in the business.

Step 2. Edit Your Wish List

Have a twelve-point wish list? Forget it. It's too much baggage. Be prepared to focus your discussion on those compensation components that are most important to you.

Some compensation components for selective consideration might be: amount of vacation time, reimbursement of moving expenses, classes, stock options, bonuses, merger and acquisition protection, longevity created by a binding employment contract, elimination of noncompete clauses upon termination, and guaranteed promotion.

Step 3. Be Prepared for the Killer Questions

Killer Question No. 1: "What is your present [or last] salary?" If you were undercompensated, be prepared to sidestep disclosing your previous salary.

Killer Question No. 2: "What are your salary expectations?" Don't throw out the first number. It will put you at a negotiating disadvantage:

If you make a wishy-washy proposal—*I think something around* $_____ *would be fair*—you may come across as a pushover.

A specific number is an announced position. You will lose face retreating from that announced position if your number is not accepted. Even worse, an overreaching number may leave a bad taste in your employer's mouth.

Come in with a low number, and you may appear desperate, weak, or lacking in the capabilities you professed to land the job.

301

Here is how to avoid the dilemma when asked your salary expectations.

Test the waters: *I believe that my skills and experience place me within the salary range the company has budgeted for the position.*

Say nothing.

It will be tough, but avoid the temptation to break the silence.

Yes, it may seem like an eternity. But wait ten seconds or so for the employer to disclose the salary range. Ideally, the silence will be broken by the employer's tipping her or his hand. If it doesn't happen, ask, *What is the range you have budgeted?*

Once disclosed, ask, *How would you place me with that salary range?*

Step 4. Back Away from a Can't-Win Battle

The employer's range may not meet your expectations.

You have two fallback options.

Fallback Option No. 1: You can indicate you were expecting a higher number: *I am disappointed. For someone with my ability and experience, I feel that a salary in the range of $_____ would be fair.*

By expressing *disappointment*, you are being neither judgmental nor threatening. You are merely conveying how you *feel*. The word *range* suggests that your proposal (which has been disguised as an expression of how you feel) is not cast in stone and sends the message that you expect nothing more than what is reasonable.

Fallback Option No. 2: Propose a performance-based pay package that includes, in addition to a base salary, financial incentives and bonuses that are paid only as agreed-on benchmarks are reached.

That alternative will be hard for the employer to turn down. Performance benchmarks can be keyed on your own performance, that of your department, or the company as a whole. They can be tied to sales, cost savings, or other goals that you are being hired to help achieve.

Be creative, be flexible: If the employer won't budge on one compensation component, introduce an alternative component.

Step 5. Negotiate How Your Next Raise Can Best Be Maximized

You can't play the game without knowing the ground rules. Ask for specific raise criteria. Consider writing a memo to your employer reiterating and confirming those criteria.

Negotiate an early review to determine whether you are on track in fulfilling the criteria.

Step 6. Negotiate a Training Program

The more your employer has invested in you, the greater the inertia to retain you. Besides, better-trained employees are more valuable.

Employers prefer employees who have a broad-based work perspective. Negotiate cross-training opportunities that will give you a broader skill and knowledge range.

Steps 7 Through 10

These steps are the same as Steps 6 through 9 in the next section, "Salary, Increases in."

Salary, Increases in

Negotiating the Best Possible Raise While Enhancing Your Job Security

A job is the ultimate invasion of your privacy and you should be compensated accordingly.

Step 1. Consider the What

Think it out: Will you ask for the raise you think you can get? Or the raise you want? Is it better to ask for more money? Increased perks? A training program? The security of a contract?

Step 2. Phrase Your Raise Request Assertively, Not Aggressively

Don't just ask "for a raise." Be prepared to make your request clear and specific—dollars, perks, benefits. Casting your raise request as an "or else" alternative will make retreating without loss of face difficult if your request is denied.

Step 3. State Why You Are Asking for a Raise

Your *why* can't be:

- *I deserve it.*

    Reason: Everyone feels they are worth more.

- *I need to buy a new car and my daughter needs braces.*

    Reason: Raises aren't doled out because things are tight at home.

- *My friend at another company does the same thing I do but is paid a lot more.*

    Reason: Employers aren't in the business of helping you keep up with your friends.

Perhaps the *why* is:

- Your creativity has been stifled by the badgering of creditors who could be paid with a raise.

304

- A raise would enable you to quit a second job and be even more productive.

- Your job calls for putting in more hours now than ever before. Your employer's business is downsizing, which may mean that more work will be expected from you.

Demonstrate that your request has been well thought out: offer your employer something in writing.

Remember those extra hours and weekends at the office? Great. Include any detail you can recall. Quantify those hours by translating them into a specific dollar request: 10 percent more work equals 10 percent more money.

Are creativity and imaginative new ideas an important part of the job? Throw in a brief description of your recent contributions.

Why not wait for your employer to make a salary proposal? It's a judgment call.

Once made, your employer's proposal becomes a psychological barrier, an announced negotiating position. A retreat from a negotiating position represents a loss of authority. Employers back away from announced positions grudgingly.

Step 4. Couple the Whys

Make one of the *whys* the escalating cost of living and the diminishing spending power of the dollar. The U.S. Bureau of Labor Statistics has a specific cost-of-living percentage increase applicable to your geographic area. If the cost of living has gone up 3 percent, then explain why 3 percent more should be tacked onto your request.

Step 5. Anticipate a Bad-News Response

Keep your cool.

You know it's coming: *Income is down, things are tight.* The choice is yours. Be prepared to walk (now is a good time to assess your negotiating leverage) or be prepared to negotiate the assumption of *new responsibilities* and a win–win *formulamatic bonus:*

> **Boss:** I hope you are not serious. Everybody knows how tight things are right now. I promise you there aren't any raises in the new budget.

If both the job and the working relationship with the boss are to be preserved, an argument must be avoided. *Linkage* and *alignment* tactics must be brought into play if you are to go back to your desk a winner.

> **Employee:** You are right. We have to stay competitive, which means operating leaner. And I know you have our collective best interests in mind. I am not asking for a raise given what's happening with our department's budget.

> **Boss:** What is it you want then?

> **Employee:** Sometime soon, when it's best for you, I would like to talk about what you think of my job performance, the ways you think I could improve, and what I could reasonably anticipate later.

It has been acknowledged that the company is not perceived as being greedy or overreaching. The further acknowledgment—that it is looking out for everyone's best interests—encourages the boss to adopt a pattern of fair dealing with the compensation issue. A mutually tense situation has been eased. At the next meeting, the boss no longer has to be defensive. No one is taking money out of the budget. The agenda for that meeting has been cast as positive: how the employee can do better for the company.

> **Employee:** Thanks for meeting with me so soon. Let me tell you about some of the things I would like to accomplish for us this year. *[Explanation follows.]* I have given a great deal of thought to our tight budget and think I could help by taking on added responsibilities that would save us money.

Discussing job goals reinforces the employee's value and importance to the company.

To energize discussions, maintain a positive environment, and capture the boss's interest, the dialogue has been focused on how the company's *need* for cost reduction can be satisfied.

The reference to *our* budget and *us* gives a sense of mutuality to the dilemma—a sense that should carry over in the quest for a solution.

The turned-down-raise issue has been judiciously avoided. But it is about to be revisited—not as a negative request for a budget-wrenching raise, but as a positive cost savings opportunity. "Added responsibilities" are a value-added plus.

> **Employee:** If I can take on *[description]* responsibilities, which will save us money, then maybe there is a way for me to be compensated out of those savings. What do you think about a formula bonus—I would only receive more if I could free up funds through my cost-cutting efforts?

There is an irrefutable logic in the proposal. It's a no-lose proposition. Asking the boss for input prompts both the boss's involvement and further dialogue.

Step 6. Negotiate Your Long-Term Company Career Path

Negotiate regular reviews to make sure you are on course. Does that upward path look like an uphill battle? Negotiate a different position within the company, where the ascent will be less challenging.

Step 7. Lock In Your Negotiating Destiny

Bosses go to expensive seminars where they are told to hire people who are smarter than they are. The more dependent your employer is on you, the more likely you will get raises and promotions. Negotiating leverage increases dramatically as dependency is developed through unique technological knowledge, close rapport with important customers, being your boss's trusted confidant and sounding board, gaining a special know-how, having the ability to cut through red tape, and so on.

Step 8. Lay the Negotiating Groundwork for Your Next Review

Keep a diary of those extra hours and weekends at the office, and note any contributions and accomplishments that were of significant benefit.

Step 9. Understand the Inner Company

Future negotiations will be even more fruitful if you understand the personal attributes that your company considers most important. They might include: a high profile in the community, sensitivity to cost-cutting opportunities, marketing savvy, the ability to take direction, the ability to lead, a polished personal style. (One client invites employees to dinner to check out their table manners and ability to make small talk.)

Steps 10 and 11

These steps are the same as Steps 5 and 6 in the previous section, "Salary, Beginning."

Store Front Lease

Negotiating a Store Front Lease

Before signing a lease, be a bit afraid. Fools rush in where wise men fear to trade.

Step 1. Know Exactly What You Are Being Offered

Is the building in compliance with all applicable safety and building ordinances, codes, and regulations relative to your type of business?

Are plumbing, electrical, mechanical, heating, air conditioning, and other building systems in good repair and condition?

Is the roof watertight and in good repair?

Are the structural elements of the building sound, including walls and foundation?

If you skip a thorough, professional physical inspection and don't check with applicable governmental authority for potential code problems or recent citations, how will you know what needs you should be addressing in your negotiations?

Step 2. Negotiate Repair and Replacement Responsibility

SG's store was a boutique just off glitzy Rodeo Drive. The lease provided that the air conditioning unit was SG's responsibility. If the unit couldn't be repaired, it was SG's obligation to replace it with a comparable new unit. In the fifty-seventh month of a sixty-month lease, the air conditioner breathed its last sigh.

Heating, air conditioning, plumbing, electrical systems, and the building's roof have to be someone's responsibility, but they don't have to be yours.

Negotiate that all repairs, except those caused by your own negligence, will be at the landlord's expense.

The landlord won't go for it? Consider negotiating one of these alternatives:

- Landlord repair responsibility for a designated period (e.g., the first year).

- Landlord responsibility for any repair in excess of X dollars.

- Limiting your responsibility for expensive replacements or major repairs (which can be defined as replacements or repairs in excess of X dollars) to the proportionate part of the cost that you will be "using." For example, if the life of the air conditioning unit is seventy-two months and you will be a tenant for just three more months, your part of the replacement obligation, if the air conditioner dies now, should be no more than $3/72$ of the air conditioner's cost.

Step 3. Negotiate Responsibility Required by Code Changes

HR's business occupied a free-standing building on Sunset Boulevard. HR's lease provided that any repair or alteration necessary to keep the building in code compliance would be HR's responsibility. A new earthquake preparedness code mandated the reinforcement of the building's structural walls. The cost of HR's compliance with the lease obligation was more than a year's rent.

There is a good chance that new building ordinances or codes will be enacted sometime during your lease term. Special-access restrooms, handicap access ramps, reinforcement of exterior walls or roof, and sprinkler systems are among the possibilities.

Negotiate that the premises will be *delivered* to you in compliance with all governmental authority and, except for improvements owned by the tenant, will be *kept* in full compliance by the landlord.

Step 4. Negotiate Signage Rights

MF was a third-floor tenant of a fashionable Westside shopping center. MF assumed that because other tenants had ground-floor signage facing the street, he too would enjoy comparable signage prominence. MF was wrong.

Determine local signage prohibitions. *Negotiate* the most signage the landlord and the law will allow. You may not want to exercise all of your signage rights, but the rights will be in place if your signage needs change.

Practice tip: An abundance of signage rights may not be important to your business but may be critical to a potential subtenant.

Step 5. Negotiate the Right to Remove Your Fixtures

The French restaurateurs invested mega dollars in kitchen fixtures, dining-room chandeliers, mirrors, and the most beautiful bar in town. After ten years, the decision was made to relocate the restaurant and to unscrew, detach, and relocate their expensive fixtures and decor items. The landlord said "no."

State law varies, but most leases provide that once fixtures, equipment, mirrors, shelves, or other tenant improvements are screwed, nailed, or attached to a floor, wall, or ceiling, they become property of the landlord. *Negotiate* the right to remove your fixtures and equipment at the end of the lease term.

Step 6. Negotiate a Nondisturbance Agreement

DM and his partners invested $500,000 in building out the prototype store of what DM hoped would be a chain. Ten months later, DM's landlord lost the building in foreclosure. The new owner canceled DM's lease.

Does your landlord have a real estate mortgage encumbering the store building?

In the event of foreclosure by the landlord's lender, your lease may be canceled and you could lose the benefit of your investment in improvements and neighborhood goodwill.

When a lender signs a *nondisturbance agreement,* the lender is promising that, in the event of foreclosure, all the terms and conditions of your lease will still be honored.

Negotiate as part of your lease that the landlord will supply you with its lender's nondisturbance agreement.

Practice alert: Does your lease have a *subrogation clause?* If so, you may be allowing a subsequent lender to have certain rights superior to yours as an existing tenant. Agree to subrogation only if a new lender will be obligated to honor your lease.

Step 7. Negotiate *How* Overages Will Be Determined

WR's barbecue restaurant's success was largely due to its incredible sauce. A food distributor offered to take the sauce to grocery shelves all over the state. WR's landlord claims he too is entitled to a piece of the sauce profits.

Is your rent a base (or minimum) against a percentage of your gross sales? If so, when the applicable percentage of sales exceeds the base rent, the difference owed the landlord is the *overage.*

Negotiate items to be excluded from the calculation of gross sales: postage; returns; sales off the store premises (fairs, bazaars, catering); catalog or mail order sales; delivery charges; sales of fixtures not part of the store's regular merchandise; sales, luxury, or similar taxes; returned merchandise; sums received in settlement for loss or damage to merchandise.

Step 8. Negotiate **When** Overages Will Be Determined

Linda owns a small gift store. Her rent is 5 percent of her monthly gross sales, with a base guarantee of $1,000 per month. Fifty percent of Linda's business is in December. Her December sales were $150,000. Linda's landlord is claiming $6,500 overage rent in addition to the $1,000 base rent.

Is your flow of business seasonal or uneven? Negotiate whether your overage will be calculated monthly, quarterly, or annually.

If, like Linda, most of your sales are during the Christmas holidays, you would not want to pay December overage against your base December rent. In this example, negotiate to determine the overage by comparing 5 percent of annual (rather than monthly) gross sales to the annual base guarantee ($12,000).

Tip: Review the "Office Lease" Section of this Playbook. It will be largely applicable to your store front lease.

If your store will be in a multistore commercial complex, pay special attention to these final steps.

Step 9. Negotiate Exclusivity

Tim had a small sporting goods store in the Marina shopping center. A popular sports shoe chain opened a store in the same center. A year later, Tim filed bankruptcy.

Negotiate that your store will be the only yogurt store, or dry cleaner, or sporting equipment store in the complex.

Practice alert: If your lease limits you to being a particular type of store, you may not be able to change businesses or sublease to a business different from your own if things don't work out as planned.

Step 10. Negotiate Special Security Needs

If your store "keeps evening hours" and is in a commercial complex, negotiate to have your special security needs paid by the landlord.

Step 11. Negotiate Rent That Fluctuates with the Complex's Vacancy Factor

John's business was instant shoe repair—heels and soles for people on the go. His business was to be generated from the mall's "foot" traffic. Too bad John couldn't hold out during the three years it took for the mall to become largely occupied.

Will your business base depend on the traffic generated by other businesses within the leasing complex?

What happens if it's a newer complex that is only half full when you move in? You would be deprived of half of your projected customer base.

Negotiate that your rent will be proportionate to the total number of square feet actually open for business in the complex each year, compared to the number of square feet available for rent.

Step 12. Negotiate Designated Customer Parking Areas

Negotiate to have parking in front of your store "reserved" for your customers. Specify how the landlord will enforce the exclusivity of this parking.

■ ■ ■

Practice alert: Larger commercial complexes usually have merchant associations. The association and its advertising programs may be of little or no benefit to your type of business. Determine whether participation is mandatory. If you join, what will be the basis for your assessment by the association: Gross sales? Store footage? Net profits?

Coming Full Circle

The soft-touch/hard-bargain methodology of the persuasion progression has come full circle. *POWER PLAYS* ends the same way Chapter 1 begins.

"Being a winner is not what you *do* but what you *are*. By *being*, you will *become*."

■ ■ ■

Your Deal-Maker's Playbook comments and suggestions are important. Please share your thoughts with me by writing to Robert Mayer, Times Business, 201 East 50th Street, New York, New York 10022.

INDEX